THE
ANNOTATED
CONSTRUCTION
LAW GLOSSARY

A. ELIZABETH PATRICK, D. ROBERT BEAUMONT
TERRENCE L. BROOKIE, HARVEY J. KIRSH
MICHAEL D. TARULLO AND KATHRYN S. SPENCER

EDITORS

FORUM ON THE
CONSTRUCTION
INDUSTRY

Defending Liberty
Pursuing Justice

Cover design by ABA Publishing.

Printed in the United States of America.

14 13 12 11 10 5 4 3 2 1

Library of Congress Cataloging-in-Publication Data

The annotated construction law glossary / edited by Lizz Patrick.
  p. cm.
  ISBN 978-1-61632-017-1
  1. Building laws—United States—Terminology. 2. Construction industry—Law and legislation—United States—Terminology. I. Patrick, Lizz. II. American Bar Association. Forum on the Construction Industry.

KF5701.A68A56 2010
343.73'078690014—dc22

2010030312

TABLE OF CONTENTS

About the Editors

A. Elizabeth Patrick

A. Elizabeth ("Lizz") Patrick is the founder of Patrick Law Group. Over the span of her career, she has prepared and negotiated hundreds of commercial, construction, and procurement contracts across the United States and abroad to assist clients with achieving objectives while minimizing the risk inherit in the process. Her experience ranges from preparing and negotiating specific and custom contracts and serving as project counsel on multimillion-dollar expansion, renovation, and new development projects to preparing and negotiating "master agreements" and "open supply" agreements for services, equipment and materials, professional services, logistics, global sourcing contracts, and specific equipment procurement and consulting contracts. She is a frequent speaker on construction contract negotiation, project administration, and related issues and has authored several articles. In recognition of her outstanding legal ability and experience, Ms. Patrick has been named in the *International Who's Who*, as well as in Chambers U.S.A. She has also been selected as a Georgia Super Lawyer, as one of the Top 50 Female Super Lawyers, and as a Law Dragons New Star. She serves on the American Arbitration Association's prestigious Roster of Neutrals, and served on the Governing Committee and as chair for Division 12 of the ABA's Forum on the Construction Industry. She is past president of the Atlanta Bar Association's Construction Law Section. She has achieved Martindale-Hubbell's highest rating of AV for legal ability and ethical standards. She received her B.A. from the University of Georgia in 1985 and her J.D. from Tulane University in 1988.

D. Robert Beaumont

D. Robert Beaumont is a senior partner and co-chair of Osler, Hoskin & Harcourt LLP's Construction and Infrastructure Group. He is a qualified and experienced professional engineer whose practice concentrates in construction law and infrastructure, procurement, and engineering matters, particularly project structuring, risk identification and allocation, contract negotiation and documentation, and financing and claims advice. He has broad experience in a wide range of major projects and has acted on behalf of the various project participants, including owners, developers, contractors, lenders, subcontractors, construction managers, architects, and engineers. His project experience, both nationally and internationally, includes major building and civil works construction and equipment procurement, industrial facilities including very extensive involvement in infrastructure, public-private partnerships, alternative financing and procurements, power generation, health facilities, and manufacturing facilities. He also advises on claims and acts with respect to dispute resolution.

Terrence L. Brookie

Terrence L. Brookie is a member in the Indianapolis, Indiana, office of Frost Brown Todd LLC. He concentrates his practice in the area of construction law, surety law, and business litigation. Mr. Brookie is a frequent speaker for construction and commercial groups and has lectured and written numerous articles for several industry groups and professional organizations in the construction industry. He is a member of the ABA's Forum on the Construction Industry (Governing Committee Member), TIPS Fidelity/Surety Law Committee, and Construction Litigation Committee. Mr. Brookie received his B.A. from Denison University in 1978 and his J.D. from Indiana University School of Law in 1981. He is a Fellow of the American College of Construction Lawyers and selected by his peers for inclusion in *The Best Lawyers in America*, 2005–2010.

Harvey J. Kirsh

Harvey J. Kirsh is a recognized authority in Canadian construction law. As a senior partner and co-chair of the Construction & Infrastructure Group of Osler, Hoskin & Harcourt LLP, he provides experience and expertise in litigating, arbitrating, and mediating complex construction claims and disputes arising out of large infrastructure, engineering, industrial, commercial, and institutional projects, both internationally and domestically. He is the founding editor of the *Construction Law Reports*, the founding editor of the *Construction Law Letter*, and the author of numerous articles and texts. Mr. Kirsh was designated as a Chartered Arbitrator by the ADR Institute of Canada, has been appointed by Infrastructure Ontario as mediator and adjudicator for its infrastructure projects throughout Ontario, and is the only Canadian ADR panel member of the Global Engineering and Construction Group of JAMS (Judicial Arbitration and Mediation Services), the largest private provider of alternative dispute resolution services in the United States. In 2009, Mr. Kirsh was also appointed chair of the Construction, Engineering and Infrastructure Panel of ADR Chambers, the leading provider of alternative dispute resolution services in Canada. Mr. Kirsh was the first president, and is a governor and a founding fellow, of the Canadian College of Construction Lawyers. Certified by the Law Society of Upper Canada as a Specialist in Construction Law, he has been prominently featured as a leading practitioner in the field of construction law in *The Best Lawyers in Canada Directory*, the *Canadian Legal Lexpert Directory*, and the *Lexpert/American Lawyer Guide to the Leading 500 Lawyers in Canada*. He is also an adjunct professor at the Faculty of Law, University of Toronto. Mr. Kirsh received his B.A. from University of Toronto in 1967, his LL.B. from Osgoode Hall Law School in 1970, and his LL.M. from Harvard Law School in 1971.

Michael D. Tarullo

Michael D. Tarullo is a principal in the law firm of Schottenstein, Zox & Dunn L.P.A. of Columbus, Ohio, and Coordinator of its Construction Industry Service Group. His law practice is concentrated in construction and construction-related matters, locally, state-wide, and federally. Prior to practicing law, he had almost 20 years of field experience in actual construction, construction-related businesses, and field construction claims evaluation and preparation. Mr. Tarullo's clients include contractors, subcontractors, suppliers, and public and private owners. Mr. Tarullo is a trained arbitrator and mediator, serving on the American Arbitration Association's select panel of construction arbitrators for complex disputes. He is active in developing practice risk prevention programs for all members of the construction industry and is a lecturer on the use of mediation and arbitration in resolving construction disputes. He is the author of "The Mediator's Role in Construction Disputes—Communicate, Challenge, and Be Creative," published for the ABA 1998 Annual Meeting; *Design/Build Procurement at the Federal Level*, published by the ABA Forum on the Construction Industry in the *Design/Build Deskbook*, and the chapter in the Forum's book entitled *Forms & Substance, Specialized Agreements for the Construction Project*, entitled "Project Site Agreements." Mr. Tarullo is a Fellow of the American College of Construction Lawyers, served as chairman of the Construction Committee of the Columbus Bar Association from 1996 to 1998, and was chairman of Division 4 of the ABA's Forum on the Construction Industry in 1999 and

2000. In 2002, Mr. Tarullo was elected to the national Governing Committee of the ABA's Forum on the Construction Industry and served as the chair of that organization in 2007 and 2008. Mr. Tarullo has actively participated in the activities of various construction trade associations throughout Ohio, in particular the Builders Exchange of Central Ohio and the Ohio Valley chapter of the Design Build Institute of America. Mr. Tarullo received a B.S. from the University of Louisville in 1972 and a J.D. from Capital Law School in 1989.

Kathryn S. Spencer

Kathryn S. Spencer is associate counsel with the Patrick Law Group. Ms. Spencer's practice focuses on construction and commercial transactional matters, particularly negotiating construction, sourcing, and procurement contracts, identifying and allocating risks, and serving as project counsel for her clients. Ms. Spencer has drafted architectural, engineering, construction, and consulting agreements required for the development of health care, hospitality, retail, and other complex projects. Ms. Spencer is the author of several articles and presentations for professional organizations in the construction industry and for use by her clients. Ms. Spencer is an active member of the ABA's Forum on the Construction Industry and the Georgia Association of Women Lawyers. Ms. Spencer received a B.A. from the University of Virginia in 1999 and a J.D. from Wake Forest University in 2005.

Contributing Authors

Lynn R. Axelroth, Ballard Spahr, LLP, 1735 Market Street, 51st Floor, Philadelphia, PA 19103; *axelroth@ballardspahr.com*

Deborah S. Ballati, Farella Braun + Martel LLP, 235 Montgomery Street, 17th Floor, San Francisco, CA 94104; *dballati@fbm.com*

Wade M. Bass, Baker Donelson Bearman Caldwell & Berkowitz, PC, 3 Sanctuary Boulevard, Suite 201, Mandeville, LA 70471; *wbass@bakerdonelson.com*

Arthur D. Brannan, DLA Piper LLP (US), One Atlantic Center, 1201 West Peachtree Street, Suite 2800, Atlanta, GA 30309; *arthur.brannan@dlapiper.com*

Daniel J. Brenner, Laurie & Brennan, LLP, Two North Riverside Plaza, Suite 1750, Chicago, IL 60606; *dbrenner@lauriebrennan.com*

Turner D. Brumby, King & Spalding LLP, 1180 Peachtree Street, N.E., Atlanta, GA 30309; *tbrumby@kslaw.com*

Lauren M. Charneski, Howrey LLP, 525 Market Street, Suite 3600, San Francisco, CA 94105; *CharneskiL@howrey.com*

W. Stephen Dale, Smith Pachter McWhorter, PLC, 8000 Towers Crescent Drive, Suite 900, Vienna, VA 22182; *sdale@smithpachter.com*

Paul E. Davis, Conner Gwyn Schenck PLLC, 3141 John Humphries Wynd, Suite 100, Raleigh, NC 27612; *pdavis@cgspllc.com*

Daniel M. Drewry, Drewry Simmons Vornehm, LLP, 8888 Keystone Crossing, Indianapolis, IN 46240; *ddrewry@drewrysimmons.com*

Michael F. Drewry, Drewry Simmons Vornehm, LLP, 8888 Keystone Crossing, Indianapolis, IN 46240; *mdrewry@drewrysimmons.com*

Tred R. Eyerly, Damon Key Leong Kupchak Hastert, Pauahi Tower, Suite 1600, 1003 Bishop Street, Honolulu, HI 96813; *te@hawaiilawyer.com*

Jennifer W. Fletcher, Sutherland Asbill & Brennan LLP, 999 Peachtree Street, N.E., Atlanta, GA 30309; *jennifer.fletcher@sutherland.com*

Gina A. Fonte, Holland & Knight LLP, 10 St. James Avenue, Boston, MA 02116; *gina.fonte@hklaw.com*

C. Allen Gibson, Jr., Buist Moore Smythe McGee P.A., 5 Exchange Street, Charleston, SC 29401; *agibson@buistmoore.com*

Anne E. Gorham, Stites & Harbison PLLC, 250 West Main Street, Suite 2300, Lexington, KY 40507; *agorham@stites.com*

Deborah S. Griffin, Holland & Knight LLP, 10 St. James Avenue, Boston, MA 02116; *deborah.griffin@hklaw.com*

A. Holt Gwyn, Conner Gwyn Schenck PLLC, 306 East Market Street, Suite One, Greensboro, NC 27401; *ahgwyn@cgspllc.com*

Stephanie J. Hall, Farella Braun + Martel LLP, 235 Montgomery Street, 17th Floor, San Francisco, CA 94104; *shall@fbm.com*

Peter C. Halls, Faegre & Benson LLP, 2200 Wells Fargo Center, 90 South 7th Street, Minneapolis, MN 55402; *phalls@faegre.com*

Suzanna Hartzell-Baird, Bose McKinney & Evans LLP, 111 Monument Circle, Suite 2700, Indianapolis, IN 46204; *Shartzell-Baird@boselaw.com*

John R. Heisse, Howrey LLP, 525 Market Street, Suite 3600, San Francisco, CA 94105; *HeisseJ@howrey.com*

Steven Henderson, Stites & Harbison PLLC, 303 Peachtree Street, N.E., Suite 2800, Atlanta, GA 30308; *shenderson@stites.com*

John W. Hinchey, King & Spalding LLP, 1180 Peachtree Street, N.E., Atlanta, GA 30309; *jhinchey@kslaw.com*

Buckner Hinkle Jr., Stites & Harbison PLLC, 250 West Main Street, Suite 2300, Lexington, KY 40507; *bhinkle@stites.com*

J. Wallace Irvin, King & Ballow, 1100 Union Street Plaza, 315 Union Street, Nashville, TN 37201; *wirvin@kingballow.com*

Ridgely J. Jackson, DLA Piper LLP (US), 203 North LaSalle, Suite 1900, Chicago, IL, 60601; *ridgely.jackson@dlapiper.com*

Brian S. Koerwitz, Woods & Aitken, LLP, 301 South 13th Street, Suite 500, Lincoln, NE 68508, e-mail: *bkoerwitz@woodsaitken.com*

Kenneth R. Kupchak, Damon Key Leong Kupchak Hastert, Pauahi Tower, Suite 1600, 1003 Bishop Street, Honolulu, HI 96813; *krk@hawaiilawyer.com*

Ty D. Laurie, Laurie & Brennan, LLP, Two North Riverside Plaza, Suite 1750, Chicago, IL 60606; *tlaurie@lauriebrennan.com*

Anthony D. Lehman, DLA Piper LLP (US), One Atlantic Center, 1201 West Peachtree Street, Suite 2800, Atlanta, GA 30309; *anthony.lehman@dlapiper.com*

Michael I. Less, Less, Getz & Lipman, PLC, 100 Peabody Place, Suite 1150, Memphis, TN 38103; *michael.less@lgllaw.com*

Jennifer S. Lowndes, Sutherland Asbill & Brennan LLP, 999 Peachtree Street, N.E., Atlanta, GA 30309; *jennifer.lowndes@sutherland.com*

H. Fielder Martin, Shapiro Fussell Wedge & Martin, LLP, One Midtown Plaza, Suite 1200, 1360 Peachtree Street, N.E., Atlanta, GA 30309; *fmartin @shapirofussell.com*

Tracy A. Marion, Shapiro Fussell Wedge & Martin, LLP, One Midtown Plaza, Suite 1200, 1360 Peachtree Street, N.E., Atlanta, GA 30309; *tmarion @shapirofussell.com*

Troy M. Miller, Bose McKinney & Evans LLP, 111 Monument Circle, Suite 2700, Indianapolis, IN 46204; *Tmiller@boselaw.com*

Christopher D. Montez, Thomas, Feldman & Wilshusen, LLP, 9400 North Central Expressway, Suite 900, Dallas, TX 75231; *cmontez@tfandw.com*

Jaimee Nardiello, Zetlin & De Chiara LLP, 801 Second Avenue, New York, NY 10017; *jnardiello@zdlaw.com*

Allen L. Overcash, Woods & Aitken, LLP, 301 South 13th Street, Suite 500, Lincoln, NE 68508; *aovercash@woodsaitken.com*

Eileen B. Quigley, Ballard Spahr, LLP, 1735 Market Street, 51st Floor, Philadelphia, PA 19103; *quigleye@ballardspahr.com*

Heather Rodriguez Pinder, Holland & Knight LLP, 200 South Orange Avenue, Suite 2600, Orlando, FL 32801; *heather.rodriguez@hklaw.com*

Jeffery M. Reichard, Nexsen Pruet, PLLC, 701 Green Valley Road, Suite 100, Greensboro, NC 27408; *jreichard@nexsenpruet.com*

David A. Senter, Nexsen Pruet, PLLC, 701 Green Valley Road, Suite 100, Greensboro, NC 27408; *dsenter@nexsenpruet.com*

Danny G. Shaw, Baker Donelson Bearman Caldwell & Berkowitz, PC, 3 Sanctuary Boulevard, Suite 201, Mandeville, LA 70471; *dshaw@baker donelson.com*

Charles M. Sink, Farella Braun + Martel LLP, 235 Montgomery Street, 17th Floor, San Francisco, CA 94104; *csink@fbm.com*

Gregory K. Smith, King & Spalding LLP, 1180 Peachtree Street, N.E., Atlanta, GA 30309; *gksmith@kslaw.com*

Liz Smith, Stites & Harbison PLLC, 250 West Main Street, Suite 2300, Lexington, KY 40507; *esmith@stites.com*

Richard F. Smith, Smith Pachter McWhorter, PLC, 8000 Towers Crescent Drive, Suite 900, Vienna, VA 22182; *rsmith@smithpachter.com*

Ron Stay, Stites & Harbison PLLC, 303 Peachtree Street, N.E., Suite 2800, Atlanta, GA 30308; *rstay@stites.com*

Harrison M. Trammell, Buist Moore Smythe McGee P.A., 5 Exchange Street, Charleston, SC 29401; *htrammell@buistmoore.com*

John H. Tarlow, Tarlow Stonecipher & Steele, PLLC, 1705 West College Street, Bozeman, MT 59715; *jtarlow@lawmt.com*

Sandra S. Varnado, Baker Donelson Bearman Caldwell & Berkowitz, PC, 3 Sanctuary Boulevard, Suite 201, Mandeville, LA 70471; *svarnado@baker donelson.com*

Laura T. Vogel, DLA Piper LLP (US), One Atlantic Center, 1201 West Peachtree Street, Suite 2800, Atlanta, GA 30309; *laura.vogel@dlapiper.com*

Margaret C. Weamer, Tarlow Stonecipher & Steele, PLLC, 1705 West College Street, Bozeman, MT 59715; *mweamer@lawmt.com*

Michael S. Zetlin, Zetlin & De Chiara LLP, 801 Second Avenue, New York, NY 10017; *mzetlin@zdlaw.com*

ACKNOWLEDGMENTS

As with any large and important undertaking, there are many people involved in making the task a success, and the production of this book is no exception but rather serves as an excellent example of teamwork and collaboration. The foundation of our success starts with the encouragement and patience of the leadership of the ABA Forum on the Construction Industry, particularly Robbie MacPherson, Adrian Bastianelli, and Andy Ness. And our contributing authors, along with their respective teams, brought construction terminology to life by providing the time, skill, and effort needed to thoroughly define each term.

I would also like to thank Harvey Kirsh and Stanley Sklar for their assistance in the early stages of developing the concept of this book, as well as acknowledge the tireless efforts of Harvey and the other members of our editorial team—Bob Beaumont, Terry Brookie, Mike Tarullo, and Kathryn Spencer. I am also grateful to Janice Garza of Frost Brown Todd LLC and Lynn Cory of Schottenstein, Zox & Dunn PLA for their assistance and dedication in proofreading, organizing, and editing the text of this book.

A. Elizabeth ("Lizz") Patrick

PREFACE

From its inception, this book was designed to be a critical resource for the legal profession and the construction industry, and to provide, in one place, annotated definitions of terms commonly used in the construction industry and the practice of construction law. Regardless of whether our reader is a young law student, a project manager, or a seasoned construction practitioner, it is our intent that *The Annotated Construction Law Glossary* will provide a fundamental understanding of each defined term.

This publishing project dates back four years, to September of 2006, when a small group of inspired construction attorneys contemplated that the creation of a glossary of construction law terms would be a welcome and useful resource and research tool for themselves and their colleagues in the profession. After outlining more substance for consideration and presentation to the Publications Committee of the ABA Forum on the Construction Industry, the project was approved and the editors' hard work began in earnest.

The prospect of creating an annotated construction law glossary was daunting, in its anticipated scope, its organizational obstacles, and its creative and practical requirements and demands. In initiating this publishing project, we were mindful of Winston Churchill's lament that writing a book begins as an adventure, but then proceeds to move from mistress to master to tyrant, and that, just as you are about to be reconciled to your servitude, you kill the monster and strew him about to the public. Well, despite a few bumps in the road over the past few years, we, the editors, are now pleased and proud to unleash this work product on an unsuspecting public. Churchill notwithstanding, we feel that it will be an excellent addition to both the evolving literature in the field and the libraries of construction attorneys, courthouses, and other institutions and individuals in both the construction industry and the legal community.

The creation of this annotated glossary is a testament to the many people who contributed to it—particularly the numerous attorney researchers and authors (expressly acknowledged elsewhere in this text) who devoted their time, skill, and effort, and whose fingerprints can be found throughout this final product.

Our initial editorial mandate was to identify and collect words and terms of use and value to our target market. In the beginning, we generally differentiated between "legal" terms (e.g., laches, quantum meruit, bad faith, consequential damages, economic loss, etc.) and "non-legal" terms (e.g., measured mile, critical path, extras, means and methods, etc.), and essentially concluded that there was no reason why the glossary should not include both universes.

We also considered sources for the definitions that were to be collected and adopted. The word "adopted" is used advisedly, since it was not our intention to create our own definitions out of whole cloth. Rather, we would access them on an unrestricted basis from legal texts, law review articles, judicial decisions, engineering texts, construction industry literature, and many other secondary sources. The editors agreed that every definition should be annotated wherever possible, so that there would be a record of attribution. Such annotation would serve to identify the source of the definition, would effectively date-stamp it, and would hopefully establish the requisite credibility, recognition, and comfort level required so that a defined word or term could be used with authority in legal opinions, court decisions, pleadings, and legal research and literature.

The initial creation of the preliminary glossary database was an enormous task. Our role as editors began with the preparation of a model template for the annotation of sample definitions for a limited number of selected construction terms. That template was for the assistance and guidance of the contributing attorney researchers and authors who agreed to work with us, and whose fine efforts we congratulate with this publication.

Over time, and multiple drafts and redrafts, the editors made ongoing judgment calls in creating, refining, and imposing guidelines and specifications relating to, among other things, the legitimacy of selected reference materials; the method of citation and footnoting; the restriction of references made to jurisdiction-specific statutes or jurisprudence of limited application elsewhere; and the length of each definition—all undertaken with the supervisory intent of seeking to enhance the quality and usefulness of the finished product. And with the clichéd components of perspiration and inspiration, we now present to you, our readers, *The Annotated Construction Glossary*.

We expect that, since a critical mass has now been attained, this glossary will be a fluid work-in-progress and that future editions are inevitable. But we leave it to the next committed groups of editors to refine and expand it over time, and, as Winston Churchill said, to kill their own monster and strew it about to their public.

Harvey J. Kirsh

ACRONYMS AND ABBREVIATIONS OF DEFINED TERMS

Acronym/ Abbreviation	Term
AAA	American Arbitration Association
AASHTO	American Association of State Highway and Transportation Officials
ABA	American Bar Association
ACEC	American Council of Engineering Companies
ADA	Americans with Disabilities Act
ADR	alternative dispute resolution
AGC	Associated General Contractors of America
AIA	American Institute of Architects
ALI	American Law Institute
ASA	American Subcontractors Association
ASC	Associated Schools of Construction
ASCE-CI	American Society of Civil Engineers—Construction Institute
BIM	building information modeling

Acronym/ Abbreviation	Term
BOO	build-own-operate
BOT	build-operate-transfer
CAD	computer assisted design
CCD	change directive/ construction change directive
CCIP	contractor-controlled insurance program
CCN	contemplated change notice
CDs	construction documents
CDB	combined dispute board
CGL	commercial general liability (insurance)
CPM	critical path method
DAB	dispute adjudication board
DB	design-build
DBB	design-bid-build
DBFOM	design-build-finance-operate-maintain
DBFOMT	design-build-finance-operate-maintain-transfer
DBO	design-build-operate

Acronym/ Abbreviation	Term
DBOM	design-build-operate-maintain
DBOO	design-build-own-operate
DDs	design development documents
DRB	dispute review board
DSC	changed conditions/differing site conditions
EJCDC	Engineers Joint Contract Documents Committee
ENE	early neutral evaluation
EPC	engineer-procure-construct
FAA	Federal Arbitration Act
FAR	Federal Acquisition Regulation
FCA	False Claims Act
FIDIC	International Federation of Consulting Engineers
GAI	general agreement of indemnity
GMP	guaranteed maximum price
ICC	International Code Council
ICDR	International Center for Dispute Resolution

Acronym/ Abbreviation	Term
IDM	initial decision maker
IPD	integrated project delivery
JAMS	Judicial Arbitration and Mediation Services, Inc.
LOC or LC	letter of credit
NCCULSL	National Conference of Commissioners on Uniform State Laws
NSPE	National Society of Professional Engineers
OCIP	owner-controlled insurance program
OSHA	Occupational Safety and Health Administration
PLA	project labor agreement
PPP	public-private partnership
REA	request for equitable adjustment
RFI	request for information
ROICC	resident officer in charge of construction
TIA	time impact analysis
UCC	Uniform Commercial Code

A

Acceleration/Constructive Acceleration. Acceleration in the construction industry context refers to increasing the pace or progress of construction in order to complete all or a portion of a project sooner than the scheduled completion date, or in an attempt to overcome previous or anticipated delays. The pace or amount of work is faster than what was contemplated in the original schedule, in an accepted bid, or as part of any other agreement between the parties. David Buoncristiani, *The Owner's Perspective, in* HANDLING CONSTRUCTION RISKS 2004: ALLOCATE NOW OR LITIGATE LATER 366 (PLI 2004). Acceleration may be either directed or constructive.

Directed acceleration typically occurs when a project owner requires that the contractor (or a contractor requires that a subcontractor) accelerate or increase the pace of the remaining work—overcome delays so that the project remains on schedule, or intentionally shorten the contract duration in the absence of any delays. When the directing party directs that the work be accelerated for its own purposes (and for reasons other than the responsibility or delays from the party being directed), the additional compensation and reimbursement for its impact costs usually are negotiated in advance of accelerating the work. If there is a dispute over the cause of directed acceleration and which party bears the costs or impact of the acceleration, the contractor (or subcontractor or other directed party), in order to recover damages, generally must establish that (1) the contract did not authorize the acceleration, (2) the contractor bears no responsibility for any project delays, (3) the owner mandated the acceleration, (4) the contractor accelerated its performance, and (5) the contractor incurred additional costs as a result of the acceleration. *Conti Corp. v. Ohio Department of Administrative Services*, No. 88-14568 1992 Ohio Misc. LEXIS 77 (Ct. Cl. 1992) at 48, citing *Norair Engineering Corp. v. United States*, 666 F.2d 546 (Ct. Cl. 1981).

When an owner (or contractor or subcontractor) fails or delays in granting a justified extension of time to a contractor (or to a subcontractor of the next lower tier), it is called a constructive acceleration. CARINA Y. OHARA ET AL., FUNDAMENTALS OF CONSTRUCTION LAW 329 (ABA 2001). The elements of constructive acceleration vary from jurisdiction to jurisdiction but generally include (1) encountering an "excusable" or "compensable" delay to the critical path that justifies an extension of the contract time; (2) a request to extend the time pursuant to the terms of the contract; (3) the requested extension being wrongfully rejected or otherwise ignored; (4) express or implied direction given to complete the contract by the original, unextended completion date; (5) timely notice of an intent to pursue an acceleration claim; and (6) that the accelerated performance resulted in damages being suffered by the accelerating party. 5 PHILLIP L. BRUNER & PATRICK J. O'CONNOR, JR., BRUNER AND O'CONNOR ON CONSTRUCTION LAW § 15.94 (2002). *See also Conti Corp.* at 48, 49. The party accelerating its work must establish that it would not have incurred the additional amounts claimed but for the acceleration. Expenses incurred because of the acceleration may be direct or indirect costs, and include items such as additional labor charges, overtime, escalated material prices, inefficiency costs, and on-site overhead. THEODORE J. TRAVNER & ANGELA M. SIST, IDENTIFYING, PROVING AND QUANTIFYING DAMAGES, IN HANDLING CONSTRUCTION RISKS: ALLOCATE NOW OR LITIGATE LATER 189 (PLI 1998).

Acceptance. The concept of acceptance in a construction project often arises upon the completion of all or a designated portion of the work, obligating the owner to decide whether the work has been properly completed, and therefore accepted. Evidence of acceptance may be given in a certificate or other writing or by virtue of making a final payment (depending on the language in the contract between the relevant parties). Contractors and subcontractors may be deemed to have accepted work or site conditions in other ways.

> By inspecting the site or underlying work and then proceeding to place its own work, a subcontractor likely will be deemed to have accepted the site and underlying work, along with the responsibility to correct its work if the underlying site or work proves unsuitable . . . or worse, its work may be rejected even though the defect lies in . . . [the underlying work].

CARINA Y. OHARA ET AL., FUNDAMENTALS OF CONSTRUCTION LAW (ABA 2001).
If the owner accepts the work, a host of rights and obligations flows from that decision. For example, upon final acceptance and inspections, the risk of loss and the obligation to maintain the work shift from the contractor to the party owning or utilizing the work. RICHARD J. BEDNAR ET AL., CONSTRUCTION CONTRACTING 817 (George Washington University 1991). Moreover, unless the contract terms specify otherwise or the owner expressly reserves its rights, acceptance of work by the owner may be a waiver of any claims for defective work, even if the defect could not be recognized at the time of acceptance. MICHAEL S. SIMON, CONSTRUCTION CLAIMS AND LIABILITY § 16.2 (Wiley Law Publications 1989). However, in many construction contracts, the impact of the acceptance of the work is negotiated and latent defects, fraud, or rights under warranties and guarantees may not automatically be released upon acceptance. *See e.g., United States v. Lembke Construction Co., Inc.,* 786 F.2d. 1386 (9th Cir. 1986). *See also* AIA Document A201-2007, General Conditions of the Contract for Construction, § 9.10.4 (2007) (acceptance and final payment does not constitute a waiver by the owner of unsettled claims, liens, security interests and encumbrances, failure of the work to comply with the requirements of the contract documents or contractual warranties). The AIA, however, takes a contrary view in the provision governing the contractor's, subcontractor's, and material supplier's acceptance of final payment. In their cases, all claims by the payee are waived except for those previously made in writing and identified as unsettled at the time of final payment. *Id.* at § 9.10.5.

Responsibilities for costs, assumption of risk, and waivers of claims are not the only implications of acceptance of all or a designated portion of a project. The commencement of limitations periods also may accrue upon the completion, acceptance, and payment for work. *Federal Insurance Co. v. Southwest Florida Retirement Center, Inc.,* 707 So. 2d 1119 (Fla. 1998).

Those confronted with the term or concept of "acceptance" should be aware that it arises in any number of construction contexts, such as whether (1) a valid and binding contract was in fact created, and (2) work not expressly provided for in a written agreement nonetheless inured to the benefit of, and was accepted by, the party disputing its obligation to pay for such work, thereby unjustly enriching that party unless it paid for the value of the work received.

Access to Site. A fundamental duty of the owner or developer of a construction project is to provide sufficient access to the project site (and to needed adjacent areas, to the extent feasible) so that those rendering services and performing work may fulfill their respective obligations. Even absent express contractual requirements, this often is an implied warranty on the part of the owner. BARRY B. BRAMBLE & MICHAEL T. CALLAHAN, CONSTRUCTION DELAY CLAIMS § 3.02 (Aspen 3d ed. 2000). Additionally, most contracts require contractors and those providing services or performing work to provide access to the site to the owner, developer, architect, and perhaps other parties (such as lenders, tenants, inspectors) while the work is in process to allow for inspection and review.

Access includes the timely acquisition of permits, easements, and other approvals necessary to enter and perform work upon the site, identification of property lines, information in order to file, record, and enforce potential lien claims, and full disclosure of any restrictions or limitations on the use of the site. If no specific time for granting access to the site is identified in the contract, the owner must make the site available within a reasonable time frame; and once the site is available to those performing the work, the owner must not interfere with ongoing access. *Id.* If there are material impairments to the use of the site or limitations that restrict access and adversely affect the ability of the contractors and design professionals to provide their services and perform their work, and such could not reasonably have been determined by authorized site inspections or by what a similarly situated contractor or architect would reasonably be expected to know, unless their respective contracts provide otherwise, the construction parties likely will be entitled to assert claims for whatever additional costs or time they incur as a result of the concealed or unknown conditions or limitations. Although a difficult standard to prove, a private owner that *intentionally* fails to disclose relevant information may be liable for fraud. A similar omission by a public owner may be treated differently, resulting in a claim for breach of contract rather than fraudulent concealment because sovereign entities and public instrumentalities or governmental agencies may be immune from such claims by statute or common law or otherwise be deemed unable to form the requisite willful intent. *Howard Contracting, Inc. v. Macdonald Construction Co. and City of Los Angeles*, 71 Cal. App. 4th 38 (1998).

Accord and Satisfaction. Accord and satisfaction is a legal principle holding that when one party to an agreement accepts from the other party less than the full amount of the debt owed to it as complete payment of the greater obligation, the terms of the original agreement are deemed modified and restated in accordance with the substitute performance. Elements of an accord and satisfaction are "(1) a disputed debt, (2) a clear and unequivocal offer of payment in full satisfaction of the debt, and (3) acceptance and retention of payment by the offeree." *T.J. Trauner Associates, Inc. v. Cooper-Benton, Inc.*, 820 F.2d 643 (3rd Cir. 1987) (interpreting Pennsylvania law). A valid accord and satisfaction has also been described as requiring a bona fide dispute, a mutual agreement or "meeting of the minds" to settle the dispute, consideration for the accord, and acceptance of the payment in satisfaction of the claim or demand. RICHARD J. BEDNAR ET AL., CONSTRUCTION CONTRACTING 676 (George Washington University 1991). No matter what the jurisdiction, there is agreement that to constitute an accord and satisfaction the transaction must result in a new contract. The new agreement is formed by the offer, acceptance, and consideration. The "accord" portion is reached by one party tendering an agreement to discharge the disputed greater obligation by tendering a lesser amount. The "satisfaction" is rendered by the acceptance of the tender, which is the legal consideration that binds the parties to the discharge of the debt. *Hoerstman General Contracting, Inc. v. Hahn*, 696 N.W.2d 708 (Mich. 2005). One typical example of accord and satisfaction occurs where the party disputing the amount of indebtedness writes on a check for a lesser amount that it is "in full settlement" or "in complete and final satisfaction of the claim." While the language must be conspicuous, crossing out or modifying the notation generally has no effect if the payment is negotiated. And once the payment is put through, the lesser amount is accepted and all other claims relating to the subject matter of the accord and satisfaction are released. *Michael L. Helton v. Philip A. Glick Plumbing, Inc.*, 672 S.E.2d 842 (Va. 2009). Thus, an accord and satisfaction may function as an affirmative defense by one party to the claim of indebtedness by another.

Additional Insured. Most parties to an architectural or construction contract carry some form of commercial general liability (CGL) insurance. To further protect themselves, it is common practice for owners, contractors, and subcontractors to require that they be named as additional insureds under the CGL, umbrella, and perhaps other insurance policies of their respective contractors and subcontractors of varying tiers. Additional insured coverage is intended to cover the vicarious liability of the additional insured arising out of the operations of the named insured. 4 PHILLIP L. BRUNER & PATRICK J. O'CONNOR, JR., BRUNER AND O'CONNOR ON CONSTRUCTION LAW § 11.154 (2010). Additional insured status increases the likelihood that claims that eventually may not be covered will, however, be defended by the applicable additional insured carrier. If the additional insured coverage is primary and noncontributory, the additional insured's own insurance will be applied only to excess coverage and may never need to be implicated. When, as is common in a construction-related accident, multiple policies may apply to a loss, the wording of the construction contract and the applicable policies will be critical in determining whose coverage applies in what order and on what basis. NEAL J. SWEENEY, CONSTRUCTION LAW UPDATE §§ 7.01–7.04, 7.08 (Aspen 2008).

Additional insured status confers several benefits. Additional insured status means that insurance limits over and above those already carried under the additional insured's own policies should be available to satisfy claims. The additional insured also should be provided a defense without the necessity of satisfying the deductible under the additional insured policy. Moreover, the payment of defense costs or damages under the additional insured policy should not affect the additional insured's experience ratings or future premiums. In many jurisdictions, the designated carrier risks bad faith claims if it fails to immediately defend the additional insured so long as the complaint at issue contains any factual allegations remotely within the protections of the insurance policy. This may be the case even though there has not yet been a determination of coverage, the complaint asserts claims outside of the coverage or within an exclusion, or the claim is groundless or ultimately held to be without merit. *BP Air Conditioning Corp. v. One Beacon Insurance Group*, 8 N.Y.3d 708, 714, 840 N.Y.S.2d 302 (2007). The additional insured also may have access to coverage for claims that manifest themselves many years later, even if the named insured has since gone out of business, so long as the additional insured endorsement provides coverage for "products/completed operations" and not just for "ongoing operations" and does not exclude the extended coverage elsewhere.

Broad endorsements providing sweeping coverage of additional insureds may not be available in all jurisdictions. Insurance may be strictly regulated in a particular state and some states require the permissible scope of coverage not to exceed the terms permitted by their respective construction anti-indemnity statutes. Other endorsements attempt to limit the additional insured's rights to those based on its vicarious liability arising out of the named insured's acts or omissions. Very precise understanding of the meaning of additional insured status and whether such is negotiable is critical in every locality that is potentially implicated.

Adjudication. An adjudication is the legal process of resolving a dispute or the process of judicially deciding a case. *APAC-Atlantic, Inc. v. Lake Developers, II, LLC*, 3:08-CV-449 2009 U.S. Dist. LEXIS 854 (E.D. Tenn. 2009). Examples of an adjudication include the entry of a decree in a court proceeding, or the judgment or decision given in the proceeding. An adjudication indicates that the claims of the parties have been considered and determined. WEST'S ENCYCLOPEDIA OF AMERICAN LAW (Thompson Gale 2d ed. 2005), *available at* www.answers.com/topic/adjudication-2. An adjudication may also be referred to as summary adjudication, summary judgment, or partial summary judgment.

Summary judgment is appropriate when it is demonstrated that there exists no genuine issue as to any material fact and that the moving party is entitled to judgment as a matter of law. If the moving party meets its initial responsibility, the burden shifts to the opposing party to establish that a genuine issue as to any material fact actually does exist. It is sufficient that the opposing party establish that the claimed factual dispute be shown to require a jury or judge to resolve the parties' differing versions of the truth at trial. *Centex Homes v. Financial Pacific Insurance Co.*, No. CV F 07-00567 AWI 2009 U.S. Dist. LEXIS 117025 (E.D. Cal. 2009).

"The adjudicative process is governed by formal rules of evidence and procedures. Its objective is to reach a reasonable settlement of the controversy at hand. . . . A hearing in which the parties are given an opportunity to present their evidence and arguments is essential to an adjudication." WEST'S ENCYCLOPEDIA, *supra*. In the construction context, adjudication often takes place before an administrative agency or under an alternative dispute resolution proceeding, such as arbitration. The arbitration proceeding may be a creature of statute or contract, or a combination of both.

Agency. Agency encompasses a wide and diverse range of relationships and circumstances. "Common-law agency" or "true agency" is defined as the fiduciary relationship that arises when one person (a "principal") manifests assent to another person (an "agent") that the agent shall act on the principal's behalf and subject to the principal's control, and the agent manifests assent or otherwise consents so to act. RESTATEMENT (THIRD) OF AGENCY §§ 1.01, 1.02 (2005).

Agency is generally a question of fact to be determined by the trier of fact. The test to be applied in determining whether there existed an agency relationship based on actual authority is whether the alleged principal exercised a right of control over the manner of the alleged agent's performance. Control must be proven; and proof of control requires more than proof of a mere right to determine if the person claimed to be an agent is conforming to the requirements of a contract. *Helen Lee v. YES of Russellville, Inc.*, 858 So. 2d 250 (Ala. 2003).

In construction projects, the question of agency often comes up when a party has engaged another individual or entity to render certain decisions or undertake specified obligations. Program Managers or Construction Managers (CMs) generally act either in an agency role, in which event the CM is a representative of the owner and acts in a consultative and advisory role but assumes no responsibility for delivering the construction of the project. The owner remains liable for the acts and omissions of the Construction Manager and for engaging a contractor or otherwise causing the project to be completed. A CM at-risk may provide preconstruction services but it is an independent contractor and is responsible for performing the work to the same extent as a traditional general or prime contractor. Design professionals and project managers or project representatives also may be engaged as agents or assume independent liability for performing certain services or work. The participants should evaluate and determine the impact of the relationships under which the parties are engaged, including their respective (1) designated rights and duties, (2) particular work and services, and (3) functions undertaken pursuant to their specific authority.

Alliancing/Alliance Agreement. Alliancing is a form of relational contracting, a project delivery method that concentrates on the relationships between the parties to a construction contract in achieving the project's requirements. It is based on the assumption that how the job is to be done is as important as the task to be completed. Relational contracting in general, and alliancing in particular, encourage the parties to a construction project to move away from the more traditional, confrontational, or adversarial form of contracting toward a more collaborative approach in which the participants work together in good faith.

It is contended by those supporting alliancing that the disputes evident in the construction industry are caused or contributed to by inappropriate allocation of risk, poor project documentation, and imprecise definitions of the parties' respective responsibilities. The alliancing method of project delivery requires improved communication, early resolution of difficulties through negotiation, and incentives for project members to behave with integrity and to make decisions on a best-for-project basis. Key elements of alliancing include assuming collective responsibility for delivering the project, accepting collective ownership of all risks associated with the project, and entering into gainshare/painshare arrangements measured against agreed-upon targets that the parties have jointly committed to achieve.

A pure alliance is an integrated team, undertaking agreed goals under an open-book approach, adopting unanimous decision-making processes on all key project issues. The concept of collective assumption of risk applies in alliance contracts where the alliance participants bear all risks equitably (although not equally regarding financial consequences).

Project alliancing is normally used for delivering larger, more complex and challenging, higher-risk projects, including those involving infrastructure and situations where budgets and schedules are limited and the project scope is unclear or uncertain. On the flip side, alliancing advocates discourage its use where project scope can be clearly defined and project risk is more easily manageable. It also is not advisable where the parties are resistant and unlikely to adopt the principles and mind-set described as the alliancing program. Mallesons Stephen Jacques, Asian Project and Construction Update (April 19, 2003), http://www.mallesons.com/publications/Asian_Projects_and_Construction_Update/6527680W.htm.

The benefits of alliancing are said to include creation of a commercial framework that aligns the interests of the parties; improved risk management, especially in environments of uncertain project requirements (but with potential for some principals to accept more and greater risks than in traditional projects), Iain Murdoch, Does Alliancing Matter?, PLC Construction, (Nov. 19, 2008), http://construction.practicallaw.com/blog/construction/plc; earlier involvement in design activities providing greater visibility of project costs and improved decision-making outcomes (although Murdoch, *supra*, also notes that alliancing requires more resources to be effective and there are greater risks of deadlocks); reductions in resources to administer proposals; improved project performance and innovation; better staff working conditions; maximizing of industry participation in tender evaluations (bids and proposals); and greater transparency. *See* Victoria, Australia, Department of Treasury and Finance, Project Alliancing, http://www.dtf.vic.gov.au/CA25713E0002EF43/pages/project-alliancing.

Some concerns have been raised that the limited number of alliancing projects, their limited scope, and the jurisdictions in which they have been undertaken (Australia, New Zealand, United Kingdom, and Canada) make it exceedingly difficult to test the various assumptions being asserted, and that (1) extensive experience, (2) establishment of metrics, monitoring of projects and wide-ranging research, and (3) broad-based, collective efforts to develop a robust form of contract are necessary before the value of alliancing may be fully understood and the essential terms of an effective alliance agreement may be formulated. *Id. See also* Murdoch, *supra*, and EVANS & PECK AND MELBOURNE UNIVERSITY, IN PURSUIT OF ADDITIONAL VALUE, A BENCHMARKING STUDY INTO ALLIANCING IN THE AUSTRALIAN PUBLIC SECTOR (2009).

Alternative Dispute Resolution (ADR). ADR refers to methods of resolving disputes other than filing a lawsuit in the traditional fashion, and many different procedures fall under the umbrella of alternative dispute resolution procedures, including arbitration, mediation, dispute review boards, project neutrals, and partnering. As a general rule, the parties to a dispute have specified an ADR method of resolution of disputes in their contracts or must both otherwise mutually agree to some form of ADR to resolve their dispute. Alternative dispute resolution is often promoted as a desirable alternative to settling construction disputes in court proceedings, given the high cost of litigation, the extensive amount of time it takes to reach a judgment, the expense of discovery and responding to motions, and the potential that the triers of fact and determiners of law may be wholly unfamiliar with the significant issues facing the construction industry. NEAL J. SWEENEY, CONSTRUCTION LAW UPDATE § 10.03 (Aspen 2008). Construction disputes often are multiparty and multi-issue, and ADR, when used creatively, is thought to serve as a vehicle to reduce dramatically the amount of time and cost associated with litigation, while at the same time enhancing the chances of salvaging or continuing future business relationships between the parties. ALBERT DIB, LEGAL HANDBOOK FOR ARCHITECTS, ENGINEERS AND CONTRACTORS 449–56 (Clark Boardman Callaghan 1993).

In construction, arbitration has been in widespread use for decades and is a feature of many standard industry contracts, including for a long time in the American Institute of Architects (AIA) form documents. However, the most recent editions of the AIA documents (2007) for the first time provide for contractual parties to select either litigation or arbitration before the AAA for resolving construction disputes. Mediation is assuming a prominent role in industry agreements, and remains an essential element of ADR in the AIA form documents.

Issues of concern to parties to ADR proceedings include (1) the risk of disclosing proprietary or confidential information without reasonable protections, (2) revealing trial strategies that prejudice a later representation, (3) the need to craft the rules and procedures under which disputes are determined or risk being subject to complex rules or discovery procedures similar to those in litigation or being bound to such minimal process that the intent of the parties cannot be realized, and (4) being bound by decision-makers ill prepared to understand or adequately address the disputes before them and permitted to issue conclusory opinions with little or no explanation and without being bound to the contract terms (nor sometimes the law). Nonetheless, if decision-makers are carefully selected and applicable rules are crafted by the parties in advance of any disputes, the opportunity to have a judgment rendered fairly, settlement reached swiftly and economically, in a forum other than litigation in court, with increasing numbers of skilled and dedicated neutrals promoting civility and advancing the success of the project and parties, continues to make ADR a popular alternative to litigation in many situations.

American Arbitration Association (AAA). The AAA was founded in 1926, following enactment of the Federal Arbitration Act, with the specific goal of helping to implement arbitration as an out-of-court solution to resolving disputes. It is a not-for-profit organization, providing a variety of dispute resolution services, as well as educational programs. AAA is one of the largest full-service alternative dispute resolution (ADR) providers, addressing disputes involving many areas, including mediation and arbitration proceedings under fast-track, regular-track, and large, complex case rules for construction, commercial, international trade, consumer, and financial services conflicts. American Arbitration Association website, www.adr.org. The AAA provides administrative services in the United States and many countries around the globe through its International Centre for Dispute Resolution (ICDR), established in 1996.

The AAA's administrative services include assisting in the appointment of mediators and arbitrators, setting hearings, and providing users with information on dispute resolution options. AAA arbitrators, or "neutrals," are lawyers as well as nonlawyers who the AAA claims possess years of industry-specific knowledge and experience. In practice, there is considerable debate whether nonlawyer panel members are as informed and capable of understanding contract provisions as the complexity of construction disputes demands today. The American Arbitration Association University (AAAU), found at www.aaauonline.org, provides information on training classes, an online bookstore, and a reference center, as well as the arbitration statutes of all 50 states, federal statutes, and international conventions on arbitration. (*See* www.construction-weblinks.com).

In agreements that include a clause referring to AAA rules, either party may file a request for arbitration or mediation with the AAA in the event of a dispute. In the absence of such a clause, parties may file a case with the AAA if there is mutual consent to do so. Administration of the case, from filing to closing, begins when a case is filed with the AAA through one of its offices nationwide or via the Internet through AAA's online system.

American Bar Association (ABA). The ABA, founded in 1878, is the largest voluntary professional association in the world. Membership is open to lawyers admitted to practice and in good standing before the bar of any state or territory of the United States. Individuals who are not admitted to practice law but have an interest in the work of the ABA are eligible for membership as associates. The mission of the ABA is to serve equally its members, the legal profession, and the public by defending liberty and delivering justice as the national representative of the legal profession. Members of the ABA may join groups within the association specific to areas of the law or business. Presently, these groups consist of 23 sections, 5 divisions, and 6 interdisciplinary forums. Each group varies in size, internal structure, and membership. The first ABA section was created in 1893 and was the Section of Legal Education and Admissions to the Bar. American Bar Association website, www.abanet.org.

In the advancement of its mission, the ABA provides law school accreditation, continuing legal education, information about the law, programs to assist lawyers and judges in their work, and initiatives to improve the legal system for the public. In order to exercise its accrediting functions, the ABA had to receive authorization from the Secretary of the U.S. Department of Education. *See e.g., Thomas M. Cooley Law School v. ABA,* 459 F.3d 705 (6th Cir. 2006); 20 U.S.C. § 1099B (2010). Accreditation by the ABA is essential for a law school's degree to satisfy the requirements of bar admission authorities nationwide. *Appeal of Murphy,* 393 A.2d 369, 372 (Pa. 1978).

American Institute of Architects (AIA). The AIA was formed in 1857. The AIA's stated goal is to serve as the voice of the architecture profession and as a resource for its members in service to society. Membership is open to individuals licensed to practice architecture in any state or territory of the United States, students, individuals who hold an architecture license or equivalent from a non–U.S. licensing authority, and individuals who share a special interest in the built environment as a professional colleague or enthusiast. The AIA also offers a special partnership with companies that are building product manufacturers, service providers to architects, or trade associations. Members may join member groups or communities within the AIA, including communities on the Web, knowledge communities, an international program, and career-stage groups.

The AIA publishes more than 100 administrative forms and contracts. The AIA published its first contract document, the Uniform Contract, in 1888. AIA contract documents are intended for nationwide use and are not specific to the law of any one state, although the AIA markets its documents as providing "a solid basis of contract provisions that are enforceable under the existing law at the time of publication." American Institutes of Architects website: www.aia .org. The drafting process is based on the input of the Documents Committee, practicing architects appointed based on their experience, regional diversity, and variety of practices.

The AIA is governed by a Board of Directors. The AIA's Code of Ethics states guidelines for the conduct of its members and is enforced by the National Ethics Council, which consists of seven members appointed by the Board of Directors. The Code of Ethics applies only to members of the AIA. *See* the American Institute of Architects' website, www.aia.org.

American Subcontractors Association (ASA). The ASA is a not-for-profit national membership trade association of approximately 5,500 subcontractors, specialty trade contractors, and suppliers in the construction industry. It is dedicated to representing its participants in the construction industry through advocacy, leadership, education, and networking. Any person, firm, or corporation that in the normal course of business furnishes subcontract labor and/or materials to the construction industry or provides a service to such subcontractors or material suppliers is eligible for regular membership in the Association. However, engineers, architects, general contractors, construction managers, and construction owners may not attain regular membership status in the ASA.

The mission of the ASA is to amplify the voice of and lead trade contractors to improve the business environment for the construction industry and to serve as a steward for the community. The Foundation of the American Subcontractors Association (FASA) is the educational arm of the ASA. It is an independent entity devoted to quality educational information and provides financial support to develop materials that promote business practices throughout the construction industry. The American Subcontractors Association website is at www.asaonline.com.

Americans With Disabilities Act (ADA). A federal statutory scheme, the ADA was enacted in 1990 and codified at 42 U.S.C. § 12181 et seq. Only Title II, which deals with provision of public services and state and local governments, and Title III, which covers public accommodations, services, and transportation provided by private entities, are applicable in a construction context generally. With respect to construction projects, the ADA, as it is usually called, requires places of public accommodation and commercial facilities to provide equivalent access to persons with disabilities.

The ADA Accessibility Guidelines (ADAAG) are developed and evaluated by the Federal Architectural and Transportation Barriers Compliance Board—also known as the Access Board—and set forth the technical requirements for various building components such as doorway widths, toilet and sink heights, and slopes for various ramp lengths. U.S. ACCESS BOARD, ADA ACCESSIBILITY GUIDELINES FOR BUILDINGS AND FACILITIES, http://www.access-board.gov/adaag/html/adaag.htm (last visited Jan. 25, 2010). ADAAG applies to places of public accommodation and commercial facilities (28 C.F.R. § 36.406) and to state and local government facilities (28 C.F.R. pt. 35) through Department of Justice regulations and to public transportation facilities through Department of Transportation regulations (49 C.F.R. PT. 37). However, private clubs—as defined by Title II of the Civil Rights Act of 1964, 42 U.S.C. § 2000a(e)—and religious entities are exempt from the requirements of Title III of the ADA. 42 U.S.C. § 12187.

The ADAAG are incorporated into the applicable building codes in each jurisdiction, which must be approved by the federal government for compliance before becoming effective. 28 C.F.R. § 36.602. States may alter the ADAAG requirements and recommendations, but only to cause the requirements to be more stringent than those set forth on the federal level. 28 C.F.R. § 36.103(c). After a building is complete, third parties with proper standing to sue may bring lawsuits against building owners for noncompliance with the ADAAG. 28 C.F.R. § 36.501.

Different standards for compliance with the ADAAG apply depending on whether the project is newly constructed or is an alteration of an existing facility. The ADA requires all buildings that are newly constructed to comply with all requirements for accessibility set forth in the ADAAG and the applicable building code. 28 C.F.R. § 36.401. The ADA also requires any alteration of places of public accommodation or commercial facilities to be made in compliance with the ADAAG to the "maximum extent feasible." 28 C.F.R. § 36.402(c). The regulations define feasibility as meaning that the alteration must comply with ADAAG unless it is "virtually impossible to comply fully with applicable accessibility standards through a planned alteration." *Id.*

Arbitration. Arbitration is a dispute resolution process by which parties agree through a contract to refer certain disputes to a panel of one or more selected persons called the arbitrator(s), who typically have specific industry knowledge, for adjudication and rendering of an award. Arbitration has been common in the construction industry for many years, and the widely used American Institute of Architects (AIA) form contracts included arbitration using the American Arbitration Association (AAA) Construction Industry Arbitration Rules as the method for dispute resolution prior to the issuance of the 2007 version. AIA Document A201-1997, General Conditions of the Contract of Construction,

§ 4.6.1 (1997). The 2007 AIA form contracts include arbitration as an option for dispute resolution. AIA Document A101-2007, Standard Form of Agreement Between Owner and Contractor, § 6.2 (2007).

Arbitration is intended to provide a private forum for the parties to resolve their dispute and attempt to avoid protracted and costly litigation. Both the courts and the Federal Arbitration Act (FAA) strongly favor arbitration and encourage enforcement of agreements to arbitrate. *See, e.g.*, 9 U.S.C. § 2 (making agreements to arbitrate "valid, irrevocable, and enforceable"); *Green Tree Financial Corp.–Alabama v. Randolph*, 531 U.S. 79, 91 (2000) ("liberal federal policy favoring arbitration agreements"); *City of Bridgeport v. Kasper Group, Inc.*, 899 A.2d 523 (Conn. 2006) (citing liberal state policies favoring enforcement of arbitration agreements).

In the international construction context, numerous organizations have promulgated their own rules for arbitrating disputes related to projects outside the United States. These organizations include, among others, the International Chamber of Commerce International Court of Arbitration, the London Court of International Arbitration, the International Centre for Dispute Resolution, the AAA, and the Singapore International Arbitration Centre. While many of these organizations do not focus specifically on construction disputes, many construction contracts for international projects will incorporate a specific organization's rules to define how any disputes that arise may be resolved through arbitration.

An arbitration award, once rendered, may be confirmed by a court of competent jurisdiction, resulting in a judgment in favor of the prevailing party. Because of the strong policy in favor of enforcing arbitral awards, the FAA, for example, provides only very limited grounds for overturning an arbitration award in a subsequent court proceeding. These grounds include instances where (1) an award was procured by corruption, fraud, or undue means; (2) there is evident partiality or corruption in the arbitration; (3) the arbitration panel refuses to hear pertinent evidence or refuses to postpone the hearing on good cause shown; or (4) the arbitration panel exceeds its powers. 9 U.S.C. § 10(a). An award may be modified in the event of an evident material miscalculation, an evident material mistake, or an imperfection in a matter of form not affecting the merits. 9 U.S.C. § 11. Even if parties to an arbitration agreement agree to broader grounds for a court to review an award, such an agreement will not be enforced under the procedures set forth in the FAA. *See Hall Street Associates, L.L.C. v. Mattel, Inc.*, 552 U.S. 576 (2008) (limiting grounds for overturning awards under the FAA to those set forth in FAA sections 10 and 11). Most states have codified similar arbitration acts or codes governing arbitration, including procedures for confirmation and challenging awards in state courts. *See* Ga. Code Ann. § 9-1-1 et seq., Fla. Stat. §§ 682.01–682.22, Utah Code Ann. 78B-1-101–78B-11-131. One should review the applicable state's arbitration code or law as part of the arbitration process, including the procedures and grounds for confirming or challenging arbitration awards and other matters governing arbitration in state courts.

Architect. An architect is a person who designs buildings and their ornamentation, drafts and issues specifications for the particular project, and provides administrative services in regard to the project's construction. In all states, either the term "Architect" or the term "Architecture" is statutorily defined, and every state requires architects to be licensed by a central licensure board. G. William Myers, State Regulation of the Design Professional, in Design Professional and Construction Manager Law 1-1 (Stephen A. Hess et al. eds., ABA 2007). For example, one state's statute defines the practice of architecture as including planning, providing preliminary studies, designs, drawings, specifications, and other design documents, and performing construction management and administration of construction contracts. 63 Pa. Cons. Stat. Ann. § 34.3 (West 2006). Architects and architecture must be differentiated from engineering design, which is meant to include work by structural, geotechnical, mechanical, and electrical engineers and their particular disciplines. G. William Myers, *State Regulation of the Design Professional, in* Design Professional and Construction Manager Law 1-1 (Stephen A. Hess et al. eds., ABA 2007).

The architect usually enters into a contract directly with the project's owner, except when the project is a design-build project and the architect is a subcontractor to or an employee of the design-builder. If using the American Institute of Architects (AIA) standard form contract, the AIA Document B141, the architect's services for the owner as a design professional are grouped into six primary categories: project administration, planning and evaluation, design, construction procurement, construction administration, and facility operation. Commentary on AIA Document B141-1997, 5 (American Institute of Architects 1999).

Architect (or Engineer) of Record. The architect (or engineer) of record is the design professional licensed in the jurisdiction in which the project is located whose name or firm's name appears on the building permit and in the public records as the design professional responsible for the project. The design professional's responsibility extends to preparing and applying his or her professional seal to the drawings, specifications, addenda, and bulletins necessary for meeting all local codes. *See Quinn Construction, Inc. v. Skanska USA Building, Inc.*, Civil Action No. 07-406 2008 WL 2389499, *1 (E.D. Pa. June 10, 2008). Placing one's professional seal on the construction drawings is a certification that the drawings and specifications are complete and accurate, and that the structure, if built as designed, will be safe. *See C.H. Guernsey & Co. v. United States*, 65 Fed. Cl. 582, 597 (2005). In some instances, the term is defined by a governmental entity's standard specifications as being the professional responsible for "develop[ing] the criteria and concept for the project, perform[ing] the analysis, and [being] responsible for the preparation of the Contract Documents." *Martin K. Eby Construction Co. v. Jacksonville Transportation Authority*, 436 F. Supp. 2d 1276, 1278 n. 7 (M.D. Fla. 2005) (quoting the Florida DOT Standard Specifications for Road and Bridge Construction).

As-Built Drawings/Record Drawings. Drawings that reflect and represent the actual conditions of the project as it was constructed are often referred to as as-built or record drawings. While the terms "as-built drawings" and "record drawings" may be used interchangeably, the two terms refer to two different sets of drawings depending on which entity—contractor or architect—prepares them. As-built drawings refer to the redline drawings prepared on-site by the contractor, while record drawings are prepared by the architect to reflect accurately the on-site changes the contractor identified in the record drawings. American Institute of Architects Knowledge Resources Team, *Terminology: As-Built Drawings, Record Drawings, Measured Drawings, in* AIA BEST PRACTICES (June 2007). An owner may specify that its contractor must provide as-built drawings for the owner's use at the end of a project. *See Carnes Co., Inc. v. Stone Creek Mechanical, Inc.*, Civil Action No. 07-0406; No. 02-C-0208-C 2003 WL 23198124, *3 (W.D. Wis. July 18, 2003). As-built drawings can be created either during or after construction and are intended to reflect all changes made during the course of construction whether as a result of change orders, to reflect construction tolerances, modifications to allow certain equipment to fit within a particular space or account for other minor changes, or otherwise. These drawings allow the end user of the project to know where plumbing pipes, ductwork, electrical wiring, and other hidden components are located. *See GilbaneBuilding Co. v. Nemours Foundation*, 568 F. Supp. 1085, 1094 (D.C. Del. 1983).

As-Built Schedule. The final project schedule reflecting the actual scope, start and completion dates, and duration of specific activities is called the final as-built schedule. An as-built schedule can be developed as the project is constructed to reflect then current "as-built" conditions. An as-built schedule can be developed after a project is complete either from a contemporaneously maintained critical path method (CPM) schedule or through a review of project records. Judah Lifschitz et al., *A Critical Review of the AACEI Recommended Practice for Forensic Schedule Analysis*, CONSTRUCTION LAW., Fall 2009, at 16. The as-built schedule is intended to detail the sequence, dates, and duration of all portions of the completed work and, from there, to determine the critical path of the project. *Id.*

Sources for an as-built schedule often include daily reports, job diaries, meeting minutes, progress reports, interviews with project personnel, and change order files. *See Youngdale & Sons Construction Co. v. United States*, 27 Fed. Cl. 516, 551 (1993). The as-built schedule may serve as the starting point for and the basis of a forensic analysis for a schedule-delay claim. Its limitations lie in the information available; for instance, an after-the-fact as-built schedule is only as accurate as the information on which it is based and, therefore, it may not accurately reflect when and in what sequence the work was performed during the course of the project. *See* Lifschitz et al., *supra.* With modern technology, however, as-built schedules can be updated on the jobsite on a daily basis to match the activities taking place on the project. ROBERT F. CUSHMAN ET AL., CONSTRUCTION DISPUTES: REPRESENTING THE CONTRACTOR § 17.06 (Aspen 3d ed. 2008).

As-Planned Schedule. A contractor's anticipated plan prior to beginning work on the project for executing the construction contract's scope of work from mobilization to completion is referred to as the original as-planned schedule. Typically, the original as-planned schedule is the authoritative record of how a contractor expects to proceed with the performance of its work and reflects the planned work activities, sequence, and manpower required for performing those activities. ROBERT F. CUSHMAN ET AL., CONSTRUCTION DISPUTES: REPRESENTING THE CONTRACTOR § 17.06 (Aspen 3d ed. 2008). To ensure that the schedule contains sufficient detail, specifications for the project's schedule may contain limitations on how long the durations for specific work may be. *Id.* An as-planned schedule can be prepared for different work scope and trade work.

The as-planned schedule generally is provided to the owner or its representative and, after approval, becomes the contractor's formal performance plan for the project. 5 PHILIP L. BRUNER & PATRICK J. O'CONNOR, JR., BRUNER AND O'CONNOR ON CONSTRUCTION LAW § 15:129 (2002). The as-planned schedule also may provide support for certain types of delay claims. Using an as-planned schedule for a delay analysis is appropriate only when the as-planned schedule includes sufficient details regarding the contractor's initial plan for carrying out the work. *Id.* Courts recognize the limitations of an as-planned schedule, however, as being "a mere projection of what might occur with respect to construction of the project and not historical fact." *Youngdale & Sons Construction Co. v. United States*, 27 Fed. Cl. 516, 551 (1993).

Assignment. The term "assignment" generally refers to the transfer of certain contractual rights, such as warranty rights or the right to receive payment, by one party to another. In the construction industry, it is not uncommon for an owner to require its contractor to assign all equipment warranties to the owner as a condition for receiving final payment. Further, some contractual termination provisions require a general contractor to assign all subcontracts to the owner in the event that the contract is terminated, which allows the owner to continue and complete the project. AIA Document A201-2007, General Conditions of the Contract of Construction, § 5.4 (2007). Another example of an assignment common in the construction industry involves factoring agreements. In a factoring agreement, a contractor assigns its right to receive certain contractual payments to a factoring company; in return, the factoring company provides the total contract amount—less a percentage of the total as the company's fee—immediately to the contractor. *See U.S. Fidelity & Guaranty Co. v. Madison Financial Corp.*, No. 01 Civ. 3998CM 2002 WL 31731020, *1 (S.D.N.Y. Dec. 4, 2002); 3 PHILIP L. BRUNER & PATRICK J. O'CONNOR, JR., BRUNER AND O'CONNOR ON CONSTRUCTION LAW § 8:64 (2002). Some contracts may contain a provision expressly prohibiting a contractor or subcontractor from assigning or transferring any of its rights in a contract to another entity. In these instances, a subcontractor may lose its right to file and perfect a lien on the project owner's property. *See Benning Construction Co. v. Dykes Paving & Construction Co.*, 426 S.E.2d 564 (Ga. 1993).

Associated General Contractors of America (AGC). The AGC is a membership trade organization with chapters located throughout the United States that represent commercial contractors, including general contractors, specialty contractors, and service providers and suppliers through lobbying and litigation, educational services, and interaction with other trade organizations. The AGC was established in 1918 by request of President Woodrow Wilson, with its stated purpose being to serve construction professionals in the United States by promoting the skill, integrity, and responsibility of its members involved in the construction industry. The Associated General Contractors of America, About AGC, http://www.agc.org/cs/about_agc (last visited Feb. 2, 2010). The AGC carries out its mission through its core services, which include

19

efforts relating to lobbying and government relations, providing educational and safety programs, and promoting better industry/owner relations. *See, e.g.*, The Associated General Contractors of America, Advocacy, http://www.agc.org/cs/advocacy (last visited Feb. 2, 2010); Education & Training, http://www.agc.org/cs/career_development (last visited Feb. 2, 2010).

As a part of AGC's mission, individual AGC chapters occasionally represent their members' interests in litigation challenging certain regulations or statutes affecting the construction industry. *See Northeastern Florida Chapter of Associated General Contractors of America v. City of Jacksonville*, 508 U.S. 656 (1993) (challenging city ordinance according preferential treatment to certain minority-owned businesses in the award of city contracts on behalf of its membership). In addition, some chapters assist their members by negotiating collective bargaining agreements with the labor unions representing workers. *See Operating Engineers Local No. 49 Health & Welfare Fund v. Ronglien Excavating, Inc.*, Civil No. 09-65 (DWF/RLE); 2009 WL 2568611, *1 (D. Minn. Aug. 18, 2009) (litigating union collective bargaining agreement negotiated by AGC); Local 513 *International Union of Operating Engineers v. Marshall Contracting, L.L.C.*, No. 4:09-CV-23 (CEJ) 2009 WL 2175979, *1 (Mo. July 2, 2009) (same).

Associated Schools of Construction (ASC). ASC is an international association representing different disciplines of academic and industry professionals supporting the development and advancement of institutional construction education and research. ASC, headquartered in Hattiesburg, Mississippi, was founded in 1965 to provide accredited colleges and universities offering four-year (minimum) degree programs having a major emphasis on building construction. *See* Associated Schools of Construction, http://www.ascweb.org (last visited Feb. 2, 2010). ASC publishes a scholarly journal entitled *International Journal of Construction Education and Research* (replacing their *Journal of Construction Education* in 2004). *See* Int'l J. Construction Educ. & Res., Aims and Scope, *available at* http://www.ascjournal.ascweb.org/purpose.html (last visited Feb. 2, 2010).

B

Backcharge. In construction, the term "backcharge" refers to costs assessed by an owner against a contractor, or a contractor against a subcontractor, to recover the expense that the owner or contractor (as applicable) would not have incurred but for the contractor's or subcontractor's actions or inactions. Typical scenarios resulting in the assessment of backcharges by a contractor against a subcontractor include (a) a contractor either performs or pays another to perform work necessary to correct work already in place that is damaged by a subcontractor (*see Brandt v. Schal Associates, Inc.*, 854 F.2d 948, 950 n.2 (7th Cir. 1988)); (b) a subcontractor delays the general contractor's work significantly (*id.*); (c) a contractor must correct a subcontractor's defective work (*see United States v. A. J. Rife*, 224 F.2d 600, (5th Cir. 1955)); (d) a contractor must supplement a subcontractor's forces or perform work itself to ensure that the subcontractor's work is performed in a timely manner (*see Oldcastle Precast, Inc. v. United States Fidelity & Guaranty Co.*, 458 F. Supp. 2d 131, 143–44 (S.D.N.Y. 2006)); (e) a subcontractor, contrary to its contractual obligation to do so, fails or refuses to maintain a clean jobsite (*id.*); or, (f) a subcontractor fails or refuses to perform warranty or punch list work and, as a result, the contractor must perform the work instead (*see United States v. Travelers Casualty & Surety Co. of America*, 423 F. Supp. 2d 1016, 1025–26 (D. Ariz. 2006)).

Bad Faith. A party acts with bad faith when it acts with a dishonest purpose, an interested motive, or ill will, or when its denial of liability is frivolous or unfounded. Typically, if there is a reasonable basis for contesting a claim or a party's actions are premised on an honest mistake concerning his or her rights or obligations, there is no bad faith. *See Lexmark Carpet Mills, Inc. v. Color Concepts, Inc.*, 583 S.E.2d 458 (Ga. Ct. App. 2003); *Rapid Group, Inc. v. Yellow Cab of Columbus, Inc.*, 557 S.E.2d 420 (Ga. Ct. App. 2001). Further, in many states, a party's bad faith may give rise to a claim in litigation for attorneys' fees or costs or have other adverse consequences. *See* O.C.G.A § 13-6-11 (example of statutory attorneys' fees provision). For instance, a project owner's bad faith—or a contractor's bad faith toward its subcontractor—may operate to defeat an attempt to enforce a no-damage-for-delay clause. *See United States ex rel. Wallace v. Flintco Inc.*, 143 F.3d 955 (5th Cir. 1998). Issues concerning bad faith also arise from time to time in the context of an insurer's failure or refusal to fulfill its obligations pursuant to an insurance policy or a surety's failure or refusal to satisfy its obligations pursuant to a performance or payment bond. 4A PHILIP L. BRUNER & PATRICK J. O'CONNOR, JR., BRUNER AND O'CONNOR ON CONSTRUCTION LAW § 12:7 (2009). Finally, if proven, bad faith may serve as a defense to a surety's demand for indemnification from its principal for payments the surety made under a payment or performance bond. *See Fidelity*

21

& Guaranty Insurance Co. v. Star Equipment Corp., 541 F.3d 1 (1st Cir. 2008); *Far West Insurance Co. v. J. Metro Excavating, Inc.*, No. 2:07-CV-11-PRC 2008 WL 859182 (N.D. Ind. Mar. 28, 2008).

Bankruptcy. Generally, a bankruptcy is a single collective judicial proceeding determining the rights of a debtor and his or her creditors arising under Title 11 of the U.S. Bankruptcy Code. The two types of bankruptcies that are encountered in a construction context generally are those arising under Chapter 7 of the Bankruptcy Code, in which the assets of the debtor are liquidated and distributed in pro rata fashion to the debtor's creditors, and those arising under Chapter 11 of the Bankruptcy Code, in which the debtor seeks to reorganize its debts and continue in business. When a petition for bankruptcy is filed, all legal activities adverse to the debtor's rights in property immediately cease pursuant to the Bankruptcy Code's automatic stay provisions. 11 U.S.C. § 362. Consequently, a debtor will be allowed to proceed with a foreclosure proceeding or repossession action, for instance, only if the bankruptcy court provides relief from the automatic stay. *Id.*

Further, creditors of the debtor are required to file their proofs of claim against the debtor's estate with the bankruptcy court in a timely manner. So as not to prefer certain creditors over others, the provisions of the Bankruptcy Code allow for the bankruptcy estate to recover certain types of payments made to creditors within a specified period of time prior to the filing of the bankruptcy petition and include those recovered payments in the estate's assets for later distribution to its creditors. 11 U.S.C. § 547(b).

In the construction context, a bankruptcy filing may have a significant impact on an ongoing construction project, since the debtor has the right either to affirm or to reject its "executory contracts." 11 U.S.C. § 365. Executory contracts include any contract involving substantial performance by both parties to the contract and under which the failure to complete performance would constitute a material breach of the contract. *Id.* Thus, if a contractor has not completed its work in connection with the construction of a building and files for bankruptcy, the contractor has the right to affirm the contract—and, as a result, cure any breaches existing at the time—and continue working on the project or to reject the contract and walk away from the project. 11 U.S.C. § 365(d)(2).

A construction contract may not be terminated solely because of the bankruptcy, making any such contractual clauses in the construction contract void and unenforceable. 11 U.S.C. § 365(e). In such instances, however, any applicable payment and performance bonds remain in effect and are not affected by the automatic stay. *See In re Kora & Williams Corp.*, 97 B.R. 258 (Bankr. D. Md. 1988). In addition, in some states, a properly filed subcontractor's or material-man's lien may be foreclosed directly against the owner of the real property if the contractor is in bankruptcy. *See, e.g.*, O.C.G.A. § 44-11-361.1(a)(4) (allowing subcontractor to forgo suit against contractor if contractor is "adjudicated a bankrupt"). If the owner is in bankruptcy, however, the automatic stay may serve to prevent the foreclosure action. *See In re Bain*, 64 B.R. 581, 583 (Bankr. W.D. Va. 1986).]

Bar Chart. In the construction industry, a bar chart is often used as a scheduling tool; typically, it has rectangular bars with lengths proportional to the values they represent. In construction scheduling, the bar chart is most often a Gantt chart, a type pioneered by Henry L. Gantt. It includes construction activities broken down into a few dozen activity bars (1) placed on a chart in time-related sequences and then colored in as the work is completed to reflect progress, and (2) overlaid with "s" curves to reflect cumulative planned and actual job progress and value of the completed work for payment purposes. A visual picture, valid at any point in time, generally establishes the order and duration in which work activities are to be performed and allows progress and payment to be monitored during performance. 5 PHILIP L. BRUNER & PATRICK J. O'CONNOR, JR., BRUNER AND O'CONNOR ON CONSTRUCTION LAW § 15:4 (2002). Because the bar chart is limited in the information it can convey, it is sometimes used on large projects to supplement (1) Critical Path Method (CPM) work activities in need of further breakdown, or (2) CPM schedules too complex to be readily understood by the trades. J.M. Wickwire & S. Ockman, *Use of Critical Path Method on Contract Claims—2000*, CONSTRUCTION LAW., Oct. 1999, at 12, 17.

Baseball Arbitration. A form of binding arbitration often used in professional sports contracts, baseball arbitration is a unique arbitration process in which the result is the one proposed either by one side or the other. It is sometimes referred to as an "either/or" arbitration because the parties submit their last best offer and demand to the arbitrator, who chooses one or the other. Baseball arbitration is useful in construction cases when the parties feel strongly about the reasonableness of their offer/demand. CARINA Y. OHARA ET AL., FUNDA-MENTALS OF CONSTRUCTION LAW 314 (ABA 2001). In "night" baseball arbitration, the figures are kept confidential from the arbitrator; once the arbitrator renders his or her decision, the figure mathematically closest to the arbitrator's award becomes the binding award.

Best Value Procurement. In the past, public construction contracts were awarded to the responsible contractor that submitted the lowest responsive bid. In the "best value" procurement, now a well-accepted component of public procurement policy, the contracting officer is permitted to make a price/technical tradeoff. Rather than making the award to the lowest-priced technically acceptable offeror, the agency has the discretion to pay a premium for a technically superior offer. Robert S. Brams et al., *Best Value in Federal Construction Contracting*, CONSTRUCTION LAW., Apr. 1999, at 25; Dean B. Thomson & Michael J. Kinzer, *Best Value in State Construction Contracting*, CONSTRUCTION LAW., Apr. 1999, at 31.

Betterment Rule. The Betterment Rule provides that damages for repair or replacement of a defectively designed or constructed item must take into account the fact that the owner had the benefit of the use of that item for a portion of its anticipated useful life. The reduction in damages is premised on the belief that an injured party should not be compensated in excess of its loss. The rule is often used as a defense against the imposition of liability for extra expenses incurred by the second party due to failure of the first party to perform some duty if the extra expense would have been incurred regardless of whether or not the first party failed in the performance of his or her duty. It also excludes enhancements beyond the original requirements or design that give the owner a "better" project than that for which the owner originally expected to pay. 6 PHILIP L. BRUNER & PATRICK J. O'CONNOR, JR., BRUNER AND O'CONNOR ON CONSTRUCTION LAW § 19:26 (2002). Such subsequent enhancements most frequently result from changes in design standards that (1) permit a better or different use of the project than originally contemplated; (2) provide a more durable project than originally contemplated; or (3) otherwise enhance the value of the property beyond its original design intent. *Crescent Coating Co., Inc. v. Berghman*, 480 So. 2d 1013, 1019 (5th Cir. 1985); *525 Main St. Corp. v. Eagle Roofing Co.*, 34 N.J. 251 (1961); *Oakwood Villa Apartments, Inc. v. Gulu*, 9 Mich. App. 568 (1968).

Bid (also known as Tender). An offer to perform the work or supply the goods described in a contract at a specified cost is a bid. More specifically, a bid is a complete and properly signed proposal to do the work, or designated portion thereof, for the sums stipulated therein, supported by data called for by the bidding requirements. CYRIL M. HARRIS, DICTIONARY OF ARCHITECTURE AND CONSTRUCTION 51 (McGraw-Hill 1975).

Bid Bond. A type of performance bond, a bid bond is a form of bid security executed by the bidder, as principal, and by a surety. Cyril M. Harris, Dictionary of Architecture and Construction 51 (McGraw-Hill 1975). It is a form of security that guarantees that the bidder who is awarded the contract will enter into the contract and furnish any performance and payment bonds that are required under the conditions of the bid or contract, or that the bidder will pay damages to the owner arising from the bidder's refusal to enter into the contract. A bid bond is designed to protect the owner in a situation where a low bidder refuses to enter into the contract in accordance with its bid. Bid bonds provide that either the entire penal sum of the bond will be forfeited or that the bond will be forfeited to the extent necessary to protect the owner from loss, i.e., the forfeiture will be the difference between the low bid and the next lowest bid. Steven G.M. Stein, Construction Law ¶ 17.01 (Matthew Bender 2009).

Bid Chiseling. Used to refer to post-bid negotiations by a prime contractor with previously chosen subcontractors who had submitted hard bids to reduce an already low sub-bid price without reduction in the scope of work, bid chiseling is an undesirable practice that can undermine an owner's expectations with respect to the cost of the work. *Oakland-Alameda County Builders' Exch. v. F.P. Lathrop Construction Co.*, 4 Cal. 3d 354 (Cal. 1971). It is a practice sometimes used by a prime contractor to reduce the price a subcontractor will charge in order to secure additional money for the prime contractor.

Bid Protest. The process whereby a disappointed bidder on a public project objects to the award of a contract to another is called a bid protest. On federal jobs, an objector can have two general bases for protest: (1) a defect in the bidding procedures or documents or (2) an irregularity in the evaluation of a bid or award of a contract. Defects of the first type include unduly restrictive specifications, ambiguous bidding documents, and improper procurement procedures. The second ground for protest, irregularities in the evaluation or award of a contract, can be divided into two subcategories: (1) irregularities that result in the improper rejection of the protester's bid, and (2) irregularities that result in the improper acceptance of another bid. These irregularities include such items as failure to sign the bidding documents properly, bids that do not conform to the Invitation for Bids (IFB), and evaluation on grounds other than those described in the IFB. Steven G.M. Stein, Construction Law ¶ 2.03[1] (Matthew Bender 2009). Any protest involving alleged defects or improprieties in bidding documents should be submitted prior to the bid opening or proposal submittal date. 48 C.F.R. § 33.103(e). The protest must be in writing. 48 C.F.R. § 33.101.

Several states have formal protest procedures whereby the disappointed bidder can seek bid protest relief on state and local projects through either the court system or administrative protest procedures. *See* THOMAS J. KELLEHER, JR., COMMON SENSE CONSTRUCTION LAW 77 (Wiley 3rd ed. 2005); *see, e.g.*, City of Atlanta, Procurement and Real Estate Code §§ 5-5111–5-5116; *Amdahl Corp. v. Georgia Department of Administrative Services*, 398 S.E.2d 540 (Ga. 1990); *Ghilotti Construction Co. v. City of Richmond*, 45 Cal. App. 4th 897 (1996); *Lawrence Brunoli, Inc. v. Town of Branford*, 722 A.2d 271 (Conn. 1999).

Bid Shopping (also see "Shopping Bids"). A practice regarded as unethical in the industry, bid shopping is utilized by successful bidders after award to improve contract profitability. It is the use of a subcontractor's low bid already received by a general or prime contractor to pressure other subcontractors into submitting even lower bids. If a lower bid is secured, the general contractor will receive a windfall profit because the savings are usually not passed on to the property owner. Ralph Nash, Jr. & Michael Love, Jr., *Innovations in Federal Construction Contracting*, 45 GEO. WASH. L. REV. 309, 315 (1977). The subcontractor whose bid is used in the initial proposal can seek to avoid bid shopping by insisting that it be irrevocably named in the contract as the project's subcontractor. BLACK'S LAW DICTIONARY 172 (8th ed. 2004).

A companion process, "bid peddling," is an attempt by a subcontractor to undercut known bids already submitted to the general contractor in order to procure the job. *Southern California Acoustics Co. v. C.V. Holder, Inc.*, 71 Cal.2d 719, 726–27 (Cal. 1969). A number of techniques have been developed to deal with the practices of bid shopping, bid peddling, and bid chiseling, although the creation of bid depositories has met with antitrust problems. *See Mechanical Contractors Bid Depository v. Christiansen*, 352 F.2d 817 (10th Cir. 1965); *but see Cullum Electrical & Mechanical, Inc. v. Mechanical Contractors Ass'n of South Carolina*, 436 F. Supp. 418 (D.S.C. 1976). A more successful approach, although it generally applies only to post-award bid shopping, is legislation requiring bidders to submit lists of proposed subcontractors and to employ only those listed. *See* Subcontractor Listing Law, CAL. PUB. CONT. CODE §§ 4101–4113 (Thompson West 2005).

Boiler and Machinery Insurance. A special form of insurance, not offered by all insurers, boiler and machinery insurance covers property boilers, pressure vessels, machinery, piping, and similar equipment during installation and until final acceptance. Standard property insurance often excludes accidental damage to such items because the risk associated with them is unique. 2 PHILIP L. BRUNER & PATRICK J. O'CONNOR, JR., BRUNER AND O'CONNOR ON CONSTRUCTION LAW § 5:226 (2002).

Bond. Generally speaking, bonds in the construction context refer to a tri-party agreement wherein a performing or obligated party (referred to often as the "principal") and an independent surety company jointly bind themselves to an "obligee" or party for whose protection the bond is being issued (such as the project owner) for the payment or performance of specified obligations of the principal. Common examples of bonds in the construction context are a bid bond, a payment bond, and a performance bond. Surety bonds involve a shifting of risk from one party to another for a fee; the fee is calculated to spread the risk out over many parties. Bonds differ from insurance in one significant respect: while insurance, generally, irrevocably shifts the risks covered by the policy to the insurance company, bonds only shift the risk to a surety company, which retains a right to seek reimbursement of any loss from the party whose performance or risk was guaranteed. STEVEN G.M. STEIN, CONSTRUCTION LAW ¶ 17.01 (Matthew Bender 2009).

Bonds often are statutorily required for public construction projects at the federal, state, and local levels. *See* 40 U.S.C. §§ 3131–3134; ALA. CODE § 39-1-1; CAL. CIV. CODE §§ 3247–3252, GA. CODE ANN. §§ 13-10-1 to 13-10-2, 13-10-40 to 13-10-6; 36-91-1to 36-91-2, 36-91-40, 36-91-70 to 36-91-75; N.C. GEN. STAT. 44A-25; S.C. ANN. § 11-25-3020.

Bonds required for private projects are essentially private contractual undertakings in which the terms of the bond will be determinative.

Bond claims, whether statutory, private, or common law, involve various notice and claim requirements, so it is important to review the statutory law and the terms of the bonds for compliance and applicability.

Breach of Contract. Failure or refusal of a party to perform its obligations under a contract is known as breach of contract. JAMES ACRET, CALIFORNIA CONSTRUCTION LAW MANUAL § 1:53 (Thomson West 6th ed. 2005). A total, major, material, or substantial breach of contract constitutes a failure to properly perform a material part of the contract. A partial or minor breach of contract is merely a slight deviation from the bargained-for performance. The differences in the types of breach are significant in ascertaining the kinds of remedies and damages available to the aggrieved party. 3 WEST'S ENCYCLOPEDIA OF AMERICAN LAW 180 (Thomson Gale 2d ed. 2005).

Brooks Act. A U.S. federal law passed in 1972, the Brooks Act regulates federal procurement of design services. 40 U.S.C.A. § 541. It requires the initial selection to be based upon demonstrated professional qualifications and experience rather than price. After the top-ranked architect is chosen, the federal agency seeks to negotiate a contract with the architect. If this negotiation is unsuccessful, the agency negotiates with the next ranked architect, and the next after that. JONATHAN J. SWEET, SWEET ON CONSTRUCTION INDUSTRY CONTRACTS: MAJOR AIA DOCUMENTS § 4.04 (2009). Some states have similar statutes. *See* CAL. GOV'T CODE §§ 4525–4529.5 (West 1995).

Build-Operate-Transfer (BOT) Contract. The build-operate-transfer (BOT) contract is a form of public-private agreement that is utilized by governmental agencies pursuant to a sponsoring or authorizing statute, also referred to as a "privatization" statute, which allows the state or political subdivision to enter into a BOT contract with an operator for the acquisition, planning, design, development, reconstruction, repair, maintenance, or financing of any public facility on behalf of the governmental body. An example of such a statutory scheme at the state level is that found in Indiana Code § 5-23-1-1–5-23-7-2. Under a BOT contract, the governmental agency retains ownership of the underlying real estate and leases the public facility from the operator. The operator constructs, operates, and maintains the facility for a set period of time, and then transfers the facility back to the governmental agency at an established future date. The BOT contract also identifies the responsibilities and cost and revenue sharing of the agency and the operator.

This delivery method also is frequently utilized by foreign governmental entities on large infrastructure projects where the entity requires assistance to finance the development. 2 PHILIP L. BRUNER & PATRICK J. O'CONNOR, JR., BRUNER AND O'CONNOR ON CONSTRUCTION LAW § 6:9 (2002). A foreign BOT highway project was mentioned in *Jovanovic v. U.S.-Algeria Business Council*, 531 F. Supp. 2d 103, 107 (D.C. 2008). Under the BOT delivery method, "a lender offers structured project financing to a contractor who largely designs, constructs, and maintains the (often public) infrastructure project." RICHARD K. ALLEN & STANLEY A. MARTIN, CONSTRUCTION LAW HANDBOOK § 41.03[B], 1661 (Aspen 2d ed. 2009). The contractor, often a group of private investors that form a special-purpose enterprise, first obtains the authority or concession to build and operate the project from the agency or entity with oversight responsibility for that particular utility or sector of the economy. 2 BRUNER & O'CONNOR, *supra*, at 508–509; ALLEN & MARTIN, *supra*, at 1663. Upon completion of construction, the contractor will operate the project and be paid for doing so for a fixed period of time. Allen & Martin, *supra*, at 1663. At the conclusion of this operation period, the financing costs and the contractor's stipulated fee or return on its investment will have been paid from the earnings of the project, and the facility is then transferred back to the governmental entity. 2 BRUNER & O'CONNOR at 508.

The BOT contract essentially bundles construction, operation, and maintenance functions together into one party, but presupposes that the contractor (the special-purpose entity) is equally adept at construction and operation/maintenance.

Build-Own-Operate (BOO). Build-own-operate (BOO) is a full privatization delivery method and a variation on build-operate-transfer (BOT). 2 PHILIP L. BRUNER & PATRICK J. O'CONNOR, JR., BRUNER AND O'CONNOR ON CONSTRUCTION LAW § 6:10 (2002). The primary distinction between BOO and BOT resides with the elimination of the transfer element. As a result, the governmental entity originally responsible for the utility or sector of infrastructure the project serves never takes legal possession or ownership of the project. *Id.* However, because the contractor (often a special-purpose entity consisting of private investors) has undertaken a project that is providing an essential service (i.e., a traditionally governmental service), the government maintains a level of involvement in the project. *See, e.g., Crowell v. Ionics, Inc.*, 343 F. Supp. 2d 1, 3–4 (D. Mass. 2004); *Maez v. Chevron Texaco Corp.*, No. C 04-00790 2006 WL 1305221, *1 (D. Cal. 2006).

Build-Own-Transfer. A build-own-transfer project delivery method is quite similar to "build-operate-transfer" (BOT), with the primary distinction being that ownership of the project resides with the special-purpose entity responsible for constructing, operating, and maintaining the facility during the concession period. The ownership of the facility is returned to the government after a fixed period of time, and the revenues generated from operating the facility are used to repay lenders and to provide a profit to the firm that built the project. J.K. YATES, GLOBAL ENGINEERING AND CONSTRUCTION § 5.7 (2007). Build-own-transfer has emerged as one of the more popular global financing arrangements, particularly in developed countries where it is used to finance infrastructure reconstruction or as an adjunct or replacement to privatization. *Id.* at 117.

Builder's Risk Insurance/All-Risk Insurance. Builder's risk insurance is a form of property loss insurance purchased to cover the risk of loss to, or damage to, the construction work while the project is under construction. Under common law, the contractor assumes the risk of loss or damage to the construction work until that work is completed and the project turned over to the owner. DAVID L. LEITNER ET AL., LAW AND PRACTICE OF INSURANCE COVERAGE LITIGATION § 45:25 (2009). Builder's risk coverage insures the named insured (such as the owner or contractor) against this liability and risk of loss. However, because commercial general liability (CGL) policies typically exclude from coverage damages to the insured's work, a separate type of insurance or coverage is required.

Builder's risk insurance typically covers property damage to the "structure under construction, materials, fixtures, supplies, machinery, and debris removal" resulting from "fire, lightning, wind and hail, leakage from fire protection equipment, smoke, aircraft and vehicles, riot, vandalism, and civil or military authority." GREGG BUNDSCHUH, OWNER'S GUIDE TO CONSTRUCTION RISK MANAGEMENT AND INSURANCE 50 (J&H Marsh & McLennan 1998).

Builder's risk coverage may be issued as part of an "all-risk" policy or as a rider to an existing property or CGL policy. LEE R. RUSS & THOMAS F. SEGALLA, COUCH ON INSURANCE, § 132:30 (West Group 3d ed. 1995). "The very purpose of a builder's risk policy is to provide protection for the building under construction. . . . Just as there are standard forms of property insurance used to insure existing buildings, builder's risk policies are used to insure the building while it is in the process of being built." *Ajax Bldg. Corp. v. Hartford Fire Insurance Co.*, 358 F.3d 795, 799 (11th Cir. 2004). While standard coverage under a builder's risk policy covers those with insurable interests for accidental damage to the project work, it typically excludes losses caused by defective design or workmanship. RICHARD K. ALLEN & STANLEY A. MARTIN, CONSTRUCTION LAW HANDBOOK § 18.03[A], 594 (Aspen 2d ed. 2009).

Building Code. Building codes are the means through which governmental entities regulate and attempt to standardize building design and construction, as well as the enforcement of applicable licensing requirements for design professionals. 5 PHILIP L. BRUNER & PATRICK J. O'CONNOR, JR., BRUNER AND O'CONNOR ON CONSTRUCTION LAW § 16:2 (2002). "[M]odern 'building codes' actually are a family of separate but related codes that address standards for buildings and for related building systems, such as mechanical systems, plumbing systems, fire retardation, energy conservation, electrical systems, and gas systems." *Id.* at 370. The model codes incorporate by reference industry standards disseminated by recognized organizations such as ASTM, AISC, ANSI, ASCE, etc. *Id.* Building codes are usually adopted and enforced at a local level.

Henry Lawrence, Jr., Building Code and Regulations, The Architect's Handbook of Professional Practice § 3.73 (AIA Press 12th ed. 1996).

Building Information Modeling (BIM). Building information modeling (BIM) is an innovation in project delivery tools wherein a model-based technology is used to create a digital representation of the building process to facilitate the exchange and interoperability of project information in a digital format. The National Institute of Building Sciences, the entity responsible for issuing the National Building Information Modeling Standard (NBIMS), has stated that "[a] Building Information Model, or BIM, utilizes cutting edge digital technology to establish a computable representation of all the physical and functional characteristics of a facility and its related project/life-cycle information, and is intended to be a repository of information for the facility owner/operator to use and maintain throughout the life-cycle of a facility." Press Release, Earle Kennett, The NBIMS Dev. Comm., The Nat'l Inst. of Bldg. Scis. (Feb. 20, 2006), *available at* http://www.graphicsystems.biz/gsi/articles/PRESS%20RELEASE%201F_16Feb2006.pdf. Although this definition references a single model, in practice the BIM is an amalgamation or federated set of models from the different project participants that together provide the entirety of the information contained in the BIM. Richard K. Allen & Stanley A. Martin, Construction Law Handbook § 41.03[B], 1661 (Aspen 2d ed. 2009). BIM covers geometry, spatial relationships, geographic information, quantities, and properties of building components and can be used to demonstrate the entire building life cycle, including the processes of construction and facility operation. BIM modeling provides for continuous and immediate analysis of project design, scope, schedule, and cost information. The technology used in BIM holds the promise of creating 3D, 4D (the implementation of time, phasing, and scheduling information), and 5D (the integration of cost information, e.g., price estimating) model of a construction project as well as the entire building life cycle.

Building Permit. A permit issued by the responsible governmental entity that authorizes construction on a new or existing building. *See* Black's Law Dictionary 208 (8th ed. 1999). The "permitting" process forms the core of building code administration and enforcement. 5 Philip L. Bruner & Patrick J. O'Connor, Jr., Bruner and O'Connor on Construction Law § 16:2 (2002). Through the building permit application and review process, the responsible governmental entity, generally at the local level, ensures that plans for construction generally comply with relevant land use and construction standards and building codes. For example, the building permit process enables the government entity to verify that the contract documents were prepared by a licensed design professional. *Id.* The project owner and contractor will contractually assign responsibility for obtaining and paying for the required building permit or permits.

C

Cardinal Change. A "cardinal change" is a term used to describe ordered work that is outside of the scope of the contract. It is a cardinal change because it fundamentally alters the original contractual undertaking. *See Edward R. Marden Corp. v. United States*, 442 F.2d 364, 369 (Ct. Cl. 1971). "Cardinal changes occur when an owner directs a contractor to make a change to a contract so substantial that performance becomes a new and substantially different undertaking between the parties." RICHARD K. ALLEN & STANLEY A. MARTIN, CONSTRUCTION LAW HANDBOOK § 21.08, 722 (Aspen 2d ed. 2009). There is no precise definition or bright-line test for when a change is contractually permitted under the unilateral change order clause, or if it is a cardinal change. *Marden*, 442 F.2d at 369; *Wunderlich Contracting Co. v. United States*, 351 F.2d 956 (Ct. Cl. 1965). As the Court of Claims set forth in *Saddler v. United States*, 287 F.2d 411 (Ct. Cl. 1961),

> the point at which a change must be considered to be beyond the scope of the contract and inconsistent with the "Changes" article is a matter of degree varying from one contract to another. We think that a determination of the permissive degree of change can be reached by considering the *totality of the change* and this requires recourse to its magnitude as well as its *quality*.

Saddler, 287 F.2d at 413 (emphasis added). A cardinal change can also occur as a result of a series of unilateral change orders, each of which alone may not represent a substantial departure from the general scope of the contract so as to be a cardinal change in and of itself, but the cumulative effect of the series of changes may exceed the general scope of the contract, thereby permitting the contractor to recover additional compensation or to refuse to perform the work. *See, e.g., J.D. Hedin Construction Co. v. United States*, 347 F.2d 235 (Ct. Cl. 1965).

The effect of a cardinal change is to discharge the contractor from its obligations under the contract. *See* BLACK'S LAW DICTIONARY 225 (8th ed. 1999); *see, e.g., O'Brien & Gere Technical Services, Inc. v. Fru-Con/Fluor Daniel Joint Venture*, 380 F.3d 447, 455 (8th Cir. 2004).

Change Directive/Construction Change Directive (CCD). The change directive (CCD) is a contractual change mechanism utilized by an owner in exercising its right to unilaterally direct changes in the work, in situations where there is not total agreement on the terms of the change. CARINA Y. OHARA ET AL., FUNDAMENTALS OF CONSTRUCTION LAW 104 (ABA 2001). The CCD is converted to a change order upon agreement by all parties as to the contract amount and/or contract time modification. *Id.* In contrast, the formal change order is used when the parties are in agreement as to the scope and pricing of the change as well as the time impact, if any. For example, Article 7 of the standard American Institute of Architects (AIA) Document A201-2007, General Conditions of the Contract for Construction, which contains a typical "changes" clause, provides for a Construction Change Directive as one of three types of contractual change documents that is signed only by the owner and need not be signed by the contractor. AIA Document A201-2007, General Conditions of the Contract for Construction, § 7.3 (2007). The contractor is required to proceed promptly with the performance of the changed work upon receipt of the change directive. *See, e.g.,* AIA Document A201-2007, § 7.1.3. The issuance of a construction change directive requires the contractor to proceed notwithstanding the fact that it disagrees with the method for determining the price for the change work. *See, e.g.,* AIA Document A201-2007, § 7.3.5. The contractor cannot wait to perform the work until there is a final determination of the value or cost to be paid it for that work.

Change Order. The construction contract between the owner and contractor sets forth in detail the contractor's performance obligations, but the parties need flexibility to adapt the contract to actual conditions encountered during construction. Although traditional contract law permits the parties to a contract to modify or change their arrangement by mutual agreement, in construction the owner needs to be able to unilaterally change the contract to accomplish his underlying purpose on the project. The contractual mechanism in construction contracts for handling contract modifications, changes, and claims for extra work in connection with them, is the "changes" clause. AIA Document A201-2007, § 7 (2007). The "changes" clause entitles the owner to unilaterally direct changes in the work without the contractor's consent and without breaching the contract, provided the change is within the general scope of the contract. *See* BLACK'S LAW DICTIONARY 247 (8th ed. 1999).

For a proposed change to be "within the general scope" of the contract, the change in the work must be regarded as fairly and reasonably within the contemplation of the parties when they entered into the contract. In exchange for this right to direct changes, the contractor is entitled to receive additional compensation for the changed or extra work. Both the contract price and the contract time to perform the work are subject to adjustment.

The changes clause establishes the procedure for the owner to make a change and for the contractor to seek compensation for the changed work to be performed. For example, Article 7 of the standard AIA Document A201-2007 requires written authorization for the change. AIA Document A201-2007, General Conditions of the Contract for Construction, § 7 (2007). The contractual document effectuating the "changes" process is the change order. Change orders are signed by both the owner and the contractor and reflect the agreement as to the change in the contract scope and price. A similar process is used for effectuating changes to subcontracts entered into between a contractor and a subcontractor or supplier.

Changed Conditions/Differing Site Conditions (DSC). Many times a contractor will experience changed conditions or differing site conditions from those anticipated or set forth in the plans and specifications. Absent a specific contractual means of receiving additional compensation in order to recover the resulting increased costs of performance caused by these conditions, the contractor must bear the loss. "The uncertainty inherent in the variability of underground soil conditions, and in the subjective judgments and interpretations about those conditions made on limited soils tests and investigations, is the construction industry's 'great risk.'" 4A PHILIP L. BRUNER & PATRICK J. O'CONNOR, JR., BRUNER AND O'CONNOR ON CONSTRUCTION LAW § 14:1 (2009).

The contractual provision that allocates this risk and allows recovery or adjustment in the contract price for changed conditions or differing site conditions is the "differing site conditions" (DSC) clause. The purpose of the differing site conditions clause is to benefit both the owner and the contractor. From the owner's perspective, the presence of the clause eliminates the risk to the owner of receiving bids that are higher than necessary in order to cover unanticipated subsurface or other differing site conditions that may not actually occur on the project. If the conditions are not encountered, then the owner has simply bought a more expensive project. With the differing site conditions clause, the owner will only have to pay for the increased cost of performance caused by differing site conditions if and when the contractor actually encounters these conditions, and if the contractor complies with the notice requirements in the clause. From the point of view of the contractor, the differing site conditions clause is beneficial because it eliminates the risk of not being compensated for unanticipated conditions encountered. With the clause, the contractor is provided a means of getting a fair adjustment in his contract price if and when differing site conditions are encountered.

Under a standard DSC, contract-based differing site conditions are classified as Type I or Type II conditions. *See, e.g.*, AIA Document A201-2007, General Conditions of the Contract for Construction, § 3.7.4 (2007). "Type I" conditions are concealed conditions below the surface or other concealed physical conditions that are materially at variance with the conditions indicated in the contract documents. These are unforeseeable conditions. "Type II" conditions consist of unknown physical conditions of an unusual nature differing materially from those ordinarily found to exist and generally recognized as inherent in the particular type of construction. Because no independent or implied right to recover costs attributable to a changed or differing site condition exists, the contractor's ultimate recovery is driven by the specific language of the differing site condition clause. RICHARD K. ALLEN & STANLEY A. MARTIN, CONSTRUCTION LAW HANDBOOK § 22.03 (Aspen 2d ed. 2009).

Chapter 11. A bankruptcy proceeding designed specifically for business entities, Chapter 11 of the Bankruptcy Code affords debtors protection whereby the company or individual is permitted to reorganize its business under the bankruptcy laws. Generally, the debtor remains in control of its business operations as a debtor in possession, subject, however, to the oversight (and jurisdiction) of the bankruptcy court. It can be either a voluntary or involuntary petition. 11 U.S.C. § 301, 303. Chapter 11 protection is most often utilized by corporate entities and is characterized by the emergence of the debtor from bankruptcy, within several months or years depending upon size and complexity, rather than liquidation. Although Chapter 11 often allows companies to maintain control of their assets and income, partial liquidation of less profitable assets is often required. *See* MICHAEL J. HERBERT, UNDERSTANDING BANKRUPTCY § 17.02 (2000).

Importantly, a bankruptcy filing under Chapter 11 triggers the automatic stay. 11 U.S.C. § 362(a). Additionally, at the time of filing, the debtor is required to notify every creditor that it has sought Chapter 11 protection. The creditors then form a Creditors Committee, which is generally made up of the 20 largest creditors. The Committee is permitted to hire an attorney and financial advisor, paid for by the debtor, to represent the interests of all the creditors. Chapter 11 also grants a U.S. Trustee the power to operate the debtor's business. 11 U.S.C. § 1108 (2009). However, except for cause, the debtor's existing management is permitted to act as the trustee. 11 U.S.C. § 1107. Thereafter, the Creditors Committee serves as a watchdog and advisor to the trustee/debtor in possession. After the Committee is established and the trustee is named, the goal of Chapter 11 proceedings is to develop a bankruptcy plan, which is typically proposed by the debtor itself. When a company emerges from Chapter 11 proceedings, virtually all existing debt is discharged. 11 U.S.C. § 1141(d)(1)(A). However, several categories of debt, such as taxes, fines, and domestic support, are nondischargeable. 11 U.S.C. § 523.

Claim. Specifically, a claim is a legal request for money, property, or other form of compensation. *See* BLACK'S LAW DICTIONARY 264 (8th ed. 2004). In the construction arena, it is generally the contractual means of presenting an amount in dispute, often a request for an increase in the contract time or price resulting from a change in the scope or price of work that does not amount to a formal change order, and/or delays or impacts to the work. Claims can arise in a number of ways, including as a result of delay and/or disruption.

Most contracts require timely notice of claims or notice of events giving rise to claims. Failure to specifically follow the notice requirements can result in waiver of the claims. *See Starks Mechanical, Inc. v. New Albany-Floyd County Consolidated School Corp.*, 854 N.E.2d 936 (Ind. Ct. App. 2006).

Collapsed As-Built Analysis. In the occurrence of delays on a construction project, a forensic scheduling analysis technique may be employed to prove responsibility for the resulting delays. This technique, termed "collapsed as-built analysis," includes a schedule that is updated with as-built dates and then "collapsed" by removing chosen activities from the schedule. The resulting analysis is intended to show what would have happened on the project if these activities had not been delayed, thereby proving which activities were the cause of the delay and what parties were responsible. In essence, the collapsed as-built analysis attempts to examine what would have transpired "but for" the alleged delaying event.

This analysis is implemented twice, once from the owner's perspective and once from the contractor's perspective. The schedule from the owner's viewpoint removes all contractor delay events from the as-built schedule and then compares the resulting schedule with the collapsed schedule. The resulting discrepancies illustrate the delays that are attributable to the contractor and may be used to calculate damages, including liquidated damages if specified. Similarly, when the analysis is run from the contractor's viewpoint, all of the owner delay events are removed and then compared with the collapsed schedule to determine the owner's liability from which the contractor's damages may be calculated. *See, e.g., Metric Construction Co., Inc. v. United States,* 81 Fed. Cl. 804, 821 (2008); Jennifer Fletcher & Laura Stipanowich, *Successful Forensic Scheduling Analysis,* 1 J. AM. C. CONSTRUCTION LAW 203 (Winter 2007) (citing Satish B. Mohan and Khalid S. Al-Gahtani, *Current Delay Analysis Techniques and Improvements,* COST ENGINEERING, Sept. 2006).

Collateral Warranty. In a general sense, a collateral warranty is a warranty given under a contract that runs in favor of a third party who is not a party to the contract. In the construction context, a collateral warranty may be given in favor of a noncontracting party who will ultimately have an interest in the completed project, such as a condominium association or an end purchaser of a commercial or industrial building. *See, e.g.,* Justin Sweet, *A View from the Tower,* CONSTRUCTION LAW., Jan. 1999, at 45 (citing David Lewis, *Investigating the JCT: Standard Forms of Agreement for Collateral Warranty,* 13 CONSTRUCTION L.J. 305 (1997)).

Combined Dispute Board (CDB). Consisting of one or three persons appointed in the construction contract and empowered to resolve disputes arising out of the construction project, a combined dispute board is constituted pursuant to the International Chamber of Commerce (ICC) rules. The CDB hears all disputes arising out of the contract in the first instance and issues a recommendation as to how the disputes should be resolved. If the parties agree, or if the CDB so decides in accordance with the rules, it may issue a decision instead of a recommendation, in which case its decision may be binding on the contracting parties, depending on the contract language. If a party disagrees with a recommendation or decision, if the CDB fails to act or fails to act timely, or for other reasons specified in the contract, the parties' dispute will be resolved finally by arbitration in accordance with the ICC Rules. *See* INT'L CHAMBER OF COMMERCE, DISPUTE BOARD RULES art. 6, *available at* http://www.iccwbo.org/court/dispute_boards/id4352/index.html#art6; Harvey J. Kirsh, *Dispute Review Boards and Adjudication: Two Cutting-Edge ADR Processes in International Construction,* 3 J. AM. C. CONSTRUCTION LAW 75 (2009).

Commercial General Liability (CGL or GL) Insurance. Known as "CGL" or "GL" coverage, commercial general liability insurance is a common form of insurance purchased by construction project participants that provides coverage both during and following completion of a construction project. This insurance covers the insured for amounts that the insured becomes legally obligated to pay to a third party as a result of a covered occurrence. CGL coverage is the most common liability policy issued today. The standard CGL policy contains three separate agreements termed coverages A, B, and C. Under Coverage A, the insured agrees to be liable for bodily injury or property damage resulting from an occurrence that takes place inside the coverage territory and during the policy period. Coverage B is labeled "personal and advertising injury liability," which may protect an insured against defamation claims and the like. Coverage C serves as a type of limited "no-fault" insurance. While the standard CGL policy provides broad coverage, it also may contain a number of specific exclusions. For instance, it is common for a CGL policy to exclude coverage for bodily injury suffered by the insured's own employees. This exclusion is based on the resulting overlap in coverage that would occur with workers' compensation. 4 Philip L. Bruner & Patrick J. O'Connor, Jr., Bruner and O'Connor on Construction Law § 11:12 (2010).

Note that CGL or GL coverage was formerly referred to as a Comprehensive General Liability Policy. *See, e.g., Breezewood of Wilmington Condos. Homeowners' Ass'n v. Amerisure Mutual Insurance Co.*, No. 08-1476 2009 WL1877465, at *6 (4th Cir. 2009) (discussing the "your work" exclusion and the subcontractor work exception under North Carolina law).

Commercial Impracticability. Under the black letter contract law of "impossibility," a contracting party cannot be held to perform its contract obligations because such performance has been rendered impossible. Similarly, a contracting party may assert the defense that it cannot be required to perform its contract obligations because performance has been rendered commercially impracticable. Courts have held a contract to be commercially impracticable when performance would be so costly that in good conscience the contracting party should not be ordered to fully perform under the contract, although some lesser aspect of performance may be required. Whether a contract requirement is impossible or commercially impracticable is a question of fact, as to which the plaintiff bears the burden of proof. *See, e.g., Blinderman Construction Co., Inc. v. United States*, 39 Fed. Cl. 529, 556 (1997) (citing *Blount Bros. Corp. v. United States*, 872 F.2d 1003, 1007 (Fed. Cir. 1989) (citing *Maxwell*

38

Dynamometer Co. v. United States, 386 F.2d 855 (Ct. Cl. 1967)); *Ehlers-Noll GMBH v. United States*, 34 Fed. Cl. 494, 499 (1995).

Common-Law Bond. Issued by a compensated surety on a private construction project, a common-law bond is a payment or performance bond required by contract. This is in contrast to a payment or performance bond required by statute to be provided on a construction project that is funded by a local, state, or federal governmental entity. In determining whether a bond is common law or statutory one must examine the obligations of the principal and its surety. Under common-law bonds, the parties are bound by their own self-imposed terms. A statutory bond, however, must be interpreted by the requirements set forth in the relevant state or federal statute. *See, e.g., Triboro Hardware & Supply Corp. v. Federal Insurance Co.*, 45 A.D.3d 134, 841 N.Y.S.2d 600 (2007) (comparing a common-law bond with a statutory bond and enforcing identical terms consistently); *Delta Fire Sprinklers, Inc. v. OneBeacon Insurance Co.*, 937 So. 2d 695 (Fl. App. 2006) (determining a bond to be statutory, and not common law, and enforcing 90-day notice requirement).

Compensable Delay. A compensable delay on a construction project is one that is not the fault of the party seeking compensation and for which the contract does not preclude compensation. Additionally, the delay must be "caused by an event within the control of the owner and beyond the control of the contractor, for which the contractor and its affected subcontractors and suppliers are entitled to an extension of contract time and damages or an equitable adjustment." 5 PHILIP L. BRUNER & PATRICK J. O'CONNOR, JR., BRUNER AND O'CONNOR ON CONSTRUCTION LAW § 15:29 (2002). *See, e.g., Metric Construction Co., Inc. v. United States*, 81 Fed. Cl. 804 (2008) (government's breach of good faith and fair dealing and constructive changes can be cause of compensable delay); *Orlosky Inc. v. United States*, 68 Fed. Cl. 296 (2005) (contractor has burden of proving compensable delay); *George Sollitt Construction Co. v. United States*, 64 Fed. Cl. 229, 238 (2005) (contractor seeking to recover for a compensable delay must show that the government was the sole proximate cause of the contractor's loss).

Competitive Negotiation. Designed to maximize competition at each step of the procurement process, competitive negotiation refers to a procedure by which owners, especially governmental entities, select contractors and other vendors for a construction project. 1 PHILIP L. BRUNER & PATRICK J. O'CONNOR,

JR., BRUNER AND O'CONNOR ON CONSTRUCTION LAW § 2:154 at n.4 (2002) (citing Ralph Nash, Jr. and Michael Love, Jr., *Innovations in Federal Construction Contracting*, 45 Geo. Wash. L. Rev. 309, 324–32 (1977)). Under this method, the owner solicits individual design and price proposals from qualified suppliers or firms (the "offerors"), conducts negotiations with the offerors concerning price and quality, and awards a contract to the offeror submitting the best overall proposal. Unlike a formal hard bid, this method permits procurement officials to conduct discussions with offerors after reviewing all proposals, enabling officials to determine precisely what is being proposed. It also allows for consideration of both the price and the quality of the product or services in determining the best offer. Because formal advertising is the statutorily preferred mode of most governmental entities, the procuring agency is often required to justify its decision to use competitive negotiation under a statutory exception to formal advertising, usually by making written determinations and findings.

Once a governmental entity has justified its decision to use the competitive negotiation process, it begins by soliciting proposals from a wide range of prospective contractors. The government's request for proposals must include its specifications as well as a summary description of the evaluation criteria it will use in selecting the winning contractor. Upon receiving the proposals, government officials will rank or score them according to the described evaluation system. Frequently, separate evaluators score different parts of the proposals, then a source selection panel accumulates and analyzes all the scores to arrive at an overall evaluation of each proposer.

After the evaluation, the government may conduct discussions with the proposers to clarify or upgrade the proposals. However, the government has discretion to award the contract to the best proposer without negotiations when "it can be clearly demonstrated from the existence of adequate competition or accurate prior experience with the product that acceptance of an initial proposal without discussion would result in fair and reasonable prices." *Id.* at 324. If the government intentionally or unintentionally undertakes discussions or negotiations with any one proposer, then it must conduct "oral or written discussions" with all the proposers within a competitive range, that is, those making "proposals which have a reasonable chance of being selected from award." *Id.* at 325. During these discussions, the government must neither reveal a competitor's price to another proposer nor disclose any other aspect of a proposal. Following discussions, the agency will request "best and final offers" from all remaining contenders. After competitors submit their final offers, the government may either award the contract to the best overall proposal or reopen negotiations. To remove the possibility of bias in the selection process, the government often withholds price information from the agency officials evaluating the proposals, disguises the names of the proposers, and vests the final selection decision in a person or board at a relatively high level in the procuring agency. *See also* Shereen Marcus, *Efficiency and Exchange: An Economic Analysis of Acquisition by Negotiation*, 32 PUB. CONT. L.J. 659 (2003); D.A. Whiteford, *Negotiated Procurements: Squandering the Benefit of the Bargain*, 32 PUB. CONT. L.J. 509 (2003) (recommending how to improve the federal bargaining process to assist the government in obtaining "best value").

Completed Operations Coverage. A type of insurance purchased by construction contractors, completed operations coverage insures damage to persons or property as a result of insured occurrences that impact construction projects following completion. Completed operations coverage will often be provided by a contractor as part of his commercial general liability coverage, in the form of a "completed operations hazard." *See, e.g., Valmont Energy Steel, Inc. v. Commercial Union Insurance Co.*, 359 F.3d 770 (5th Cir. 2004).

Liability policies often contain either an exclusion for injury encompassed by a so-called completed operations hazard or a separate policy limit for claims encompassed by the completed operations hazard. The standard policy definition of *completed operation hazard* has been interpreted narrowly. It has been held that the standard definition applies only to construction or maintenance type work. Moreover, the fact that servicing of an otherwise completed system remains to be done, or that some aspect of the job was unwittingly not done, does not render the operation incomplete. Work is complete when the people involved with performing and receiving it believed that the work was completed. Similarly, it has been held that an insured's work is complete when an insured abandons the work, even if the project remains unfinished. The fact that there is generally coverage for and a separate policy limit for the completed operations hazard does not mean that claims encompassed by the hazard do not have to satisfy the basic insuring clause or are not subject to the exclusions in the policy. ALLAN D. WINDT, 2 INSURANCE CLAIMS & DISPUTE: REPRESENTATION OF INSURANCE COMPANIES & INSUREDS § 11:20 (5th ed. 2009).

Computer Assisted Design (CAD). Sometimes also known or referred to as "computer aided design," computer assisted design refers to the use of computerized technology for the design of objects, real or virtual, including the design of buildings or structures. CAD is commonly used in the process of creating construction drawings in two dimensions or construction modeling in three dimensions. "Computer-aided design (CAD) systems are commonplace tools in most design firms. [CAD] technology provides a number of benefits including accuracy and consistency in the preparation of drawings and facilitating the making of changes in drawings in later phases." 5 PHILIP L. BRUNER & PATRICK J. O'CONNOR JR., BRUNER AND O'CONNOR ON CONSTRUCTION LAW § 17:78 (2010). One of the first CAD software programs available for personal computers was AutoCad, released for use with the IBM PC in late 1982. AutoCad runs exclusively on Microsoft Windows operating systems.

Conciliation. A form of alternative dispute resolution (ADR), conciliation is the process of settling a dispute through nonconfrontational or extrajudicial means. Under this ADR method, a third party or third parties, who are usually—but not necessarily—neutral, hear both sides of a dispute and then issue a nonbinding opinion as to how the dispute should be resolved. Conciliation is less structured than mediation and is frequently employed under federal labor laws such as the Railway Labor Act. *See* 45 U.S.C. § 151–188. Parties to construction contracts also make use of this method by including it in the contract as a required step to resolving a dispute prior to instigating a legal action.

Concurrent Delay. When there are two unrelated yet simultaneous delays, one on the part of the owner and one on the part of the contractor, the resulting delay in the construction project is said to be concurrent. Concurrent delays occur "where both parties are responsible for the same period of delay," as opposed to sequential delays where one party and then the other causes different delays seriatim or intermittently. *See e.g., R.P. Wallace, Inc. v. United States,* 63 Fed. Cl. 402, 409–10 (Fed. Cl. 2004) (citing *Essex Electro Engineers v. Danzig,* 224 F.3d 1283, 1295–96 (Fed. Cir. 2000) (distinguishing concurrent and sequential delays)). Courts have held that a contractor cannot generally recover for concurrent delays "for the simple reason that no causal link can be shown: [an] act that delays part of the contract performance does not delay 'the general progress of the work' when the 'prosecution of the work as a whole' would have been delayed regardless of the [other]'s act." *Clearwater Constructors, Inc. v. United States,* 71 Fed. Cl. 25, 36 (Fed. Cl. 2006).

ConsensusDOCS. ConsensusDOCS produces a series of contracts that can be used by owners, architects, general contractors, subcontractors, design/builders, and others involved in the construction industry. In general, ConsensusDOCS are developed around a general contracting series, a design/build series, a subcontracting series, and a construction and program management series. There are more than 70 contract forms and other documents that are useful in the construction contracting process in the ConsensusDOCS family. These documents are available at http://consensusdocs.org and can be purchased through various packages or subscriptions. They are promoted by ConsensusDOCS as "[t]he only standard construction contracts written and endorsed by owners, contractors, subcontractors, designers and surety professionals." ConsensusDOCS, ConsensusDOCS Construction Contracts, http://www.consensusdocs.org (last visited Jan. 26, 2010).

It is notable that for many years the Associated General Contractors of America (AGC) endorsed the American Institute of Architects (AIA) standard form agreements. However, as the cycle of revisions to the AIA documents was instituted, the AGC decided not to participate in the drafting of the 2007 version and, instead, joined with 21 other industry associations to develop this new set of form construction contracts. The ConsensusDOCS that were the result of that collaboration were first published in 2007. The following associations have endorsed the ConsensusDOCS contracts: American Subcontractors Association (ASA), Associated Builders and Contractors, Inc. (ABC), Associated General Contractors of America (AGC), Associated Specialty Contractors, Inc. (ASC), Association of the Wall and Ceiling Industry (AWCI), Construction Industry Roundtable (CIRT), Construction Owners Association of America (COAA), Construction Users Roundtable (CURT), Finishing Contractors Association (FCA), Lean Construction Institute (LCI), Mechanical Contractors Association of America (MCAA), National Association of Electrical Distributors (NAED), National Association of State Facilities Administrators (NASFA), National Association of Surety Bond Producers (NASBP), National Electrical Contractors Association (NECA), National Insulation Association (NIA), National Roofing Contractors Association (NRCA), National Subcontractors Alliance (NSA), Painting and Decorating Contractors of America (PDCA), Plumbing Heating and Cooling Contractors Association (PHCC), Sheet Metal and Air Conditioning Contractors' National Association (SMACNA), and Surety & Fidelity Association of America (SFAA). *Id.*

Consequential Damages. Also referred to as "indirect damages" or "special damages," consequential damages are damages for breach of contract that do not flow directly from the alleged breach, but are an indirect source or a result of such breach. THOMAS J. KELLEHER, JR., COMMON SENSE CONSTRUCTION LAW, A PRACTICAL GUIDE FOR THE CONSTRUCTION PROFESSIONAL 392–93 (Wiley 3rd ed. 2005). Typical examples of consequential damages in construction claims include loss of profits, loss of financing, loss of business opportunity, and loss of bonding capacity. Consequential damages are often more difficult to prove because the causal link between the damage and the alleged breach may be uncertain, and the damages may be speculative. In most situations, recovery of consequential damages requires proof that the damages were "reasonably foreseeable," the loss flowed proximately from the alleged breach, and the amount of damages can be reasonably ascertained and not remote or speculative. *See, e.g., Kline Iron & Steel Co. v. Superior Trucking Co.,* 201 S.E. 2d 388 (S.C. 1973).

Various jurisdictions differ on how consequential damages are defined and under what circumstances they can be recovered, so a careful review of the applicable law is necessary to understand what damages might be included in this definition. CARINA Y. OHARA ET AL., FUNDAMENTALS OF CONSTRUCTION LAW 338 (ABA 2001). Consequential damages in the context of contractor's unexcused delays are often addressed in construction contracts by specifying liquidated damages to cover these types of losses. Additionally, due to their uncertainty as to amount and risk, some agreements provide that the parties waive claims against each other for consequential damages arising out of or related to the contract. 2 PHILIP L. BRUNER & PATRICK J. O'CONNOR, JR., BRUNER AND O'CONNOR ON CONSTRUCTION LAW § 5:115 (2002). The "waiver of consequential damages" provision is an example of a disincentive provision, which is a provision that shields a party from some or all of the consequences of its performance failures. *Id.* at § 5:20. There are two types of waiver clauses: assumption (which serves to identify and define all potential consequential damages and assumes that risk, in the name of the owner) and protective (which assigns consequential damages to the party causing those damages). *Id.* at § 5:115. Both the American Institute of Architects (AIA) and ConsensusDOCS standard agreements between owner and contractors contain express waivers of consequential damages. *See* AIA Document A201-2007, General Conditions of the Contract for Construction, § 4.3.10 (1997); ConsensusDOCS Standard Agreement and General Conditions Between Owner and Contractor (Where the Contract Price is a Lump Sum) § 6.6 (2007).

Constructability Review. A third-party review of the project plans and specifications instituted by the owner before receipt of contractor bids, made in an effort to recognize areas of possible conflict or uncertainty and for purposes of revising the design to address such conflicts, is often referred to as a constructability review. CARINA Y. OHARA ET AL., FUNDAMENTALS OF CONSTRUCTION

LAW 338 (ABA 2001). The constructability review is frequently done by a contractor who is experienced with the type of project being designed. The reviewer may be allowed to provide a bid to perform the work.

Construction Documents (CDs). CDs are the last sets of design documents generated by the architect and/or engineer based on the design development documents. CDs can be used for pricing, bidding, and construction of the project, and include the drawings, plans, and specifications for the permitting and construction of a project. According to the American Institute of Architects (AIA), construction documents "shall include the Drawings and Specifications that establish in detail the quality levels of materials and systems required for the project." AIA Document B141-1997, Standard Form of Agreement Between Owner and Architect with Standard Terms and Conditions, § 2.4.4.1 (1997).

Construction Management (Agency). The agency model of construction management is similar to the role served by a design professional in project development. 2 PHILIP L. BRUNER & PATRICK J. O'CONNOR, JR , BRUNER AND O'CONNOR ON CONSTRUCTION LAW § 6:12 (2002). Under the agency model, the construction manager is frequently referred to as a "pure" construction manager. CARINA Y. OHARA ET AL, FUNDAMENTALS OF CONSTRUCTION LAW 182 (ABA 2001). Stated simply, in this model the construction manager acts as the owner's agent. BRUNER & O'CONNOR at § 6:12 The construction manager can mediate disputes between the contractor and the designer in a way most beneficial to the owner. OHARA et al. at 182.

The construction manager does not enter into contracts directly with trade contractors and is not responsible for the project deliverable, but instead devotes its resources to making certain that the construction proceeds efficiently. BRUNER & O'CONNOR at § 6:12. The construction manager has no economic interest in the contractor's ability to generate a profit, but may prove costly to the owner because a potentially large management fee is owed to the construction manager regardless of the project's success. OHARA ET AL. at 182.

During the design process, the construction manager may provide constructability reviews, cost estimations, and life-cycle costing analyses. BRUNER & O'CONNOR at § 6:12. During the bidding process, the construction manager typically advises the owner on bid package preparation, contractor selection, and bid review. *Id.* During the construction phase, the construction manager focuses on contract administration, quality assurance, budget and schedule adherence, and change order management. *Id.*

Construction Management (Agency v. At-Risk). The owner contracts with a construction expert who is at risk for completion of the project in the construction manager at-risk model. CARINA Y. OHARA ET AL., FUNDAMENTALS OF CONSTRUCTION LAW 183–84 (ABA 2001). The construction manager at-risk model is comparable to the traditional design-bid-build approach, where there is a separate contractor and designer, with the primary difference being that the construction manager at-risk is typically involved before the construction phase to provide preconstruction services. *Id.* A construction management at-risk agreement is frequently priced on a guaranteed maximum price (GMP) basis. *Id.*

The primary difference between the two construction manager models is that a construction manager at-risk is responsible for the deliverable, whereas, under the agency model, a construction manager is not. *Id.* The construction manager at-risk's profitability is linked to the success of the project, whereas a construction manager utilizing agency construction management is paid its contract price regardless of the project's success. *Id.* Although the construction manager at-risk model creates an incentive for positive construction results, the potential for loss of profits can generate a conflict of interest between the construction manager at-risk and the owner. *Id.*

Construction Pyramid. In a typical traditional construction project, the owner of the project will contract separately with an architect and a general contractor to provide the design and construction services for the project. The architect and general contractor in turn will utilize the services of lower-tier consultants and subcontractors who in turn may have subconsultants, suppliers, or sub-subcontractors. This creates a construction pyramid with the entities at the base of the pyramid working together to create the finished product for the owner. The following is an example of a construction pyramid:

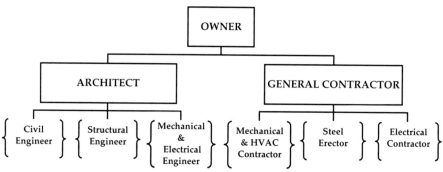

In the majority of construction projects today, the risk associated with the project is also allocated much like a pyramid. Grant A. Simpson & James B.

Atkins, *The Power of One: The Effective Owner-Architect-Contractor Team*, 14 AIAR-CHITECT, Apr. 27, 2007, http://info.aia.org/aiarchitect/thisweek07/0427/0427p_bp_full.cfm (last visited Jan. 26, 2010). The owner takes the most financial risk because it owns the finished project and it obtains the most benefit from the project. *Id.* The contractors take the next most risk with accountability for the cost and duration of construction, and their benefits are in proportion to that risk. *Id.* The designers take the least risk of these three parties with the least benefits, taking principal responsibility for the cost of design, although some responsibility for construction cost is possible. *Id.* The contractors and designers share the long-term risk of construction and design deficiencies.

Constructive Change. Stated succinctly, constructive change is typically a contractor claim for additional compensation or contract time, stemming from the owner's actions that have effectively altered the contract, without following the contract's formal changes provision. CARINA Y. OHARA ET AL., FUNDAMENTALS OF CONSTRUCTION LAW 339 (ABA 2001). "Certainty of change is a constant of the construction process." 1 PHILIP L. BRUNER & PATRICK J. O'CONNOR, JR., BRUNER AND O'CONNOR ON CONSTRUCTION LAW § 4:1 (2002). "Construction 'rarely proceeds as planned,' because 'there are always unexpected events and conditions that occur during construction and impact the contractor's ability to complete the project as planned.'" *Id.; see also* ASSOCIATED GENERAL CONTRACTORS OF AMERICA, CONSTRUCTION PLANNING & SCHEDULING 4–5 (1997).

A constructive change can take the form of

> (1) owner-initiated changes in project requirements that materially affect design or construction performance or completion; (2) circumstances beyond the control of the parties, such as unforeseen site or weather conditions; (3) differences between contractually estimated and actually furnished material quantities; (4) directions necessary to remediate design deficiencies, unavailability of specified products or suitable materials, unexpected construction hindrances or interferences, or impractability of specified design requirements or construction methods; and (5) contractor-initiated 'value engineering' changes accepted by the owner.

BRUNER & O'CONNOR at § 4:1; JOHN CIBINIC, JR. & RALPH C. NASH, JR., ADMINISTRATION OF GOVERNMENT CONTRACTS 381–485 (3d ed. 1995); GOLDBERG & BANKS, *Changes and Extras, in* CONSTRUCTION LAW HANDBOOK 769 (1999);

RALPH C. NASH, JR., *Changes and Claims, in* CONSTRUCTION CONTRACTING (1991).

Consulting Engineer. Unlike the primary engineer for a construction project, a consulting engineer is an individual with engineering training who is retained to perform a discrete portion or aspect of the engineering work for the project under the supervision of the primary licensed engineer, render an opinion on engineering work related to the project, or provide advice regarding a specific engineering task or event. *See* CYRIL M. HARRIS, DICTIONARY OF ARCHITECTURE AND CONSTRUCTION 250 (McGraw-Hill 4th ed. 2006) ("An engineer, usually employed by the owner or architect to perform specific tasks of engineering design for a portion of the construction contract."). Some authorities define a consulting engineer as a "licensed engineer, employed to perform specific engineering tasks." KORNELIS SMIT ET AL., MEANS ILLUSTRATED CONSTRUCTION DICTIONARY 137 (R.S. Means Co. 1991). However, a consulting engineer does not necessarily need to be licensed. Licensure requirements for a consulting engineer will vary based on the scope of work to be performed, the level of supervision and authority granted to the consulting engineer, and jurisdictional requirements. While a consulting engineer may not be required to be licensed, the work of an unlicensed consulting engineer may be subject to greater scrutiny and expose the entity that retained and relied upon the consulting engineer to greater liability if there is subsequent litigation related to the project.

Contemplated Change Notice (CCN). A contemplated change notice (CCN) is used typically by the owner, or the owner's agent, to request a cost estimate from the project's contractor for a proposed change to the plans and specifications for the project before a formal change order is issued. "A form issued to a construction contractor as a means for obtaining [its] quotation on the price change associated with a contemplated change in work included in [its] contract." LEN F. WEBSTER, THE WILEY DICTIONARY OF CIVIL ENGINEERING AND CONSTRUCTION 141 (Wiley 1997); *see also* OLIVER LINDIWIG, LOTUS ILLUSTRATED DICTIONARY OF MANAGEMENT 52 (Lotus Press 2006). More specifically, a CCN includes any type of notice of proposed or considered change(s) to the scope of work, construction plans, or construction drawings, issued by the owner or the owner's agent for the sole purpose of determining the potential cost and effect of a proposed change. It should be noted, however, that a contemplated change notice is not a change order and does not bind either party to the proposed change absent the execution of a formal change order as required by the construction documents. Canadian Mechanical Contracting Education Foundation, National Change Notice Procedure Guide § 1 (Canadian Mechanical Contracting Education Foundation 2001).

Contract Administration. The duties and responsibilities of contract administration are usually defined in the various project contracts. The contract administrator is also identified in the contract and is, most typically, the architect or engineer. During the contract administration phase of the project, the contract administrator often serves as the owner's representative and point of contact with the contractor with respect to designated matters. Carina Y. Ohara et al., Fundamentals of Construction Law 66 (ABA 2001). The contract administrator frequently provides services to assess the progress and quality of the finished work; to determine if the work is being performed in compliance with contract and code requirements; to certify progress payments; and generally to attempt to protect the owner's interests in the project. *Id.*

Contract Documents. The contract documents refer to the agreements and other documents that define the relationship and responsibilities of the parties for constructing a project, and the documents depicting the work to be performed by the contractor. Carina Y. Ohara et al., Fundamentals of Construction Law 25 (ABA 2001). The contract documents for construction of a project normally include the agreement between the contractor and the owner; the general and supplementary conditions; the plans and specifications for the project; and any later alterations (change orders) to the contract. *Id.* at 95.

Contract Price/Contract Sum. The stated contract price or contract sum in a construction contract or agreement is the amount of money representing the total consideration for which a contractor agrees to complete the work described in the construction contract. The contract price or contract sum can be adjusted only by change order. *See* J. Stewart Stein, Construction Glossary: An Encyclopedic Reference and Manual 753 (Wiley 2d ed. 1993). The contract price or sum can be structured in a number of different ways, such as a fixed or lump-sum price, time and materials, unit prices, or defined costs of the work with a fee for overhead and profit (with or without a guaranteed maximum price).

Contracting Officer (Federal). According to the Federal Acquisition Regulations, a federal contracting officer is a person with the authority to enter into, administer, and/or terminate contracts and make related determinations and findings for the federal government. Federal Acquisition Regulations for National Aeronautics and Space Administration § 2.101 (Mar. 31, 2009). Included in this group are certain authorized representatives of the contracting officer acting within the limits of their authority as delegated by the contracting officer. *Id.* Federal contracting officers are required to have specific authority to enter into contracts. James W. Norment, *Are You Ready for Federal Government Contracting?*, LOCAL TECH WIRE, Aug. 14, 2007, http://localtech-wire.com/business/local_tech_wire/opinion/story/1703158/. This authority is evidenced by a "warrant," which is written permission from the head of the applicable agency for the contracting officer to enter into contracts up to a certain amount. *Id.*

In the event that a contracting officer agrees to a contract greater than that amount, the contract is invalid regardless of whether the contractor has knowledge that the contracting officer has surpassed his or her limit. *Id.* In other words, the federal government is not bound by the acts of its contracting officers beyond the scope of their actual authority. *See Harbert/Lummus v. United States*, 142 F.3d 1429, 1432 (Fed. Cir. 1998). A contractor on a federal government contract is responsible for the knowledge of a contracting officer's authority and the limits of that authority. *Id.* Such a contractor takes on the risk of accurately determining the authority of the contracting officers who purport to act for the federal government, and this risk remains with the contractor even when the contracting officers themselves may be unaware of the limitations of their authority. *Harbert/Lummus*, 142 F.3d at 1432 (quoting *Trauma Service Group v. United States*, 104 F.3d 1321, 1325 (Fed. Cir. 1997)).

Contractor. While the exact definition may vary by state law, a contractor is typically an individual or entity who is engaged for the construction of or improvements to real property. More generally, it is "the individual, firm, or corporation undertaking the execution of the work under the terms of the [construction] contract and acting directly or through its agents or employees; a person or company who agrees to furnish the materials and labor to do [construction] work for a certain price." NAT'L ASS'N OF WOMEN IN CONSTR., GREATER PHOENIX, ARIZ. CHAPTER #98 (NAWIC), CONSTRUCTION DICTIONARY: CONSTRUCTION TERMS & TABLES 135 (NAWIC 9th ed. 1986). The contractor may also be described as "the party to the contract for construction, pledged to the owner to perform the work of construction in accordance with the contract documents." KORNELIS SMIT ET AL., MEANS ILLUSTRATED CONSTRUCTION DICTIONARY 137 (R.S. Means Co. 1991).

The contractor will generally hire trade contractors or subcontractors to actually perform large portions of the scope of work on the project. Under state contractor registration statutes, a "contractor" is typically a business that facilitates a construction project and pays its bills, but may not do any actual construction work itself. 13 AM. JUR. 2D *Building and Construction Contracts* § 130 (2009); *Interstate Commercial Building Services, Inc. v. Bank of America National Trust & Savings Ass'n*, 23 F. Supp. 2d 1166 (D. Nev. 1998) (applying Nevada law). However, many contractors do self-perform some portions of the work.

A property owner is not automatically transformed into a "contractor" just because it takes on the duties throughout a construction project that are traditionally the responsibilities of a general contractor. 13 AM. JUR. 2D *Building and Construction Contracts* § 130 (2009); *Winter v. Smith*, 914 S.W.2d 527 (Tenn. Ct. App. 1995).

Contractor-Controlled Insurance Program (CCIP). Also known as a "wrap-up" policy, a contractor-controlled insurance policy (CCIP) is an insurance policy obtained by the contractor to provide coverage for all of the major participants in a large construction project or series of related similar projects. CCIP insurance policies are typically valued in excess of $100,000,000. The goal of the policy is to reduce the cost associated with numerous policies for a single project and also avoid potential litigation expense associated with multiparty, multi-insurer construction lawsuits seeking recovery for the various liabilities and claims for indemnification among and between the owner, project manager, architect, engineer, subcontractors, contractors, and suppliers. CCIPs may "provide general liability insurance to all parties, workers compensation, personal injury, employer's liability and property coverage. They may also include professional liability, environmental liability, and builders risk coverage." Walter J. Andrews & Ruth S. Kochenderfer, *Deconstructing Wrap Up Policies*, 15 COVERAGE 16 (ABA Litigation Section, May/June 2000); *see also* WM. CARY WRIGHT, CONSTRUCTION INSURANCE—UNDERSTANDING THE ANATOMY OF THE STANDARD CGL POLICY AND TERMS OF THE BUILDER'S RISK, PROFESSIONAL LIABILITY AND OCIP POLICIES § 3.23 (Florida Bar Advanced Construction Law and Certification Review Course, 2009).

Contractual Liability Coverage. In addition to the standard workers' compensation insurance and commercial general liability coverage, some contracts also call for contractual liability coverage. This is typically special insurance coverage for a contractual indemnity obligation undertaken by a contractor in favor of the owner. This coverage can usually be provided by endorsement to the commercial general liability insurance policy. CARINA Y. OHARA ET AL., FUNDAMENTALS OF CONSTRUCTION LAW 284 (ABA 2001).

Correction Period. In the construction context, the correction period refers to the time period required under construction contracts within which a contractor, subcontractor, or vendor must correct or repair a defect or deficiency in the work or items supplied after the responsible party has received notification of the defect or deficiency. It is not the whole period from completion to the date the defect is discovered, but a period of time that is specified in the construction contract. Typically the correction period after project completion is at least one year after substantial completion to repair or replace any work discovered to be nonconforming. *See* 2 PHILLIP L. BRUNER & PATRICK J. O'CONNOR, JR., BRUNER AND O'CONNOR ON CONSTRUCTION LAW § 5:239; 3 BRUNER & O'CONNOR at § 9.62 (2002) and cases cited therein. The contract between the parties or the project specifications may require specific correction or "warranty" periods for certain components or portions of the work, such as roofing, plumbing, mechanical, and electrical systems.

Cost-Plus Contract/Cost-Reimbursable Contract. A cost-plus or cost-reimbursable contract refers to a construction contract where compensation is to be paid to the contractor based on defined costs incurred in the performance of the work plus an agreed-upon lump-sum amount or proportional sum (usually based on a percentage of the costs of the work to be reimbursed) to compensate the contractor for its overhead costs and as the contractor's profit for performance (with the overhead and profit amount or percentage being commonly referred to as the contractor's "fee"). This form of compensation structure can be with or without a cap or maximum contract amount or "guaranteed maximum price." This type of contract is favored where the scope of work is indeterminate or highly uncertain and the kinds of labor, material, and equipment needed also are uncertain. *See* LEN F. WEBSTER, THE WILEY DICTIONARY OF CIVIL ENGINEERING AND CONSTRUCTION 149 (Wiley 1997). For cost-plus contracts it is crucial to maintain complete and detailed records of all time and materials expended by the contractor on the work. Typically, wages for labor and taxes; benefits; insurance costs based on those wages; rented equipment; subcontract costs; project insurance costs; bonding costs; building permit costs; costs of contractor-owned equipment; on-site overhead costs such as a job trailer, electricity, water, telephone lines and the like; and material costs are reimbursed, whereas home office overhead costs are not reimbursed. *See* 2 PHILLIP L. BRUNER & PATRICK J. O'CONNOR, JR., BRUNER AND O'CONNOR ON CONSTRUCTION LAW § 6:81 (2002).

CPM Schedule. A critical path method (CPM) schedule is a schedule developed from the activity-oriented time-control system and time analysis of a network of logically connected activities—the critical path method—that outlines the steps needed to complete a project. *See* J. STEWART STEIN, CONSTRUCTION GLOSSARY: AN ENCYCLOPEDIC REFERENCE AND MANUAL 18 (Wiley 2d ed. 1993).

Critical Path Method (CPM). Many construction contracts require use of the critical path method, a system of construction management that involves the complete planning and scheduling of a project in the form of an arrow diagram that shows each project activity, its appropriate place in the timetable based on sequence of work, and its importance relative to other tasks and the anticipated completion of each sequence of work. *See* KORNELIS SMIT ET AL., MEANS ILLUSTRATED CONSTRUCTION DICTIONARY 145 (R.S. Means Co. 1991).

> A CPM is a standard construction device used to plan the activities of a construction project in a logical, orderly sequencing manner citing durations for the different activities from the beginning of the job to the end. A CPM is created by dividing the entire project into discrete and quantifiable steps; in turn, each step is allotted an estimated time for completion. Ultimately, each step is arranged into a chronological sequence, thus revealing the anticipated length and structure of the entire construction schedule. In addition to serving as a road map for the contractors to determine when and where their work fits into the overall construction sequence, the CPM also assists contractors in assessing their hiring and material purchasing needs.

Roberts & Schaefer Co. v. Hardaway Co., 152 F.3d 1283, 1287 (11th Cir. 1998).

> Essentially, the critical path method is an efficient way of organizing and scheduling a complex project which consists of numerous interrelated separate small projects. Each sub-project is identified and classified as to the duration and precedence of the work. . . . [T]he data is then analyzed, usually

by a computer, to determine the most efficient schedule for the entire project. Many subprojects may be performed at any time within a given period without any effect on the completion of the entire project. However, some items of work are given no leeway and must be performed on schedule; otherwise, the entire project will be delayed. These latter items of work are on the "critical path." A delay, or acceleration, of work along the critical path will affect the entire project.

Haney v. United States, 676 F.2d 584, 595 (Ct. Cl. 1982). *See also* 5 PHILLIP L. BRUNER & PATRICK J. O'CONNOR, JR., BRUNER AND O'CONNOR ON CONSTRUCTION LAW §§ 15:5–8, 10, 127 (2002).

D

Daily Reports. Business records prepared daily, usually by a construction superintendent, clerk of the works, or owner's representative who is present on the project site on a daily basis, are referred to as daily reports. These reports record both routine and irregular observations. Routine observations often include date; hours of work; weather conditions at various times during the workday; attendance or absence of personnel, subcontractors, professionals and visitors; meetings occurring on-site; equipment brought on or taken off the site; deliveries of materials; progress and areas of work. Irregular observations often include meetings occurring on-site; achievement of progress milestones; significant disruptions; accidents and injuries. Parties often use daily reports to support or contest claims for adjustments in contract price and/or time. *See generally* 1 PHILLIP L. BRUNER & PATRICK J. O'CONNOR, JR., BRUNER AND O'CONNOR ON CONSTRUCTION LAW §§ 4:54, 4:55 n.1; 2 BRUNER & O'CONNOR at § 6:84; 5 BRUNER & O'CONNOR at § 15:124 (2002).

Default. When a contracting party commits a material breach or series of breaches of its contractual obligations, which breach goes to the heart of the contract and deprives the other contracting party of the essential bargained-for benefit of the contract, the breaching party is said to be "in default," or to have committed a default. The result of a default is that the nondefaulting party has the right to terminate the contract and, if it has a performance bond, to call upon the surety to respond under its bond. *See* 5 PHILLIP L. BRUNER & PATRICK J. O'CONNOR, JR., BRUNER AND O'CONNOR ON CONSTRUCTION LAW § 18:1 at nn.6–7 and cases cited therein (2002).

Defective Specification. This term refers to a specification by a design professional, including a contractor or supplier with design responsibility, that, when followed by the contractor, proves to be inadequate, inaccurate, impossible to meet, or otherwise defective. Examples include failure to design in accordance with applicable building codes (*see Johnson v. Salem Title Co.*, 425 P.2d 519 (Or. 1967)) and failure to specify flashing to prevent roof leakage (*see Kubby v. Crescent Steel*, 466 P.2d 753 (Ariz. 1970)). Defective specifications are distinguished from defective work or defective products. *See Engelhardt v. Rogers Group, Inc.*, 132 F. Supp. 2d 757, 759 (E.D. Ark. 2001) ("Plaintiffs do not argue that the asphalt itself was defective, or that it was defectively applied to the surface of the road; instead, they insist that Rogers Group was negligent in using the Type III asphalt even though that is what the contract required."). The designer can be subject to liability to the owner or other party that engaged the designer, to the contractor whose costs were increased by the defect, or to persons suffering bodily injury or property damage caused by the defect. *See* 5 PHILLIP L. BRUNER & PATRICK J. O'CONNOR, JR., BRUNER AND O'CONNOR ON CONSTRUCTION LAW § 17:40 (2002). A project owner can also be subject to liability to the contractor for breach of an implied warranty of the adequacy of plans and specifications. *See United States v. Spearin*, 248 U.S. 132 (1918).

Defective Work/Defect. Work or work product that fails to comply with contract requirements is referred to as "defective work" or simply as a "defect." Defects usually result in a deficiency in function, performance, strength, durability, or appearance of the work product. *See* KORNELIS SMIT ET AL., MEANS ILLUSTRATED CONSTRUCTION DICTIONARY 157 (R.S. Means Co. 1991). *See also* definitions of "Critical nonconformance," "Major nonconformance," and "Minor nonconformance" in FAR 46.101, 48 C.F.R. § 46.101. Compare definition of goods as "conforming" under U.C.C. § 2-106(2). Defective work can also result in injury or damage to persons or property.

Contracting parties can be held responsible for correcting the defective work and/or held liable for damages caused by defective work for which they are responsible, by virtue of contract, statute, regulation, or common law. *See* Joseph G. Wagman & Judy H. Chen, *Liability for Defective Work—Drafting Contract Provisions from the General Contractor's Perspective*, CONSTRUCTION LAW., May 1990, at 1. Such liability can be avoided or mitigated by contractual indemnity, exoneration, and limitation of liability provisions and by liability insurance coverage. Wagman & Chen at 34–37.

Delay Claim. A delay claim is one arising from a time impact to the critical path of the planned project schedule and ultimate completion dates provided in the contract between the parties. Claims asserted by contractors against the project owners commonly include delay claims for owner-caused or owner-responsible delay to the contractor. The basis for the claim may include interference with the contractor's work; delayed or restricted access to the site; the owner's failure to coordinate the work; defective, deficient, or incomplete drawings and specifications; changes in the work; delays in making changes, responding to legitimate questions, or approving shop drawings; and/or failure to make timely progress payments. Damages the contractor commonly seeks to recover include costs of extended performance, increased overhead costs (jobsite and office), and escalation in and additions to labor, material, and equipment rental costs. *See* LESLIE O'NEAL COBLE ET AL., ABA FORUM ON THE CONSTRUCTION INDUSTRY, CONSTRUCTION DAMAGES AND REMEDIES 199–201 (ABA 2004).

The project owner may also assert a claim for damages caused by the contractor's late completion of work. The owner's damages commonly include the owner's additional project financing costs, loss of use, lost profits, additional overhead expenses, and additional project management expenses. *Id.* at 165.

Design-Bid-Build (DBB). The traditional method for project delivery in North America during most of the 20th century was design-bid-build.

With this project delivery system, the project owner retains an engineer or an architect in a separate contract to design the work. After the design is completed to the extent required by the design contract (there are numerous situations where the design need not be fully complete at this juncture), a set of plans, specifications, and general construction contract administration terms is advertised by the owner for bid within the construction industry. Construction contractors submit a price to the owner, and the project, if a public project, is awarded to the lowest responsive and responsible bidder. *See Associated Subcontractors of Massachusetts, Inc. v. University of Massachusetts Building Authority*, 810 N.E.2d 1214 (Mass. 2004). In many jurisdictions, owners who advertise their design for bid in a design-bid-build arrangement impliedly warrant to the bidding contractors that the plans are adequate, accurate, and complete. *See Greenbriar Digging Service L.P. v. South Central Water Ass'n*, Civil Action No. 3:07-CV-601, 2009 WL 812241 (S.D. Miss. March 26, 2009); *Interstate Contracting*

Corp. v. City of Dallas, 407 F.3d 708 (5th Cir. 2005). Bidding contractors likewise impliedly warrant to bidding subcontractors that the plans are adequate, accurate, and complete.

Design-bid-build has also been described as a "segmented delivery strategy in which design is fully separated from construction." JOHN B. MILLER, PRINCIPLES OF PUBLIC AND PRIVATE INFRASTRUCTURE DELIVERY 50 (Kluwer Academic Publishers 2000). The Federal Brooks Act of 1972, 40 U.S.C. §§ 1101–1104 (2009), entrenched design-bid-build as the only viable delivery model in federal procurement for the remainder of the 20th century, because it effectively required that all design services be procured through negotiation without regard to price. This requirement forced government agencies to always procure design and construction services separately, since by rule they had to proceed under different procurement paths—one by negotiation, the other by competitive bidding. The Brooks Act acted as a bar to design-build delivery. *Fluor Enterprises, Inc. v. United States*, 64 Fed. Cl. 461 (2005).

Design-Build (DB). With the design-build method of project delivery, both the design and construction services are procured from a single entity (which might be a single construction firm with in-house design professionals or a team of construction and design professionals assembled for a project) in a single procurement process. *See* ROBERT F. CUSHMAN, CONSTRUCTION BUSINESS HANDBOOK § 6.02[D], 154 (Aspen 2004).

Design-build was the only delivery model known prior to the late 19th century in federal public works procurement, because the concept of separating design services from construction services had not yet matured. Slowly over the next half-century, the marriage of design and construction services began to erode as, following the private sector, Congress first authorized, and then required, preconstruction preparation (and near completion) of design, including drawings and specifications.

Following the Federal Property and Administrative Services Act of 1949, 41 U.S.C. §§ 251–266 (2009), construction services could be procured only through competitive bidding, but design services could be procured through the more flexible negotiated procurement, following the preferred practice in private projects. This dichotomy resulted in more widespread use in the federal government of design-bid-build deliveries for public works as federal agencies took advantage of the opportunity to procure design services through negotiation.

The Federal Brooks Act of 1972, 40 U.S.C. §§ 1101–1104 (2009), entrenched design-bid-build as the only viable delivery model in federal procurement for the remainder of the 20th century, because it effectively required that all design services be procured through negotiation without regard to price. This requirement forced government agencies to always procure design and construction services separately, since by rule they had to proceed under different procurement paths—one by negotiation, the other by competitive bidding. The Brooks Act acted as a bar to design-build delivery. *Fluor Enterprises, Inc. v. United States*, 64 Fed. Cl. 461 (2005).

Design-build procurement method differs from traditional competitive sealed bidding (design-bid-build) in two important ways. First, under the design/build method, there is only one contract for both the design and the construction of the project. Second, the design/build method allows for subjective evaluations to be made when awarding the contract. Price does not have be the sole or primary criterion for evaluating the proposals. It is design-build's lack of objective, bright-line, and completed design and procurement criteria that raises concerns about its use. In the public arena, critics claim that design-build also vests too much discretion with the governing body regarding when and to whom public contracts are awarded. Because price is not a controlling factor in public design-build source selection, the public entity may not always receive the lowest, most competitive price possible. *Sloan v. Greenville County*, 590 S.E.2d 338, 343–44 (S.C. App. 2003).

Design-Build-Finance-Operate-Maintain (DBFOM). The design-build-finance-operate-maintain (DBFOM) approach bundles the responsibilities for designing, building, financing, operating and maintaining the project's completed facility and transfers them to the project's private sector partners. There is a great deal of variety in DBFOM arrangements in the United States, and especially the degree to which financial responsibilities are actually transferred to the private sector. One commonality that cuts across all DBFOM projects is that they are either partly or wholly financed by debt leveraging revenue streams dedicated to the project. Direct user fees (tolls) are the most common revenue source. Other revenue sources range from lease payments to shadow tolls and vehicle registration fees. Future revenues are leveraged to issue bonds or other debt that provides funds for capital and project development costs. They are also often supplemented by public sector grants in the form of money or contributions in kind, such as rights-of-way. In certain cases, private partners may also be required to make equity investments. In DBFOM projects, the public sector often depends upon life-cycle costing of the constructed asset to achieve desired value calculation.

Design-Build-Finance-Operate-Maintain-Transfer (DBFOMT). The design-build-finance-operate-maintain-transfer (DBFOMT) partnership model is the same as a DBFOM except that the private sector owns the asset until the end of the contract, at which time the ownership is transferred to the public sector. While common abroad, DBFOMT is not often used in the United States today.

Design-Build-Operate (DBO). In the design-build-operate model, a single contract is awarded for the design, construction, and operation of a capital improvement. The title to the facility remains with the public sector unless the project is a design-build-operate-transfer or design-build-own-operate project. The DBO method of contracting is contrary to the separated and sequential approach ordinarily used in the United States by both the public and private sectors. The separated and sequential method involves one contract for design with an architect or engineer, followed by a different contract with a builder for project construction, followed by the owner's taking over the project and operating it.

A design-build approach creates a single point of responsibility for design and construction and can speed project completion by facilitating the overlap of the design and construction phases of the project. On a public project, the operations phase is normally handled by the public sector under a separate operations and maintenance agreement. Combining all three phases into a DBO approach maintains the continuity of private sector involvement and can facilitate private sector financing of public projects supported by user fees generated during the operations phase. The public entity is also relieved from the staffing responsibilities of operation. *See* FIDIC International Federation of Consulting Engineers, Design-Build-Operate Contract (1st ed. 2009).

Design-Build-Operate-Maintain (DBOM). The design-build-operate-maintain (DBOM) model is an integrated partnership that combines the design and construction responsibilities of a design-build procurement with those of an operations and maintenance contract. These project components are procured from the private sector in a single contract with financing secured by the public sector. The public agency maintains ownership and retains a significant level of oversight of the operations through provisions within the DBOM contract.

Design-Build-Own-Operate (DBOO). A variation of the design-build project delivery system is the design-build-own-operate system. This form of project delivery is seen more often in public-private partnerships (P3s or PPPs), but is not the exclusive province of P3s. There are numerous variations of design-build-own-operate, including design-build-operate, design-build-finance-operate-maintain, design-build-operate-maintain, and design-build-finance-operate-maintain-transfer.

See GOV'T ACCOUNTING OFFICE, PUBLIC-PRIVATE PARTNERSHIPS: TERMS RELATED TO BUILDING AND FACILITY PARTNERSHIPS (1999), *available at* http://www.gao.gov/special.pubs/Gg99071.pdf.

Design Development Documents (DDs). The term "DD" refers to design documents generated by the architect and/or engineer, which provide greater detail and information than the schematic design documents yet remain incomplete. The level of detail in the documents is ultimately determined by the owner's request, but design development documents typically include the mechanical, electrical, plumbing, and architectural details. AIA KNOWLEDGE RESOURCES STAFF, AIA BEST PRACTICES: DEFINING THE ARCHITECT'S BASIC SERVICES (July 2007), *available at* http://www.aia.org/aiaucmp/groups/ek_members/documents/pdf/aiap026834.pdf. The conflicts in mechanical, electrical, and structural components that were undetected in the schematic design documents should be resolved at the design development phase. *See* WERNER SABO, LEGAL GUIDE TO AIA DOCUMENTS 41 (5th ed. Aspen 2008). According to the AIA, these documents

> shall illustrate and describe the refinement of the design of the Project, establishing the scope, relationship, forms, size and appearance of the Project by means of the plans, sections and elevations, typical construction details, and equipment layouts . . . [and] shall include specifications that identify major materials and systems and establish in general their quality levels.

AIA Document B141-1997, Standard Form of Agreement Between Owner and Architect with Standard Terms and Conditions, § 2.4.3.1 (1997).

Design Documents. The primary documents used to define and describe a project are identified as the project's design documents. In general terms, any item that can be used to depict the whole or a portion of the project can be part of the project's design documents. The definition of design documents can take on added importance if, for example, issues arise on a project regarding the scope of the contracted work. Development of the design documents is typically done in stages referred to as the schematic design documents, design development documents, and construction documents, with the construction documents typically being the "final" design documents that are submitted for obtaining the necessary approvals and permits from governmental jurisdictions, and by the contractor for the construction of a given project.

The AIA describes "design documents" as representations, in any medium of expression now known or later developed, of the tangible and intangible creative work performed by the architect and the architect's consultants under their respective professional services agreements. The AIA further labels design documents "instruments of service," which is a term of art in intellectual property law. Under this nomenclature, the ownership of the intellectual property rights in the design documents remains with the architect, regardless of design modification (whether by the architect or others), use of the completed project, even termination of the architect from the project. Instruments of service under the AIA definition "include, without limitation, studies, surveys, models, sketches, drawings, specifications, and other similar materials." AIA Document A201-2007, General Conditions of the Contract for Construction, § 1.1 (2007).

The issue of who owns the intellectual property of the design of the project is one that the parties should address contractually at the outset of project development. Designers commonly desire to maintain ownership of the design and allow the design to be used only for that project's construction. Design ownership rights may be transferred or retained by contract, and are generally as negotiable as other contractual rights such as price and fee.

Design Professional. The term commonly used to identify the person or persons responsible for the design of a construction project is "design professional." Included within this definition are licensed practitioners of architecture (including landscape architecture) and professional engineers (including land surveying) who provide certain creative elements used in the construction of a project. *Design Professional Rights and Obligations, in* 1 CONSTRUCTION AND DESIGN LAW § 4.1 (1989) (Michie Co. 1984). Where a contract uses the word "architect" or "engineer," it generally means a licensed architect or engineer as well as their consultants.

> A design professional is typically responsible for the preparation of plans and specifications (information) that are supplied to and used by potential bidders in formulating a bid for a project. Additionally, a design professional may make

representations to a contractor while performing administrative responsibilities, which are either assumed or specifically made a part of his or her contract with the owner. The design professional is paid a fee for using his or her skills and training to provide information that is relied on by others prior to and during construction.

Excavation Technologies, Inc. v. Columbia Gas Co., 936 A.2d 111, 115 (Pa. Super. Ct. 2007).

Diary (of Superintendent). In the context of the construction industry, the term "diary" means a person's (commonly the superintendent's) daily record in written form in which the site supervisor records on-site project activities and occurrences. *See County Excavation, Inc. v. State of New York*, 255 N.Y.S.2d 708 (Ct. Cl. 1964) and *United Construction Co., Inc. v. United States*, 10 Cl. Ct. 257 (1986).

The site diary is kept by project superintendents (or, in larger projects, assistant superintendents) to record all activities on-site including weather, visitors, special meetings and operatives on-site, manpower levels, work undertaken (including locations), progress made, and health and safety issues. Most recorders are required to record this information on a daily basis. This information has traditionally been kept in a notebook; however, with the onset of electronic communications, the industry has moved toward creating and maintaining this information in paperless form, electronically recorded and archived in the home office and at the project site. Many contractors utilize a formalized process whereby the recording superintendent completes a diary form electronically and then sends it both to the project's site file and to the contractor's home office to be kept in its separate records.

On every project it is essential that a day-to-day record of site activities be prepared and maintained (there are few excuses for "lost" daily reports). Because the site diary is a contemporaneous record of events, it is the best evidence in written form of what happened at the time. Site diaries may be utilized mid-project to verify health and safety audits/inspections, quality inspections, and progress reports, and need to be kept post-project for claims and disputes. *See Belcon, Inc. v. D.C. Water & Sewer Authority*, 826 A.2d 380 (D.C. 2003). Currently the process for recording information in site diaries varies across the industry.

Many general contractors also require their trade subcontractors to keep site diaries to document project progress, including amount of subcontractor manpower (supervisors and laborers) on-site, equipment used, and materials delivered and incorporated, for the same reasons set forth above. *See CC-Aventura, Inc. v. Weitz Co., LLC*, No. 06-21598-CIV 2007 WL 2700603 (S.D. Fla. Sept. 12, 2007).

Site diaries are most often referred to when there is a query (or dispute) as to what actually took place on-site. The usefulness of the information in response to such a query (and/or dispute) is in direct proportion to the thoroughness of detail of the site diary entry.

Dispute Adjudication Board (DAB). A dispute adjudication board (DAB) is a jobsite dispute adjudication process, typically composed of three independent and impartial construction professionals who are experienced and knowledgeable in the commercial and technical aspects of the project. The DAB members are selected by the contracting parties, and the DAB procedures and powers are spelled out beforehand in the construction contract. The DAB will normally be appointed at the commencement of the project, with the objective that its members become familiar with the technical and contractual characteristics of the project and continue to monitor its progress until completion. The significant difference between a DAB and most other alternative dispute review techniques is that the DAB is appointed at the commencement of a project before any disputes arise and, by undertaking regular visits to the site, is actively involved throughout the project. A DAB has "real-time" value. The idea behind a standing DAB is that it would be called upon early in the evolution of a project dispute that cannot be resolved by the parties and be asked to make decisions on how a dispute is to be resolved. DABs and DRBs (Dispute Review Boards) operate similarly. Like a DRB, a DAB is established to promote resolution of disputes while construction is still under way. Unlike a DRB, a DAB renders a decision following an evidentiary hearing; DRBs issue recommendations. The parties decide the effect of the DAB's decision and the protocol and scope of decisional review.

Dispute Review Board (DRB). A dispute review board (DRB) is a panel of experienced, respected, and impartial construction professionals acting as project reviewers. The DRB is normally organized before construction begins and meets regularly on-site at certain intervals. The cost of the DRB is normally shared by the owner and contractor, and the DRB's procedures and powers are spelled out beforehand in the construction contract. Typically, the DRB receives copies of the contract documents and is kept informed of project developments. The DRB meets with representatives of the owner and contractor during its regular site visits, hears concerns and complaints, and encourages resolution of disputes at the site project management level. *See* INTERNATIONAL CHAMBER of Commerce Dispute Resolution Board Rules (2004); American Arbitration Association, AAA Dispute Resolution Board Operating Procedures and AAA Dispute Resolution Board Guide Specification (2000).

The DRB process is intended to help the parties head off project problems before they escalate into major disputes. When the parties cannot themselves resolve a dispute arising from either the direction of the work or the interpretation of contract responsibilities, it can be referred to the DRB. An in-person hearing is usually convened, during which each party explains its position and answers questions from the other party and the DRB. In arriving at a recommendation, the DRB considers the relevant contract provisions and other documents, correspondence, testimony, and other particular circumstances of the dispute. The DRB's report is a nonbinding explanation of a decision and recommendation for resolution of the dispute. The report includes an explanation of the DRB's evaluation of the facts and contract provisions and the reasoning that led to the report's conclusions. Robert F. Cushman et al., Construction Dispute Resolution Formbook 209 (Wolters Kluwer 1997).

Acceptance by the parties of the DRB's recommendation is the rule rather than the exception. Although the decision is generally nonbinding, the parties often defer to the judgment of the Board; to do otherwise would defeat the purpose of having a DRB. The parties' acceptance of the DRB's recommendation is facilitated by the parties' confidence in the DRB, the technical expertise of its members, and their firsthand understanding of project conditions, as well as the DRB method providing the parties with due process and a fair opportunity to be heard.

Disruption/Inefficiency/Loss of Efficiency/Loss of Productivity. Unanticipated events that occur on a project can cause impacts to the planned performance of a contractor or subcontractor. These impacts are often described as disruption that causes inefficiency (loss of efficiency) or loss of productivity. These terms describe components of claims of contractors and subcontractors for extra costs resulting from unforeseen delay to or acceleration of their work alleged to have been caused by someone higher in the contractual chain. For general contractors, the claim is normally against the project owner or those for whom the owner is responsible. For a first-tier subcontractor, the claim could arise from the actions of the owner, but also from the actions of the general contractor, for instance, who orders the subcontractor to accelerate its work and/or work in many areas at the same time.

The delay to or acceleration of a contractor's work affects the contractor's variable costs, which include the contractor's labor, equipment, and job overhead. Of these, the major variable risk component by far is the contractor's management, supervision, and labor costs (including those of its principal sub-contractors). Claims based on increases in a contractor's management and labor costs due to delay or acceleration are commonly measured by the disruption of the contractor's workforce in terms of loss of labor efficiency and productivity. Labor productivity is expressed in man-hours per unit of work produced (labor productivity = man-hours/unit of work). If more man-hours are needed to produce a unit of disrupted or impacted work than prior to an alleged disruption, the result is a loss of productivity. WILLIAM SCHWARTZKOPF, CALCULATING LOST LABOR PRODUCTIVITY IN CONSTRUCTION CLAIMS 3–5 (Aspen 2d ed. 2004).

E

Early Finish. In the construction industry proper scheduling of the numerous different parts of the work taking place sequentially or simultaneously is vital to a successful project. One common scheduling method is known as the critical path method (CPM). In a CPM schedule, the phrase "early finish," "earliest finish," or "early finish date" refers to the first possible point at which the as-yet-to-be-completed elements of a scheduled activity (or, depending on the particular context, the entire project as a whole) may potentially be completed. The early finish date is arrived at through usage of the project schedule network logic, as well as accurately factoring in any known or predictable scheduling constraints.

The earliest time an activity may be completed is equal to the early start of the activity plus its remaining duration. While the early finish date can be created and/or established at an early point in the project planning process, the early finish date will likely be modified multiple times throughout the life cycle of the project, particularly as (i) the project advances into different stages, (ii) unanticipated delays occur, and (iii) changes are made to the project scope of work. These modifications are typically noted on the monthly project schedule updates (in ideal cases, including being ahead of schedule). *See* 5 PHILLIP L. BRUNER & PATRICK J. O'CONNOR, JR., BRUNER AND O'CONNOR ON CONSTRUCTION LAW § 15:8 (2002).

Early Neutral Evaluation (ENE). Early neutral evaluation (ENE) is a method of dispute resolution akin to a mini-trial. The U.S. District Court, Northern

District of California, ADR Program (ADR Local Rule 5) describes ENE as follows:

> The goals of ENE are to: enhance direct communication between the parties about their claims and supporting evidence; provide an assessment of the merits of the case by a neutral expert; provide a "reality check" for clients and lawyers; identify and clarify the central issues in dispute; assist with discovery and motion planning or with an informal exchange of key information; and facilitate settlement discussions.
>
> ENE aims to position the case for early resolution by settlement, dispositive motion or trial. The Northern District ENE may serve as a cost-effective substitute for formal discovery and pretrial motions. Although settlement is not the major goal of ENE, the process can lead to settlement.

The evaluator, an experienced attorney with expertise in the case's subject matter, hosts an informal meeting of clients and counsel at which the following occurs: (1) each side—through counsel, clients, or witnesses—presents the evidence and arguments supporting its case (without regard to the rules of evidence and without direct or cross-examination of witnesses); (2) the evaluator identifies areas of agreement, clarifies and focuses the issues, and encourages the parties to enter procedural and substantive stipulations; (3) the evaluator writes a private evaluation that includes an estimate, where feasible, of the likelihood of liability and the dollar range of damages; an assessment of the relative strengths and weaknesses of each party's case; and reasoning that supports his assessment. The evaluator has no power to impose settlement and does not attempt to coerce a party to accept any proposed terms. The parties' formal discovery, disclosure, and motion practice rights are fully preserved. The confidential evaluation is nonbinding and is not shared with the trial judge.

The American Arbitration Association, in its publication *AAA Resolution Services—Early Neutral Evaluation: Getting an Expert's Assessment* (2005), describes the ENE process as a forum that "encourages direct communication between adversarial parties about possible claims and supporting evidence—particularly important in situations where the disputants are far apart in their views on the evidence and how the law applies to the facts in question or what the case is worth . . . ." The Early Neutral Evaluation process can be triggered by written agreement in the parties' contract or by mutual agreement if such a settlement procedure is not contemplated by their contract.

Once the process has been initiated, the parties are given a list of potential neutral evaluators who possess the required expertise to hear the dispute. The parties then mutually agree upon an evaluator. The evaluator first arranges with the parties an appropriate schedule for exchanging written initial statements. Generally, an initial statement describes the substance of the dispute, the party's view of the critical liability and damages issues, important evidence, and any other information that may be useful to the evaluator. The evaluator and the parties normally also agree to the length and extent of the initial written statements.

At the evaluation (generally, in-person), each party presents its claims or defenses and describes the principal evidence on which its claims or defenses are based. The evaluation session is informal and the rules of evidence do not apply. There is no formal examination or cross-examination of witnesses, and the presentations and discussions are not recorded. Generally, a written evaluation is rendered approximately 14 days after the evaluation concludes.

Easement (or Right of Way). Construction projects often impact adjacent property, making it critical for project owners and contractors to make sure they have appropriate rights to use or impact adjacent property. Often the use or impact for a construction project requires only limited rights, not outright ownership and control of the adjacent property. One important form of a limited right to use or impact the property of another is an easement. "An easement is merely the right to use the land of another." *Drees Co. v. Thompson*, 868 N.E.2d 32, 41 (Ind. Ct. App. 2007). "An easement is neither an estate in land nor the "land" itself. It is, however, property or an interest in land. Thus, an easement is real property." 25 Am. Jur. 2d *Easements and Licenses* § 2 (2010).

Failing to have the requisite rights to use or impact adjacent property can create liability or severe problems for participants in a construction project, including liability for trespass, requirements to tear down buildings constructed on adjacent property, work shutdowns, and the need to use more expensive alternative methods of construction. Easements or some other form of permission to use adjacent property could be needed for a number of situations. The project may need to run permanent utility lines over adjacent property in order to have service for the project; the contractor may need to construct temporary scaffolding on adjacent property; limited space on-site may require the use of adjacent property for storage or staging areas; access for construction equipment may require use of adjacent property; the contractor may need to swing the boom of its crane and the loads it lifts through the airspace above adjacent property; shoring may impact or require the use of adjacent property; or the contractor or owner may need to temporarily or permanently divert runoff onto adjacent property. Easements are an important form of property right that can be used to provide the necessary permission to use adjacent property in these situations. *See generally* CARINA Y. OHARA ET AL., FORMS & SUBSTANCE: SPECIALIZED AGREEMENTS FOR THE CONSTRUCTION PROJECT (ABA 2007).

Economic Loss Doctrine. Many jurisdictions have adopted this doctrine, which is a rule of law barring a claimant from recovering purely economic losses from a defendant with whom the claimant did not have contractual privity unless the claimant suffered personal injury or physical property damage. The modern version of the doctrine was articulated in *Seely v. White Motor Co.*, 63 Cal. 2d 9, 45 Cal. Rptr. 17, 403 P.2d 145 (1965), a case involving a claim by the buyer of goods. Economic losses are losses that are financial; economic losses include losses for such things as diminished value, additional or increased costs of construction, costs of corrective work, costs to replace defective products, unpaid contract balances, and overhead and profit. Physical injuries such as bodily injury or physical property damage are not economic losses. Most other types of damages are economic losses. As one court described it, "'Economic losses' occur when there is no personal injury and no physical harm to other property." *Gunkel v. Renovations, Inc.*, 822 N.E.2d 150, 153–54 (Ind. 2005).

In construction, there are many parties involved in a project, all interdependent on each other even though they do not all have contracts with everyone involved on the project. A major issue is whether to apply the economic loss doctrine to protect a party on a construction project from the claims of another harmed by the actions of the party for purely economic losses even though there was no contract between the two. A number of jurisdictions have used the economic loss doctrine to bar recovery of economic losses when the claimant did not suffer personal injury or physical property damage and did not have a contract with the defendant. *See, e.g., BRW, Inc. v. Dufficy & Sons, Inc.*, 99 P.3d 66 (Colo. 2004) (subcontractor's tort claims against engineer and inspector for economic losses were barred by the economic loss doctrine); *Gunkel v. Renovations, Inc.*, 822 N.E.2d 150 (Ind. 2005) (homeowners were barred from recovering for economic losses from mason for economic losses under tort theory, but were allowed to recover under claim for breach of contract); *Lord v. Customized Consulting Specialty, Inc.*, 643 S.E.2d 28 (N.C. Ct. App. 2007) (homeowners were barred by economic loss doctrine from recovering from truss subcontractor in negligence for damages to the trusses themselves as those were economic losses, but they were allowed to recover for physical damage to other portions of their homes); *Rotonda Condominium Unit Owners Ass'n v. Rotonda Associates*, 380 S.E.2d 876 (Va. 1989) (economic loss doctrine precluded condominium homeowners' association from recovering economic losses from condominium developer under tort theories and left as the association's only recourse recovery under breach of contract or statutory warranties); *Alejandre v. Bull*, 153 P.3d 864 (Wash. 2007) (economic loss doctrine barred claims by home purchasers against developer for fraud and misrepresentation).

A number of other jurisdictions reject the economic loss doctrine in connection with service providers and have allowed contractors or others to sue service providers, such as architects and engineers, for economic losses without being in privity of contract and without suffering personal injury or property damage. *See, e.g., Moransais v. Heathman*, 744 So. 2d 973 (Fla. 1999) (economic loss doctrine did not bar homeowner's claims for negligent inspection against an engineer despite the lack of a contract between the two parties); *A.R. Moyer, Inc. v. Graham*, 285 So. 2d 397 (Fla. 1973) (a general contractor who may foreseeably be injured and sustain economic losses caused by an architect or engineer's negligent performance of a contractual duty may recover from the architect or engineer even though the contractor is not the one that has the contract with the architect or engineer), limited by *Casa Clara Condominium Ass'n v. Charley Toppino & Sons, Inc.*, 620 So. 2d 1244 (Fla. 1993) (economic loss doctrine barred claims for purely economic losses by homeowners against a product supplier (a concrete supplier) with whom they did not have a contract); *Farrell Construction Co. v. Jefferson Parish*, 693 F. Supp. 490 (E.D. La. 1988) (contractor allowed to pursue negligence claims for economic losses against engineer despite lack of privity); *Prichard Bros., Inc. v. Grady Co.*, 428 N.W.2d 391 (Minn. 1988) (contractor allowed to pursue negligence claims for economic losses against engineer despite lack of privity); *Jim's Excavating Services, Inc. v. HKM Associates*, 878 P.2d 248 (Mont. 1994) (contractor could recover for purely economic losses from an engineer for negligent design and supervision even though the contractor did not have a contract with the engineer); *John Martin Co. v. Morse/Diesel, Inc.*, 819 S.W.2d 428 (Tenn. 1991) (subcontractor allowed to pursue claim for negligence against construction manager despite the fact there was no contract between the two).

Eichleay Formula. The Eichleay formula is commonly used to measure the amount of damages recoverable for extended home office overhead in a suspension of work or delay claim asserted by a contractor. The formula is named after a federal government contract case, *Appeal of Eichleay Corp.*, 60-2 B.C.A. (CCH) ¶ 2688, 1960 WL 538 (ASBCA 1960), which recognized the use of this formula to measure damages in a federal government contract case, although previous cases had also employed the same formula. *See, e.g., Fred R. Comb Co. v. United States*, 103 Ct. Cl. 174, 181, 183–84 (1945); *Houston Ready-Cut House Co. v. United States*, 119 Ct. Cl. 120, 172–73, 192–93 (1951).

The courts have recognized that a contractor needs to recover its home office overhead by allocating these costs to the various contracts that the contractor has, even though these costs are not directly attributable to a particular contract.

> Suspension or delay of contract performance results in interruption or reduction of the contractor's stream of income from payments for direct costs incurred. This in turn causes an interruption or reduction in payments for overhead, derived as a percentage of direct costs, which is set by the contract. Home office overhead costs continue to accrue during such periods, however, regardless of direct contract activity. Consequently, this decrease in payments for direct costs creates unabsorbed overhead, unless home office workers are laid off or given additional work during such suspension or delay periods. When the period of delay is uncertain and the contractor is required by the government to remain ready to resume performance on short notice (referred to as "standby"), the contractor is effectively prohibited from making reductions in home office staff or facilities or by taking on additional work.

Wickham Contracting Co. v. Fischer, 12 F.3d 1574, 1577–78 (Fed. Cir. 1994). "The Armed Services Board of Contract Appeals devised the *Eichleay* formula to provide a fair method for allocating home office overhead costs, otherwise inallocable, to specific contracts." *Wickham Contracting Co.*, 12 F.3d at 1578.

The formula is as follows:

(1)	Total contract billing/ Total billings for contract period	×	Total home office overhead for contract period	=	Overhead allocable to the contract
(2)	Allocable overhead/ Days of performance	=	Daily contract overhead		
(3)	Daily contract overhead	×	No. days delay	=	Amount claimed

First, the formula calculates the amount of the claimant's overhead that would have been allocated to the contract had there been no delay. Second, the formula calculates what the daily allocation of overhead to the contract would have been had there been no delay. Third, the formula multiplies the daily overhead calculation by the number of days of delay in order to calculate the amount of the claim for extended home office overhead due to the delay. "The Eichleay formula estimates unabsorbed overhead by determining a daily overhead dollar amount for a particular contract and multiplying that amount by the number of days of delay." *Mech-Con Corp. v. West*, 61 F.3d 883, 886 (Fed. Cir. 1995).

Generally, in order to use the Eichleay formula, a contractor must prove that it was required to be on standby for the duration of the delay and could not obtain replacement work. "[A] contractor must show: (1) a government-imposed delay; (2) that the contractor was on 'standby'; and (3) that the contractor was unable to take on other work." *Mech-Con Corp.*, 61 F.3d at 886. *See also* 6 PHILLIP L. BRUNER & PATRICK J. O'CONNOR, JR., BRUNER AND O'CONNOR ON CONSTRUCTION LAW § 19:85 (2002 & Supp. 2009). Many federal and state courts have recognized the use of the Eichleay formula, although there has also been some criticism and some disfavored "modified" Eichleay formulae. *See* 6 PHILLIP L. BRUNER & PATRICK J. O'CONNOR, JR., BRUNER AND O'CONNOR ON CONSTRUCTION LAW § 19:85 (2002 & Supp. 2009).

Employer. In the United States, the term "employer" means the party that employs workers. In the international construction contracting context, the term means the party that "employs" or contracts with the contractor or the engineer—in other words, the project owner. WENDY KENNEDY VENOIT ET AL., INTERNATIONAL CONSTRUCTION LAW 71 n.1 (ABA 2009).

Employer's Liability Insurance. A workers' compensation policy includes employer's liability insurance. Coverage A or Part One of the workers' compensation policy provides the coverage to protect the insured from liability under the applicable workers' compensation laws. Coverage B or Part Two of the workers' compensation policy is the employer's liability insurance. Employer's liability insurance provides coverage for employment-related bodily injury or disease not covered by workers' compensation laws. A claim that might be covered by the employer's liability insurance is a claim by an employee for a disease that at least in part arose out of the employment but does not come within the definition of occupational disease in the applicable workers' compensation law. Another example might be a claim where an employee of a contractor sues the project owner for an injury alleged to result from an unsafe condition on the owner's property, and the owner then sues the contractor that employed the claimant for contribution or indemnification alleging negligence on the part of the contractor, referred to as an "action over" claim. *See generally* WILLIAM J. PALMER ET AL., CONSTRUCTION INSURANCE, BONDING, AND RISK MANAGEMENT 128–29 (McGraw-Hill 1996); PATRICK J. WIELINSKI ET AL., CONTRACTUAL RISK TRANSFER: STRATEGIES FOR CONTRACT INDEMNITY AND INSURANCE PROVISIONS XIV.E.1–.3 (International Risk Management Institute 1995 & Supp. 2009).

Engineer. An engineer is a professional who provides design and other services based on the application of mathematics and engineering science. All states require engineers to be licensed in order to practice engineering, subject to exceptions, and define "engineer" and what it means to practice engineering by statute. An example is:

> "Engineer" means a person who, by reason of intensive preparation in the use of mathematics, chemistry, physics, and engineering sciences, including the principles and methods of engineering analysis and design, is qualified to perform engineering work as defined in this part 1. "Engineering" means analysis or design work requiring intensive preparation and experience in the use of mathematics, chemistry, and physics and the engineering sciences.

COLO. REV. STAT. ANN. § 12-25-102(3), (4) (Supp. 2009).

> "Practice of engineering" means the performance for others of any professional service or creative work requiring engineering education, training, and experience and the application of special knowledge of the mathematical and engineering sciences to such professional services or creative work, including consultation, investigation, evaluation, planning, design, and the observation of construction to evaluate compliance with plans and specifications in connection with the utilization of the forces, energies, and materials of nature in the development, production, and functioning of engineering processes, apparatus, machines, equipment, facilities, structures, buildings, works, or utilities, or any combination or aggregations thereof, employed in or devoted to public or private enterprise or uses.

COLO. REV. STAT. ANN. § 12-25-102(10) (Supp. 2009). *See also* HUGH BROOKS, ENCY-CLOPEDIA OF BUILDING AND CONSTRUCTION TERMS 166 (Prentice-Hall, Inc. 1983).

The requirements for obtaining an engineering license in most states include such things as minimum age, formal education and type of degree, years of experience, recommendations, proof of good moral character, passing an examination, and paying a fee. Depending on the jurisdiction, there can also be significant restrictions on corporate form, ownership, and control of companies that provide engineering services; and the consequences of violating licensing statutes can include criminal penalties and the inability of an engineer to enforce his contract or be paid for any of his services. STEVEN G.M. STEIN, CONSTRUCTION LAW ¶ 1.01 [1] (Matthew Bender 2009). *See, e.g., Ellers, Oakley, Chester & Rike, Inc. v. St. Louis Air Cargo Services, Inc.*, 984 F.2d 1108 (10th Cir. 1993) (engineer that violated licensing requirements could not recover payment for his services under his contracts, which as a result was unenforceable or under equitable principles that people should pay for value received).

Engineer-Procure-Construct (EPC). An EPC contract is a design-build contract generally used for industrial or process plants where the contractor agrees to design the plant, procure the equipment and materials, construct the plant, and turn it over to the owner after starting up and commissioning the plant and demonstrating that it operates as promised. Such contracts are often referred to as EPC contracts because the design professionals involved are engineers, and equipment components are of such importance that procurement of the equipment receives special emphasis. *See* WENDY KENNEDY VENOIT ET AL., INTERNATIONAL CONSTRUCTION LAW 77–78, 88–90 (ABA 2009); Joseph A. Huse & Jonathan Kay Hoyle, *FIDIC Design-Build, Turnkey and EPC Contracts*, 16 INT'L CONSTRUCTION L. REV. 27, 35–36 (1999).

Equitable Lien. A right that is not recognized by statute as a lien, but can be enforced out of doctrines of equity to have a claim satisfied from a specific piece of property or specific funds, is referred to as an equitable lien. An example of a situation that might create an equitable lien in certain jurisdictions is where a contractor works on a project, but is not paid, and the lender with a mortgage takes over the project in the foreclosure of the mortgage but does not disburse the loan proceeds. In some jurisdictions, the courts will grant the contractor an equitable lien in the undisbursed loan proceeds if the court concludes that, under the circumstances, it would be unfair for the lender to seize the collateral made valuable by the contractor's efforts and also keep the loan proceeds that were supposed to be disbursed to pay the contractor. *See, e.g., Swinerton*

& Walberg Co. v. Union Bank, 101 Cal. Rptr. 665 (Ct. App. 2d Dist. 1972); *Emerald Designs, Inc. v. Citibank F.S.B.*, 626 So. 2d 1084 (Fla. Dist. Ct. App. 4th Dist. 1993); *Tradesmen International, Inc. v. Lockheed Martin Corp.*, 241 F. Supp. 2d 1337 (D. Kan. 2003). *See generally* 6 PHILLIP L. BRUNER & PATRICK J. O'CONNOR, JR., BRUNER AND O'CONNOR ON CONSTRUCTION LAW § 8:149 (2002 & Supp. 2009).

Escalation. Increases in the cost of materials or services are often characterized as escalation. When price increases are difficult to predict, it is risky for contractors or suppliers to commit to a price for performance that extends very far into the future. Such circumstances can make a fixed-price contract less profitable for a contractor or supplier when the escalation is unexpected, and can even bankrupt contractors and suppliers. The longer the duration of the contract or the more volatile the inflation, the greater the risk to the contractor or supplier in agreeing to a price. Under those circumstances, one method for contractors and suppliers to protect themselves is to include price escalation clauses (also referred to as "escalator clauses") in their bids and contracts. Price escalation clauses provide that the contract price will be increased in the costs to the contractor for the materials or services included in the scope of the clause increase, usually by more than a certain percentage. W.E. Shipley, *"Escalator" Price Adjustment Clauses*, 63 A.L.R. 2d 1337 (2009).

Estoppel. Estoppel means a bar on asserting certain rights or defenses or denying or claiming certain facts or legal arguments. For example, when a contractor's bid is accepted by an owner, the law in many states holds that any subcontractor on whose bid the contractor relied is bound by its bid to the general contractor by the principle of estoppel. *See, e.g., Drennan v. Star Paving Co.*, 333 P.2d 757 (1958); *Preload Technology, Inc. v. A.B. & J. Construction Co.*, 696 F.2d 1080 (5th Cir. 1983).

Excusable Delay. Construction contracts typically require the parties to perform by certain deadlines. Failure of one party, often the contractor or a subcontractor, to meet a deadline can constitute a breach of contract and create liability to the other party unless the delay is excusable. Whether a delay is excusable is usually determined by the terms of the contract, or if the delay is not contemplated by the contract, then by the application of various legal principles. Sometimes the contractor or other performing party is not only entitled to an excuse from performing on time, but also may be entitled to an adjustment or extension of the time or performance and compensation for the delay. As one commentator has observed, "A compensable delay is one for which the contractor may recover from the owner its resulting increased costs. All compensable delays are also excusable delays; however, not all excusable delays are also

74

compensable delays." STEVEN G.M. STEIN, CONSTRUCTION LAW ¶ 6.09 (Matthew Bender 2009). *See also* 5 PHILLIP L. BRUNER & PATRICK J. O'CONNOR, JR., BRUNER AND O'CONNOR ON CONSTRUCTION LAW § 15:42–15:49 (2002 & Supp. 2009).

Expert. Generally, a person with special knowledge, skill, experience, training, or education who can provide more insight into the facts and data available than the typical person is referred to as an expert.

> Ordinarily, a determination that the care, skill, and diligence exercised by a professional engaged in furnishing skilled services for compensation was less than that normally possessed and exercised by members of that profession in good standing and that the damage sustained resulted from the variance requires expert testimony to establish the prevailing standard and the consequences of departure from it in the case under consideration.

City of Eveleth v. Ruble, 302 Minn. 249, 254–55, 225 N.W.2d 521, 525 (1974) (holding also that some acts of negligence were so obvious that expert testimony was not required for them). In a trial, one must meet the requirements of the rules of evidence before the court will allow expert testimony.

> If scientific, technical, or other specialized knowledge will assist the trier of fact to understand the evidence or determine a fact issue, a witness qualified as an expert by knowledge, skill, experience, training, or education, may testify thereto in the form of an opinion or otherwise, if (1) the testimony is based on sufficient facts or data, (2) the testimony is the product of reliable principles and methods, and (3) the witness has applied the principles and methods reliably to the facts of the case.

FED. R. EVID. 702. When there is an "expert determination" process, the person selected to make the determination is the "expert" for the purposes of that process.

Expert Determination. A dispute resolution process known as expert determination is one in which the parties contractually agree to select an independent third party, or panel of independent third parties, to study the facts and data involved in the dispute and issue a decision as an expert, and not as an arbitrator, to resolve the dispute. The parties can choose to have the decision be final and binding or simply advisory. The expert determination process is typically less formal than an arbitration and may not involve a hearing. Dispute review boards can be considered a form of expert determination. Outside of North America, final and binding expert determinations have been used more often and have had more attention. *See generally Donald L. Marston, Final and Binding Expert Determination as an ADR Technique*, 2001 INT'L CONSTRUCTION L. REV. 213.

Extended (or Unabsorbed) Home Office Overhead. Extended (or unabsorbed) home office overhead refers to indirect costs resulting from an extension of the construction contract's performance period attributable to compensable delay, suspension, or disruption. See 6 PHILLIP L. BRUNER & PATRICK J. O'CONNOR, JR., BRUNER AND O'CONNOR ON CONSTRUCTION LAW § 19:85 (Supp. 2009).

> Home office overhead costs are those that are expended for the benefit of the whole business, which by their nature cannot be attributed or charged to any particular contract. In contracting with the government, a company necessarily includes a portion of home office overhead expenses, which it calculates based on the contract's duration, in its estimate of costs to perform the contract. When the government delays or disrupts contract performance, ultimately requiring that it be extended, the contractor's stream of income from the government for the direct costs it has incurred under the contract is reduced or interrupted. However, home office overhead continues to accrue throughout both the original and extended performance periods, regardless of direct contract activity.

Altmayer v. Johnson, 79 F.3d 1129, 1132–33 (Fed. Cir. 1996) (internal citations and quotations omitted). Extended (or unabsorbed) home office overhead costs are typically calculated using the *Eichleay* formula. *See* 6 PHILLIP L. BRUNER & PATRICK J. O'CONNOR, JR., BRUNER AND O'CONNOR ON CONSTRUCTION LAW § 19:85 (Supp. 2009). "The *Eichleay* formula approximates extended home office overhead costs by calculating a daily overhead dollar amount for the contract in question and multiplying that figure by the number of days of delay." *Altmayer v. Johnson*, 79 F.3d at 1133.

Extras/Extra Work Order. "'[E]xtras' means work or costs arising outside of and entirely independent of the contract; that is, something not required in its performance, not contemplated by the parties, and not controlled by the contract." *Candee Construction Co. v. Department of Transportation*, 447 N.W.2d 339, 343 (S.D. 1989). *See also* JUSTIN SWEET, LEGAL ASPECTS OF ARCHITECTURE, ENGINEERING AND THE CONSTRUCTION PROCESS § 21.04, 456–57 (5th ed. 1994). Some jurisdictions have enumerated distinct elements to define extra work:

> Under Illinois law, in order for a contractor to recover money for "extra work," it must show by clear and convincing evidence that the work was 1) outside the scope of the original contract; 2) ordered at the direction of the owner; 3) agreed to be paid for by the owner either by words or by conduct; 4) not voluntarily furnished by the contractor; and 5) not rendered necessary by fault of the contractor.

Brant Construction Co. v. Metropolitan Water Reclamation District, 967 F.2d 244, 246 (7th Cir. 1992).

> If a change is considered outside the scope of the contract and, hence, an extra, the contractor or subcontractor must not only comply with the provisions of the contract in regard to documenting and authorizing the extras, but the contractor must be prepared to inform the owner of the cost of the extra. The usual recovery price, unless an "extras formula" is agreed to in the contract, is the reasonable value of extra work.

2 STEPHEN G.M. STEIN, CONSTRUCTION LAW ¶ 4.02 (Matthew Bender 2009). An "extra work order" is often the document prepared by an owner and contractor to memorialize the extra work.

F

False Claims Act (FCA). The False Claims Act (FCA) (*see* 31 U.S.C. §§ 3729 to 3733) imposes civil and criminal penalties on persons who knowingly present false or fraudulent monetary claims to the federal government or who knowingly use a false record to avoid or decrease a monetary obligation to pay the federal government. 1 WEST'S FEDERAL ADMINISTRATIVE PRACTICE § 616 (West Group 4th ed. 2002); *see also* 31 U.S.C. §§ 3729 to 3733. While different courts have applied differing elements for liability under the FCA, typical elements include (1) whether "there was a false statement or fraudulent course of conduct; (2) made or carried out with the requisite scienter; (3) that was material; and (4) that caused the government to pay out money or to forfeit moneys due (i.e., that involved a claim)." *United States ex rel. Longhi v. United States*, 575 F.3d 458, 467 (5th Cir. 2009).

For purposes of FCA liability, the terms "knowing" and "knowingly":

    (A)   mean that a person, with respect to information—

        (i)   has actual knowledge of the information;

        (ii) acts in deliberate ignorance of the truth or falsity of the information; or

        (iii) acts in reckless disregard of the truth or falsity of the information; and

    (B)   require no proof of specific intent to defraud. 31 U.S.C. § 3729(b)(1). A party found to violate the FCA

> is liable to the United States Government for a civil penalty of not less than $5,000 and not more than $10,000, as adjusted by the Federal Civil Penalties Inflation Adjustment Act of 1990 . . . , plus 3 times the amount of damages which the Government sustains because of the act of that person.

31 U.S.C. § 3730(d). In addition, a party found to violate the FCA may be subject to reimburse certain types of attorneys' fees and expenses. *Id.*

Fast-Track Rules. In the construction context, fast-track rules or procedures refer to specified rules or a process whereby a dispute which has been submitted to arbitration are subject to a faster or quicker track or time period for resolution for specified types of disputes. Typically, fast-track procedures can apply to disputes where the dollar amounts are relatively low and the issues may be relatively straightforward. For instance, the American Arbitration Association (AAA) established "Fast Track Procedures" for certain types of construction disputes that are designed for cases involving claims between two parties where no party's disclosed claim or counterclaim exceeds $75,000, exclusive of claimed interest, attorneys' fees, arbitration fees, and costs. The procedures provide for a 45-day "time standard" for hearing process completion, with the expedited procedures for arbitrator selection. AAA Construction Industry Arbitration Rules and Mediation Procedures, Fast Track Procedures, F-1–F-13 (2010), *available at* http://www.adr.org.

Judicial Arbitration and Mediation Services, Inc. (JAMS) also has streamlined rules for fast-track arbitrations. In general, under JAMS rules, streamlined rules may be employed when no disputed claim or counterclaim exceeds $250,000, not including interest or attorneys' fees. JAMS Streamlined Arbitration Rules & Procedures, *available at* http://www.jamsadr.com.

Federal Acquisition Regulation (FAR). The Federal Acquisition Regulation (FAR) is the primary regulation used by all federal executive agencies in their acquisition of supplies and services. The FAR became effective on April 1, 1984, and is issued within applicable laws under the joint authorities of the Administrator of General Services, the Secretary of Defense, and the Administrator for the National Aeronautics and Space Administration, under the broad policy guidelines of the Administrator, Office of Federal Procurement Policy, Office of Management and Budget. The FAR precludes agency acquisition regulations that unnecessarily repeat, paraphrase, or otherwise restate the FAR; limits agency acquisition regulations to those necessary to implement FAR policies and procedures within an agency; and provides for coordination, simplicity, and uniformity in the federal acquisition process. It also provides for agency and public participation in developing the FAR and agency acquisition regulation. 48 C.F.R. § 1 et seq.; FAR Prologue. The purpose of the FAR is to deliver on a timely basis the best-value product or service to the government, while maintaining the public's trust and fulfilling public policy objectives. 48 C.F.R. § 1.102; FAR 1.102. The FAR is codified at Title 48 of the U.S. Code. The FAR contains many of the "standard" contract terms used in government contracts.

Federal Arbitration Act (FAA). The Federal Arbitration Act (FAA), 9 U.S.C. § 1–14, is a federal law that establishes a national policy favoring arbitration and a procedures to be applied when the parties contract for that mode of dispute resolution. "The Act, which rests on Congress' authority under the Commerce Clause, supplies not simply a procedural framework applicable in federal courts; it also calls for the application, in state as well as federal courts, of federal substantive law regarding arbitration." *Preston v. Ferrer*, 552 U.S. 346, 128 S. Ct. 978, 981 (2008).

Section 2 of the Federal Arbitration Act "declares a national policy favoring arbitration of claims that parties contract to settle in that manner." *Id.* at 983. Specifically, Section 2 provides that

> [a] written provision in any . . . contract evidencing a transaction involving commerce to settle by arbitration a controversy thereafter arising out of such contract or transaction . . . shall be valid, irrevocable, and enforceable, save upon such grounds as exist at law or in equity for the revocation of any contract.

9 U.S.C. § 2. This section makes private agreements to arbitrate specifically enforceable, so long as the agreement evidences a transaction involving interstate commerce. 13D CHARLES ALAN WRIGHT & ARTHUR R. MILLER, FEDERAL PRACTICE AND PROCEDURE § 3569 (3d ed. 2009). The Supreme Court has broadly interpreted this language, holding that the FAA applies to all contracts within the power of Congress to regulate under its Commerce Clause power. *See Allied-Bruce Terminix Cos., Inc. v. Dobson*, 513 U.S. 265, 277 (1995).

This expansive interpretation of the FAA favoring private agreements and streamlined proceedings is vital to the construction industry because

> submission of disputes for decision to and by selected peers knowledgeable in industry customs and practices universally has been viewed as an option far superior to submission of disputes to judges and juries who knew little about the construction process. Many judges themselves have recognized the wisdom of submitting complex construction disputes to arbitrators or mediators rather than to the courts.

6 PHILLIP L. BRUNER & PATRICK J. O'CONNOR, JR., BRUNER AND O'CONNOR ON CONSTRUCTION LAW § 20:1.50 (Supp. 2009).

Fiduciary. "A person who is required to act for the benefit of another person on all matters within the scope of their relationship" is considered a fiduciary. BLACK'S LAW DICTIONARY (8th ed. 2004). A fiduciary has a duty to act loyally for the principal's benefit, which "requires that the agent subordinate [its] interests to those of the principal and place the principal's interests first as to matters connected with the agency relationship." RESTATEMENT (THIRD) OF AGENCY § 8.01 cmt. b (2006).

Final Completion. In the construction industry setting, the date on which all work to be performed under a construction contract is 100 percent complete, including all punch list and corrective work items that remained after achievement of substantial completion of the work, is referred to as "final completion."5 PHILLIP L. BRUNER & PATRICK J. O'CONNOR, JR., BRUNER AND O'CONNOR ON CONSTRUCTION LAW § 15:16 (2002) (internal citations omitted); *see also* CONSTRUCTION MANAGEMENT ASSOCIATION OF AMERICA, CONSTRUCTION MANAGEMENT STANDARDS OF PRACTICE (Construction Management Association of America, 2008 ed.) (defining "final completion" as "[t]he date on which the terms of all construction contracts have been satisfied"). Final completion typically triggers the obligation of the owner or other obligated party to make final payment, including retainage.

Final Payment. In the construction context, final payment is the payment of the entire contract price, including all retainage, to which the contractor is entitled only after the architect issues the final certificate of payment and the contractor submits all supporting documentation to close out the project. FREDERICK GOULD & NANCY JOYCE, CONSTRUCTION PROJECT MANAGEMENT 294–95 (Pearson Prentice Hall 3d ed. 2009).

"Most construction contracts are drafted so that the owner's act of making final payment to the contractor is not construed to be a waiver of claims for defective or nonconforming work." 4A PHILLIP L. BRUNER & PATRICK J. O'CONNOR, JR., BRUNER AND O'CONNOR ON CONSTRUCTION LAW § 13:76, 552 (2009).

> As a general rule, something more than merely making final payment is necessary to establish that the owner has waived the right to claim for defective work. If the owner makes final payment to the contractor and there is any indication that defective work was discussed and the contractor indicated that it would be taken care of, then waiver is seldom found.

Id. (internal citation omitted). On the other hand, the contractor's acceptance of final payment waives all claims against the owner, "except those previously made in writing and identified as unsettled at the time of final application for payment." *Id.* at n.1.

Final Release v. Partial Release. A release is a "[l]iberation from an obligation, duty, or demand; the act of giving up a right or claim to the person against whom it could have been enforced." BLACK'S LAW DICTIONARY (8th ed. 2004). A final release is most often executed by a contractor only after the contractor's work under its contract has been fully performed and as a condition precedent to receiving final payment. By way of contrast, a partial release is generally submitted by the contractor in its monthly pay applications to the owner, and contains language under which the contractor releases the owner "from all rights to liens and claims 'to date.'" 1 PHILLIP L. BRUNER & PATRICK J. O'CONNOR, JR., BRUNER AND O'CONNOR ON CONSTRUCTION LAW § 4:48 (2002).

A release, whether final or partial, will generally be enforced by the courts to the extent that its language is clear and unambiguous. *See, e.g.,*

Vulcan Painters, Inc. v. MCI Constructors, Inc., 41 F.3d 1457, 1461 (11th Cir. 1995) (enforcing unambiguous final release executed by subcontractor in favor of primary contractor).

Fixed-Price Contract/Lump-Sum Contract. A firm-fixed-price contract provides for a price that is not subject to any adjustment on the basis of the contractor's actual cost experienced in performing the contract, although it is subject to adjustment by change order. "This contract type places upon the contractor maximum risk and full responsibility for all costs and resulting profit or loss. It provides maximum incentive for the contractor to control costs and perform effectively and imposes a minimum administrative burden upon the contracting parties." 48 C.F.R. § 16.202-1; *see also Bowsher v. Merck & Co., Inc.*, 460 U.S. 824, 826 n.1 (1983) ("A pure fixed-price contract requires the contractor to furnish the goods or services for a fixed amount of compensation regardless of the costs of performance, thereby placing the risk of incurring unforeseen costs of performance on the contractor rather than the [owner].").

The fixed-price or lump-sum contract is one preferred method of contracting in the construction industry because it allows the owner to plan future financial commitments with a greater degree of certainty. *See* 1 PHILLIP L. BRUNER & PATRICK J. O'CONNOR, JR., BRUNER AND O'CONNOR ON CONSTRUCTION LAW § 2:16 (2002). Although this method permits the owner to know to the greatest extent possible the final cost of the project before the work begins, it requires that the project be clearly defined at the time the contract is executed. "The risk for the owner is that the contract is only as good as the accuracy of the contract documents. If the scope of the project changes or if errors exist in the documentation the contract will need to be renegotiated, possibly exposing the owner to increased costs." FREDERICK GOULD & NANCY JOYCE, CONSTRUCTION PROJECT MANAGEMENT 93 (Pearson Prentice Hall 3d ed. 2009).

Float/Total Float/Free Float. The amount of time a project activity can be delayed without adversely affecting the project's completion date represents schedule float. An activity that has float has a window within which its start or conclusion can be delayed without delaying the project's completion. Any delay to an activity with no float will delay project completion. *Weaver-Bailey Contractors, Inc. v. United States*, 19 Cl. Ct. 474, 481, 1990 WL 10845 (1990), *reconsideration denied*, 20 Cl. Ct. 158, 1990 WL 45589 (1990); 5 PHILLIP L. BRUNER & PATRICK J. O'CONNOR, JR., BRUNER AND O'CONNOR ON CONSTRUCTION LAW § 15:9 (2002); *see* MICHAEL T. CALLAHAN & H. MURRAY HOHNS, CONSTRUCTION SCHEDULES 25–27 (LEXIS Publishing 2d ed. 1998).

Float is used within the context of critical path method scheduling when identifying critical path activities (those without float) and non–critical path activities (those with float). The cushion of float for a particular activity can be consumed by events during construction, such that a noncritical activity can become critical if its float is exhausted and a further delay to that activity will delay project completion. *Blinderman Construction Co., Inc. v. United States*, 39 Fed. Cl. 529, 579–80 (1997), *aff'd without opinion*, 178 F.3d 1307 (Fed. Cir. 1998); *Haney v. United States*, 676 F.2d 584, 595–96 (Ct. Cl. 1982). Float is generally considered to be an "expiring resource" available on a first-come first-served basis to any project party acting in good faith. Jon M. Wickwire & Stuart Ockman, *Use of Critical Path Method on Contract Claims—2000, in* 19 CONSTRUCTION LAW., Oct. 1999, at 12, 13.

"Total float" and "free float" are sometimes used for further distinction. Total float is equivalent to float; the amount of time an activity can be delayed without adversely affecting the project's completion date. *Blinderman*, 39 Fed. Cl. at 579–80. Free float focuses on the relationship of successive noncritical activities to one another, and is "the amount of time that an activity's start can be delayed without affecting the early start of the successor activity." BRUNER & O'CONNOR, *supra*, § 15:9.

Flow-down Provision. A flow-down provision is a clause found in many contracts between prime contractors and subcontractors incorporating obligations and responsibilities from the prime contract (i.e., the owner-contractor contract) into the subcontract. The clause requires the subcontractor to assume obligations and responsibilities toward the prime contractor that the prime contractor has already assumed toward the owner. *Plum Creek Wastewater Authority v. Aqua-Aerobic Systems*, 597 F. Supp. 2d 1228, 1233 (D. Colo. 2009) (quoting ROBERT F. CUSHMAN ET AL., THE CONSTRUCTION INDUSTRY FORMBOOK § 5.08 (Shepard's 1979)). *See also Brown v. Boyer-Washington Boulevard Associates*, 856 P.2d 352 (Utah 1993); *Industrial Indemnity Co. v. Wick Construction Co.*, 680 P.2d 1100, 1103 (Alaska 1984); *United Tunneling Enterprises, Inc. v. Havens Construction Co.*, 35 F. Supp. 2d 789, 795 (D. Kan. 1998).

Specific benefits, when appropriately incorporated by reference, can flow down as well. When this is the case, the subcontractor has the same rights and remedies available to it that the prime contractor has against the owner. *Steadfast Insurance Co. v. Brodie Contractors, Inc.*, No. 4:07CV00058, 2008 WL 4780099, 2008 U.S. Dist. LEXIS 88448 (W.D. Va. Oct. 31, 2008) (not reported in F. Supp. 2d) (discussing the flow-down of a statute of limitations to the subcontract); *Wasserstein v. Kovatch*, 618 A.2d 886 (N.J. Super. App. Div. 1993) (discussing the flow-down of an arbitration to a subcontractor), *cert. denied*, 627 A.2d 1145 (N.J. April 13, 1993); *Turner Construction Co. v. Midwest Curtainwalls, Inc.*, 543 N.E.2d 249 (Ill. Ct. App. 1989) (discussing an arbitration clause's incorporation into the subcontract and flow down to the subcontractor).

Force Account. A force account is a time and materials–based method for computing the cost of work in which predetermined compensation rates are applied to the actual labor and equipment time spent in order to compensate the contractor for additional work performed. A force account clause, included in the contract between owner and contractor, typically contains detailed formulas regarding rates of compensation for men, materials, and equipment. *See, e.g., Pacific Alaska Contractors, Inc. v. United States*, 193 Ct. Cl. 850, 855–56 (1971); *see also* 2 PHILLIP L. BRUNER & PATRICK J. O'CONNOR, JR., BRUNER AND O'CONNOR ON CONSTRUCTION LAW § 6:84 (2002). The clause is triggered when additional work is required (for example, because of differing site conditions. *See, e.g., Foundation International, Inc. v. E.T. Ige Construction, Inc.*, 78 P.3d 23 (Haw. 2003), *judgment aff'd*, 78 P.3d 23 (Haw. 2003), *reconsideration denied*, 81 P.3d 1216 (Haw. 2003); *Clark-Fitzpatrick, Inc./Franki Foundation Co. v. Gill*, 652 A.2d 440 (R.I. 1994); *Lester N. Johnson Co., Inc. v. City of Spokane*, 588 P.2d 1214 (Wash. App. 1978), *review denied*, 92 Wash. 2d 1005 (1979)), and the parties cannot otherwise agree upon compensation for the additional work. *Westinghouse Electric Supply Co. v. Fidelity & Deposit Co.*, 560 F.2d 1109 (3d Cir. 1977); *Harrison & Burrowes Bridge Constructors, Inc. v. New York*, 839 N.Y.S.2d 854 (App. Div. 2007); *Lester N. Johnson Co.*, 588 P.2d 1214.

Once the force account clause is triggered, detailed records regarding the use of men, materials, and equipment for the additional work must be kept. A representative for the owner and one for the contractor typically each keep and compare daily records. The formulas contained within the force account clause are then used to determine compensation. *See, e.g., Weeshoff Construction Co. v. Los Angeles County Flood Control Dist.*, 88 Cal. App. 3d 579 (1979); *see also* BRUNER & O'CONNOR, *supra*, § 6:84.

Force Majeure. Force majeure is a control-based principle used to allocate the risk of time-impacting events in order to ensure that neither party is responsible for losses caused by risks over which it has no control. This principle, when expressly included in a construction contract, excuses nonperformance for unforeseeable, unavoidable events outside either party's control, the effects of which the party is unable to overcome. *Fru-Con Construction Corp. v. United States*, 44 Fed. Cl. 298, 314 (1999). *See also United States v. Brooks-Callaway*

Co., 318 U.S. 120 (1943); CALAMARI & PERILLO, CONTRACTS § 13.19 (Thomson/West 5th ed. 2003) (discussing force majeure clauses in American contract law). Such events can include "acts of God, acts of public enemy, acts of the owner or its agents, fires, floods, epidemics, strikes, unusually severe weather, unavoidable casualties, and unusual delay in deliveries." 5 PHILLIP L. BRUNER & PATRICK J. O'CONNOR, JR., BRUNER AND O'CONNOR ON CONSTRUCTION LAW § 15:22 (2002). *See also* AIA Document A201-2007, General Conditions of the Contract for Construction, § 8.3.1 (2007); 48 C.F.R. § 52.249-10(b)(1) (2009).

Foreman. A foreman is one level within the hierarchical division of labor and supervision associated with construction projects. Situated above workers but below superintendents, foremen oversee the work of those beneath them. *See generally* JOSEPH P. FREIN, § 2-8 *Job Supervision, in* HANDBOOK OF CONSTRUCTION MANAGEMENT AND ORGANIZATION 19–20 (Van Nostrand Reinhold Co. 2d ed. 1980) (discussing general construction supervision, including how the foreman fits within that system and older, skill-based methods of selecting foremen). *See, e.g., Local No. 207, International Ass'n of Bridge, Structural & Ornamental Iron Workers Union v. Perko*, 373 U.S. 701, 704 n.1 (1963) (noting that in the instant case, a superintendent supervised the entire construction project and a foreman was responsible for receiving his orders from the superintendent and transmitting them to the crew he oversaw), *reh'g denied*, 372 U.S. 872 (1963).

There are different types of foremen. Nonworking foremen have duties that are purely supervisory in nature. Working foremen, on the other hand, perform some kind of labor in addition to their supervisory duties. *See, e.g.,* 29 C.F.R. § 5.2(m) (2009). *See also Hayes v. City of Pauls Valley*, 74 F.3d 1002 (10th Cir. 1996) (differentiating between executive and working foremen under the Fair Labor Standards Act); *Schockley v. City of Newport News*, 997 F.2d 18, 26 (4th Cir. 1993) (stating that the labor law classifications of executive and working foremen help distinguish managerial supervisors from "mere supervisor[s] of subordinate employees").

Fragnet. A fragnet (fragmented network) is a method used within the context of critical path method (CPM) scheduling to quantify delay; it is sometimes referred to as "time impact analysis." RICHARD K. ALLEN & STANLEY A. MARTIN, CONSTRUCTION LAW HANDBOOK § 23.06 (Aspen 2d ed. 2008). A fragnet represents a specific delay due to changes such as additional work or logic revisions to the original schedule. Each fragnet is a segment of the CPM network and "break[s] one or more activity shown on a CPM diagram into a finer level of detail to develop the individual sub-activities necessary for completion of the activity shown on the critical path." JON M. WICKWIRE ET AL., CONSTRUCTION SCHEDULING: PREPARATION, LIABILITY, AND CLAIMS § 9.08(Q) (Aspen 2d ed. 2003 & Supp. 2008); *see also* 5 PHILLIP L. BRUNER & PATRICK J. O'CONNOR, JR., BRUNER AND O'CONNOR ON CONSTRUCTION LAW § 15:128 (2002). As a project progresses and conditions change, fragnets are applied and reviewed in conjunction with the CPM schedule. The comparison provides a more complete picture, identifying delays and their effects upon the project's critical path. WICKWIRE ET AL., *supra*, § 9.08(Q).

Because fragnets offer a more refined picture of what is actually occurring within a project, they can be helpful as a litigation tool when asserting a claim for damages due to delay. *Id.* It is important to note, however, that the usefulness of fragnets presupposes that the baseline CPM schedule is properly updated as conditions change and the original CPM schedule is revised. *See, e.g., Robust Construction,* 05-2 B.C.A. (CCH) ¶ 33,019 (A.S.B.C.A. 2005); *Fru-Con Construction Corp.,* 05-1 B.C.A. (CCH) ¶ 32,936 (A.S.B.C.A. 2005) *clarified on denial of reconsideration,* 05-2 B.C.A. (CCH) ¶ 33,082; *Youngsdale & Sons Construction Co. v. United States,* 27 Fed. Cl. 516 (1993); *see also* ALLEN & MARTIN, *supra,* § 23.06; ROBERT F. CUSHMAN ET AL., PROVING AND PRICING CONSTRUCTION CLAIMS § 9.07 (Aspen 3d ed. 2001 & Supp. 2009).

Fraud/Promissory Fraud. Fraud is a tort composed of five elements: (1) defendant makes a false representation of material fact to plaintiff, (2) defendant knows or believes the representation to be false, (3) at the time of the false representation, defendant intends to induce plaintiff to act in reliance, (4) plaintiff reasonably relies upon defendant's false representation, and (5) plaintiff is damaged as a result of reasonably relying upon defendant's representation. *See* STEPHEN G.M. STEIN, CONSTRUCTION LAW ch. 2, at § 5B.01 (Matthew Bender & Co., Inc. 2009); PROSSER & KEETON, THE LAW OF TORTS ch. 18, at 728 (West Pub. Co. 5th ed. 1984).

Promissory fraud is a subset of fraudulent misrepresentation containing the same five elements and one additional requirement: defendant (at the time he makes false representations of fact to plaintiff in a successful effort to induce plaintiff into entering an agreement) must intend to not perform under the promise. In other words, when defendant misrepresents facts to plaintiff in order to induce plaintiff to contract with him, defendant additionally lies about his own intention to follow through on the promise. Defendant never intends to keep or act on the promise, regardless of the truth or falsity of his representation and regardless of whether it is possible for him to perform the contract. *See Tyson Foods, Inc. v. Davis,* 66 S.W.3d 568 (Ark. 2002); *Lazar v. Superior Court,* 909 P.2d 981 (Cal. 1996); *Steinberg v. Chicago Medical School,* 371

N.E.2d 634 (Ill. 1977); RESTATEMENT (SECOND) OF TORTS § 525 (1976). The simple failure of one party to keep a promise does not necessarily create a cause of action for promissory fraud; proof of intent not to perform is required. *See, e.g., Trade Finance Partners v. AAR Corp.*, 573 F.3d 401 (7th Cir. 2009).

Frustration of Performance. This is a legal doctrine that excuses nonperformance of a party's contractual obligations because changed circumstances outside of the contracting party's control make the party's performance "virtually worthless" to the point of it being "unjust or commercially senseless to require performance." RESTATEMENT (SECOND) OF CONTRACTS § 265 (1981); MICHAEL T. CALLAHAN, CONSTRUCTION CHANGE ORDER CLAIMS § 10.02 (Aspen 2d ed. 2005 & Supp. 2009). Triggering the frustration of performance doctrine does not require impossibility or impracticability of performance. *Id.*

This doctrine is not highly favored and is not commonly applied in construction cases. *See generally* CALLAHAN, *supra*, § 10.02. *See, e.g., United States v. Southwestern Electric Cooperative, Inc.*, 869 F.2d 310 (7th Cir. 1989) (holding a contract was not void due to frustration of performance and stating that frustration of performance is a doctrine that should not be liberally applied in Illinois courts); *Dudley v. St. Regis Corp.*, 635 F. Supp. 1468 (E.D. Mo. 1986) (stating that the doctrine of "commercial frustration" should be limited in application in order "to preserve the certainty of contracts"); *Conlon Group, Inc. v. City of St. Louis*, 980 S.W.2d 37 (Mo. App. 1998) (stating that for the sake of preserving the certainty of contracts, courts should limit their application of the doctrine of frustration).

G

General Agreement of Indemnity (GAI). Because of contractors' frequent need to file performance or payment bonds, thereby securing their work with a surety's guarantee, contractors (principals) frequently execute general agreements of indemnity with bonding companies (sureties). 3 PHILLIP L. BRUNER & PATRICK J. O'CONNOR, JR., BRUNER AND O'CONNOR ON CONSTRUCTION LAW § 10:102 (2002). Such agreements define the rights and obligations existing within the principal-surety relationship, contractually augmenting the surety's common-law rights of reimbursement, exoneration, subrogation, and contribution. RICHARD K. ALLEN & STANLEY A. MARTIN, CONSTRUCTION LAW HANDBOOK § 36 (Aspen 2d ed. 2008).

Although the Model General Agreement of Indemnity exists, its use is not required. J. Paul McNamara & Daniel Mungall, *Project Update 1975: Guide for the Drafter of a Contract Bond Indemnity Agreement*, 42 DEF. COUNS. J. 291 (1975); Edward G. Gallagher, *Illustrative Provisions of a General Indemnity Agreement Taken in Connection with Contract Surety Bonds*, 62 DEF. COUNS. J. 260 (1995). While the nonstandardized details of general agreements of indemnity vary, they tend to focus upon common objectives including providing a contractual right of recovery against the principal, facilitating bond claims, requiring collateral as a security deposit, easing burdens of proof with regard to recovery for losses, and providing a security interest in the principal's equipment and machinery. EDWARD G. GALLAGHER, THE LAW OF SURETYSHIP 487 (ABA 2d ed. 2000); *see also* BRUNER &. O'CONNOR, *supra*, § 10:102.

General Conditions. The term "general conditions" has two different meanings when used in the construction industry context. One use of the term refers to the general terms and conditions contained in a construction contract that will govern the requirements of performance of a contractor, as contrasted with the specific terms such as details of the compensation to be paid to the contractor, the specific schedule requirements, and the scope descriptions of the work to be performed. A document forming the basis of the construction contract, the general conditions "set the minimum performance requirements of a contract and define the legal basis of the agreement between the contractor and the owner. They also define the general rights and responsibilities of the parties." RICHARD K. ALLEN & STANLEY A. MARTIN, CONSTRUCTION LAW HANDBOOK § 44.02 (Aspen 2d ed. 2008).

The general conditions may be specifically drafted by the parties. There are, however, three major forms often used: (1) the American Institute of Architects' General Conditions of the Contract for Construction, AIA Document A201-2007, (2) the ConsensusDOCS, endorsed by the Associated General Contractors of America Standard Form of Agreement and General Conditions between Owner and Contractor Document 200 (ConsensusDOCS 200), and (3) the Engineers Joint Contract Documents Committee Document C-700 (2007 edition). Three different groups with different perspectives and interests publish the three major forms, but all general conditions forms share the common goal of addressing fundamental issues pertaining to setting the parameters of the work and the project at issue. 1 PHILLIP L. BRUNER & PATRICK J. O'CONNOR, JR., BRUNER AND O'CONNOR ON CONSTRUCTION LAW § 5:21 (2002).

The term "general conditions" also is commonly used in the construction industry to refer to supervisory or management expenses that make up a contractor's contract price (particularly when compensation is based on a "cost-plus" or "guaranteed maximum price" structure). These costs are contrasted with the actual costs to be paid to subcontractors by the contractor or for other "direct costs" for materials or equipment that will be incorporated into the project as part of the work that is to be performed for the specific project.

Geotechnical Reports/Findings. Engineers conduct subsurface testing at construction sites in order to collect data regarding soil structure, which is then compiled into a report. This testing often includes the use of soil borings, a process by which a machine removes a cylindrical core of subsurface soil. With all geotechnical testing, scientific standards are used to determine soil type. The U.S. government and military specifically use the Unified Soil Classification System in order to classify soil according to particle size, liquid limit, plastic limit, and plasticity index. This allows engineers to identify not only the type of soil in a particular location (e.g., peat, silt, clay, sand, gravel, cobbles, boulders), but also its structural properties and stability. 4A PHILLIP L. BRUNER & PATRICK J. O'CONNOR, JR., BRUNER AND O'CONNOR ON CONSTRUCTION LAW § 14:2 (2009); P. Cunin, *Soils Part I: Aspects and Physical Properties, in* THE CONSTRUCTION SPECIFIER, May 1968, at 86. *See also* ASTM Standard D2487-98, Standard Classification of Soils for Engineering Purposes (Unified Soil Classification System) (2001).

The results of the tests are used by both contractors and design engineers. Absent language in the bid document to the contrary, bidding contractors can rely upon the geotechnical results in order to more accurately estimate the type of equipment and the quantity of labor necessary to perform that particular project. This helps bidding contractors to submit a more accurate bid for the project. It also aids in relieving bidders of the necessity of including a large contingency amount to protect against the risk of encountering different subsurface conditions than anticipated. *See Foster Construction C.A. & Williams Bros. Co. v. United States*, 435 F.2d 873, 887 (Ct. Cl. 1970). *See also United States v. Atlantic Dredging Co.*, 253 U.S. 1 (1920); *Travelers Casualty & Surety Co. of America v. United States*, 75 Fed. Cl. 696, 712–15 (2007); *Shank-Artukovich v. United States*, 13 Cl. Ct. 345, 354 (1987), *aff'd without opinion*, 848 F.2d 1245 (Fed. Cir. 1988). Design engineers use the results of geotechnical testing when, for example, designing a foundation or structural system on that plot of land, *see* BARRY B. BRAMBLE & MICHAEL T. CALLAHAN, CONSTRUCTION DELAY CLAIMS § 16.04(A) (Aspen 3d ed. Supp. 2009), or when checking to ensure that soil compaction requirements contained within the contract have been met. *See, e.g., W.M. Schlosser, Inc. v. United States,* 50 Fed. Cl. 147, 149, 153 (2001) (noting that the quality of soil required is contractually defined).

Although technology has grown more sophisticated, the current nature of the subsurface tests performed still does not permit a perfect image of sub-surface conditions. Test results are open to interpretation and the act of inter-preting them is considered an art. BRUNER & O'CONNOR, *supra,* § 14.2; Cunin, *supra,* at 86. This presents a tension between project owners and contractors when the anticipated soil conditions contained in the geotechnical reports do not correspond to actual soil conditions on-site. When this occurs, contrac-tors use the changed conditions doctrine to claim damages for extra expenses incurred. *See, e.g., Comtrol Inc. v. United States,* 294 F.3d 1357 (Fed. Cir. 2002); *P.J. Maffei Bldg. Wrecking Corp. v. United States,* 732 F.2d 913 (Fed. Cir. 1984).

Guaranteed Maximum Price (GMP) Contract. An agreement in which the contractor is compensated for its cost plus a fee, with the total paid not to exceed a set price ceiling, is a GMP contract. The parties estimate the cost to complete the work according to the plans and specifications contained in the contract and, from that, calculate the fee owed to the contractor. This forms the basis for the price ceiling (guaranteed maximum price) that the owner will pay to the contractor. 2 PHILLIP L. BRUNER & PATRICK J. O'CONNOR, JR., BRUNER AND O'CONNOR ON CONSTRUCTION LAW § 6:82 (2002); RICHARD K. ALLEN & STAN-LEY A. MARTIN, CONSTRUCTION LAW HANDBOOK § 6.08 (Aspen 2d ed. 2008).

When a GMP contract is used, the actual cost of the construction is in no way guaranteed. Rather, GMPs simply allocate the risk of increased cost to the contractor rather than to the owner. Although he is burdened by having to pay out of pocket for any additional costs above the GMP that are required to com-plete the project, the contractor is benefited in that he receives a fee along with reimbursement for actual cost—up to, but not exceeding, the amount of the GMP. BRUNER & O'CONNOR, *supra,* § 6.82; ALLEN & MARTIN, *supra,* § 6.08. *See TRW, Inc. v. Fox Development Corp.,* 604 N.E.2d 626 (Ind. Ct. App. 1992), *reh'g denied* (Feb. 19, 1993). *See also Davis Construction Co., Inc. v. Palmetto Proper-ties, Inc.,* 281 S.C. 415 (1984); *Holder Construction Group v. Georgia Tech Facilities, Inc.,* 640 S.E.2d 296 (Ga. Ct. App. 2006). While the contractor bears the risk of going over the estimated cost of completion, absent a special savings clause, the contractor does not benefit from coming in under budget. ALLEN & MAR-TIN, *supra,* § 6.08(B); BRUNER & O'CONNOR, *supra,* § 6.82.

Even with a GMP contract, however, a contractor may be entitled to be paid for additional work outside of the scope contemplated by the original contract by change order or otherwise. In such instances, the work was not contemplated, and therefore was not included within, the estimates and, ultimately, the GMP. *See, e.g., Triad Electric & Controls, Inc. v. Power Systems Engineering, Inc.,* 117 F.3d 180 (Tex. Ct. App. 1997). Alternatively, courts have recognized that the scope of work may not be determined prior to setting a GMP, but that such instances merely increase the risk to the contractor without preserving a right to compensation for additional work as it becomes included within the scope of the contract. *See, e.g., Bouten Construction Co. v. M&L Land Co.,* 877 P.2d 928 (Idaho Ct. App. 1994), *reh'g denied* (Feb. 8, 2000).

H

Hazardous Materials/Hazardous Substances. Materials or substances that, despite reasonable precautions, present a risk of bodily injury or death are considered hazardous. RICHARD K. ALLEN & STANLEY A. MARTIN, CONSTRUCTION LAW HANDBOOK § 11.04(B)(5) (Aspen 2d ed. 2008); AIA Document A201-2007, General Conditions of the Contract for Construction, § 10.3.1 (2007); 2 PHILLIP L. BRUNER & PATRICK J. O'CONNOR, JR., BRUNER AND O'CONNOR ON CONSTRUCTION LAW § 5:205 (2002).

Hazardous materials, like asbestos, BRUNER & O'CONNOR, *supra,* § 7:9, contaminated underground storage tanks, *id.* § 7:91, lead paint, *id.* § 7:92, and contaminated soil, *id.* § 7:93, can be preexisting at a construction or remodeling site. *Id.* § 5:203. Owners also have a duty to indemnify contractors, subcontractors, and architects for losses resulting from work affected by the hazardous materials, when the losses did not occur solely through the fault of the damaged party (e.g., contractor) and when the damaged party immediately stopped work upon identification of the hazardous materials. *Id.* § 5:205; AIA Document A201-2007, § 10.3.1.

If the contract does not require the use of hazardous materials, the contractor bears liability for any hazardous materials he introduces into the worksite. On the other hand, if the contract requires the contractor to use specified hazardous materials, the owner bears liability provided that the specified materials are properly used and handled. BRUNER & O'CONNOR, *supra,* § 5:206; AIA Document A201-2007, § 10.3.4. Additionally, the owner must indemnify the contractor for any remediation the contractor must complete due to use of the contract-required materials. BRUNER & O'CONNOR, *supra,* § 5:207; AIA Document A201-2007, § 10.3.5. When it is unclear which party assumed the risk with respect to particular hazardous materials, courts will sometimes look to differing site conditions clauses for guidance in assigning liability. *See, e.g., R.J. Wildner Contracting Co. v. Ohio Turnpike Commission*, 913 F. Supp. 1031 (N.D. Ohio 1996).

Hindrance. Hindrance is synonymous with an impediment or obstacle and is sometimes used interchangeably, or in conjunction, with "delay," "disruption," or "interference." In ordinary usage, to "delay" means "to stop, detain or hinder for a time." MERRIAM-WEBSTER'S COLLEGIATE DICTIONARY 329 (11th ed. 2003). In construction, however, "hindrance" is distinguished from "delay." A hindrance may impact method or sequence of construction, while delay extends the project duration, although hindrance can certainly cause compensable impact. 5 PHILLIP L. BRUNER & PATRICK J. O'CONNOR, JR., BRUNER AND O'CONNOR ON CONSTRUCTION LAW § 15:57 (2002).

Construction contracts carry an implied warranty not to hinder or interfere with performance, which is also expressed as the implied duty to cooperate. BRUNER & O'CONNOR, *supra*, § 4:31 n.3 (2002) (citing the "doctrine of prevention" articulated in 13 WILLISTON ON CONTRACTS § 39-3 (4th ed. 2000)). Breach of this implied warranty takes multiple forms, including failures to provide timely access to the project site, to completing precedent work as planned, to correcting design errors promptly and to timely respond to submittals or requests for information (RFIs). *Id.*

Impact. The effect that an event has on cost or time is generally described as an impact. Impacts can occur in different forms. Some of the most common examples are delay, working out of sequence, change in work methods, unanticipated comebacks, stacking of trades, crowding of the workforce, interference, productivity loss, overtime, lack of material or equipment, inadequate time extensions, adverse weather, late responses, and restricted site access. JON M. WICKWIRE ET AL., CONSTRUCTION SCHEDULING: PREPARATION, LIABILITY AND CLAIMS § 8.10 (Aspen 2d ed. 2003).

Impacts may be subdivided into direct impacts and cumulative impacts. Michael F. D'Onofrio, The Cumulative Impact of Changes, Stadiums, Arenas, Malls and More: The Community Impact Project (2001) (ABA Forum on the Construction Industry Program, New Orleans, La.). "Direct impact" refers to the immediate disruption resulting from a discrete event. Direct impacts are usually foreseeable, can be related to a specific event, and thus the time and cost can be directly calculated. *Centex Bateson Construction*, 99-1 B.C.A. 30, 153 (VABCA 1998).

"Cumulative impact" has been equated with "disruption" and refers to the impact on unchanged work not attributable to any single change but rather to multiple, and sometimes undifferentiated, events. *Bell BCI Co. v. United States*, 570 F.3d 1337, 1340 (Fed. Cir. 2009); *Aetna Casualty & Surety Co. v. The George Hyman Construction Co.*, No. 93-CV-4570 1998 U.S. Dist. LEXIS 22627 (E.D. Pa. May 13, 1998). Unlike direct impacts, cumulative impacts are unforeseeable and incapable of direct estimation or quantification. *See, e.g., Amec Civil, LLC v. DMJM Harris, Inc.*, Civil Action No. 06-64 (FLW) 2009 U.S. Dist. LEXIS 55410 (D.N.J. June 30, 2009); *J.A. Jones Construction Co.*, ENG CBA 6348, 2000-2 BCA (CCH) P 31,000 (2000); *Haas & Haynie Corp.*, 84-2 B.C.A. 17, 446 (GSBCA 1984).

Cumulative impacts may take the form of "cardinal change." *See Atlanta Dry Dock Corp. v. United States*, 773 F. Supp. 335 (M.D. Fla. 1991). Cardinal change occurs outside the scope of the contract; "thus it is not governed by the 'changes clause,' and cannot be remedied under the contract." 1 PHILLIP L. BRUNER & PATRICK J. O'CONNOR, JR., BRUNER AND O'CONNOR ON CONSTRUCTION LAW § 4.13 (2002). In theory, however, cardinal change and cumulative impact are not the same. The former relies on proof of abandonment of the contract or changes beyond the scope of the contract. *L. K. Comstock & Co. v. Beacon Construction Co.*, 932 F. Supp. 906 (E.D. Ky. 1993). These two elements are not necessary to prove cumulative impact.

Cumulative impact claims have failed when challenged by accord and satisfaction. *Bell BCI Co. v. United States*, 570 F.3d 1337 (Fed. Cir. 2009). And, even though a "cumulative impact" may be distinguishable from a "delay," a no-damage-for-delay clause has been successfully utilized to defeat a cumulative impact claim. *Dugan & Meyers Construction Co. v. Ohio Department of Administrative Services*, 864 N.E.2d 68 (Ohio 2007).

I

Impact Claim. An impact claim is a claim arising from impacts on a construction project that seeks recovery of time and/or money from direct or cumulative impacts. The claim is often associated with losses of labor productivity. To recover on an impact claim, the contractor or other claiming party must prove a causal connection between accumulated events that give rise to contract "growth" and the effect of those events on other work. *See Hensel Phelps*

Construction Co., 01-1 BCA 31249 (GSBCA 2001); *see also Centex Bateson Construction*, 99-1 B.C.A. 30, 153 (VABCA 1998).

Impacted As-Planned Analysis. An impacted as-planned analysis is one of several forms of critical path method (CPM) schedule analyses. Jennifer W. Fletcher & Laura J. Stipanowich, *Successful Forensic Schedule Analysis*, J. AM. C. CONSTRUCTION LAW., Winter 2007, at 229–234. It is also known as the "what if" method. 5 PHILLIP L. BRUNER & PATRICK J. O'CONNOR, JR., BRUNER AND O'CONNOR ON CONSTRUCTION LAW § 15:134 (2002). The analysis is intended to demonstrate how the contractor's as-planned or adjusted as-planned CPM schedule was affected by selective impacts asserted to be the owner's responsibility. JON M. WICKWIRE ET AL., CONSTRUCTION SCHEDULING: PREPARATION, LIABILITY AND CLAIMS § 9.08 [F] (Aspen 2d ed. 2003).

Once a widely used technique, this method is no longer favored because it does not "require the contractor to accept responsibility for its own delays and to give the owner credit for delays that might not be the responsibility of either the contractor or the owner, such as weather and strikes." *Id.* Courts have rejected the analysis. *See, e.g., Gulf Contracting, Inc.*, ASBCA Nos. 30,195, 32,839, 33,867, 89-2 BCA ¶ 21,812 (1989) (analysis totally unreliable because it did not account for all delays). *See also Titan Pacific Construction Corp. v. United States*, 17 Cl. Ct. 630, 1989 WL 78828 (1989), *aff'd*, 899 F.2d 1227 (Fed. Cir. 1990).

Implied. Implied contract terms are inferred when the terms are deemed to be obvious or integrally involved with a contractual relationship. *General Finance Corp. v. Dillon*, 172 F.2d 924, 927–28 (10th Cir. 1947). When a bargain has been sufficiently defined to be a contract, but is missing a term essential to the determination of rights and duties, the court may supply such term as is reasonable under the circumstances. RESTATEMENT (SECOND) OF CONTRACTS § 204 (1978). Examples of implied terms are the warranty of accuracy and suitability of plans, *Spearin v. United States*, 248 U.S. 132 (1918); the warranty of good faith and fair dealing, *RAM Engineering & Construction, Inc. v. University of Louisville*, 127 S.W.3d 579 (Ky. 2003); the disclosure of essential information, *Helene Curtis Industries, Inc. v. United States*, 312 F.2d 774 (Ct. Cl. 1963); and the warranty of workmanlike construction, *Pittsburgh National Bank v. Welton Becket Associates*, 601 F. Supp. 887 (W.D. Pa. 1985). Sections 2-314 and 2-315 of the Uniform Commercial Code codify implied warranties of merchantability and fitness for a particular purpose that are applicable to the sale of materials and equipment utilized for construction projects.

Impossibility of Performance. Tracing its origins to English common law, the doctrine of impossibility of performance excuses contract performance when the circumstances underlying the contract have changed through no fault of the party seeking relief. *See* David E. Rosengren & Jared Cohane, *The Impossibility Doctrine—Still Hazy after All These Years*, J. AM. C. CONSTRUCTION LAW (Summer 2008). Initially recognized as an excuse for physical or legal improbability, the doctrine has expanded to situations that frustrated performance to the degree that performance became "commercially impracticable." *Id.*; RESTATEMENT (SECOND) OF CONTRACTS § 261 (1978). In the modern view, impracticability has been interpreted to include excessive financial loss on the contract. *See Aluminum Co. of America v. Essex Group, Inc.*, 499 F. Supp. 53 (W.D. Pa. 1980). The modern view also recognizes "frustration of purpose" as an excuse for nonperformance, provided the foundation is "substantial." RESTATEMENT (SECOND) OF CONTRACTS § 265 (1978). These concepts also apply to sales of goods within the scope of the Uniform Commercial Code § 2-615.

Incentive/Disincentive Clause. Contractual provisions that encourage early contract completion by offering a financial incentive for completion ahead of schedule and/or imposing damages for delays in performance are known as incentive/disincentive clauses. R. Harper Heckman & Benjamin R. Edwards, *Time Is Money: Recovery of Liquidated Damages by the Owner*, CONSTRUCTION LAW., Fall 2004, at 28. These clauses are distinguishable from liquidated damage provisions. The former is designed to motivate a contractor to complete a project ahead of schedule, while the latter is designed to allow an owner to recover costs associated with the contractor's failure to complete the project on time. *See* Federal Highway Administration Technical Advisory T 5080.10: Incentive/Disincentive (I/D) for Early Completion (Feb. 8, 1989), *available at* http://www.fhwa.dot.gov/construction/contracts/t508010.cfm.

Incentive provisions have become fairly common on public transportation projects. Agencies will often use incentives on projects involving high traffic volumes where it is critical to minimize delays to the traveling public by completing the project early (or at least on time). The measures used range from a simple incentive/disincentive clause based on a specified contract completion date to other, unique measures, such as lane rental fees imposed to encourage contractors to limit road closures and interruptions to the traveling public. *See* SIDNEY SCOTT & KATHRYN MITCHELL, TRAUNER CONSULTING SERVICES, INC., ALTERNATIVE PAYMENT AND PROGRESS REPORTING

Methods—Task #2, *available at* http://www.fhwa.dot.gov/programadmin/contracts/etgpayment.pdf.

Incentive/disincentive clauses are also often used on private commercial construction projects. For example, owners may include some type of shared savings provision in guaranteed maximum price (GMP) contracts. 2 Steven G.M. Stein, Construction Law § 3A.04 [1] (Matthew Bender 1986). An incentive is offered to the contractor by allowing it to share in any savings if the project is completed at a cost less than the GMP. Likewise, the contract may specify that the contractor is fully responsible for all project costs that exceed the GMP. Owners may also offer an incentive for early project completion. Standard agreements published by the Design-Build Institute of America (DBIA) provide for an early completion bonus that is based on the number of days that substantial completion is achieved before the specified completion date in the contract. 1 Steven G.M. Stein, Construction Law § 3.09 [3][f][x] (2009) (Matthew Bender 1986).

Incentives. Any factor (financial or otherwise) that enables or motivates a particular course of action is considered an incentive. Incentives applicable to any given construction project may be positive or negative and take varied forms.

Incentives are usually intended to motivate the contractor to meet or surpass performance goals. 2 Phillip L. Bruner & Patrick J. O'Connor, Jr., Bruner and O'Connor on Construction Law § 5:20 (2002). The most widely used negative incentive is a liquidated damages clause assessing the contractor a specified monetary sum for each day the contractor is late in completing the contract. This sum is in lieu of actual damages. An early completion bonus is the positive alternative to liquidated damages. *Id.* "Value engineering" is another type of positive financial incentive to motivate a contractor to suggest cost-saving alternatives to a project's original design. For example, highway contractors may submit bids proposing an equivalent or better option to something proposed in the contract at a reduced cost to the owner (e.g., Kentucky Transportation Cabinet, 2008 Standard Specifications for Road and Bridge Construction § 111—Value Engineering, *available at* http://transportation.ky.gov/construction/spec/spec08.htm). If the proposal is accepted, the contractor and the owner share in the savings. This approach is designed to reduce overall construction costs by encouraging contractors to look for cost-saving alternatives that produce equivalent results.

From the owner's perspective, state and federal governments may offer incentives to promote a particular type of project or to utilize sustainable construction and design techniques. For example, the federal government's Low-Income Housing Tax Credit program is designed to encourage the construction of affordable rental housing for low-income households. Paul Duncan, Carol Rosenberg & Kim Rueben, *Tax Incentives for Economic Development: What Is the Low-Income Housing Tax Credit?, in* The Tax Policy Briefing Book: A Citizens' Guide for the 2008 Election and Beyond (Tax Policy Center, Urban Institute & Brookings Institution 2008, updated 2009), http://www.taxpolicy center.org/briefing-book/key-elements/economic-development/low-income -housing.cfm. This program allows developers to claim tax credits over a 10-year period equal to the present value of up to 70 percent of the project costs. *Id.* There are also a number of different incentives (in the form of tax credits) that are offered on the state and federal levels that are designed to promote energy efficiency and the use of sustainable construction techniques. *See generally* Database of State Incentives for Renewables & Efficiency, http://www.dsireusa.org/.

Indemnify v. Hold Harmless v. Defend. An indemnification clause may include the terms "hold harmless" and "defend" in conjunction with "indemnify." For example:

> Design-Builder, to the fullest extent permitted by law, shall indemnify, hold harmless and defend Owner, its officers, directors, employees and agents from and against claims, losses, damages, liabilities, including attorneys' fees and expenses, for bodily injury, sickness or death, and property damage or destruction (other than to the Work itself) to the extent resulting from the negligent acts or omissions of Design-Builder, Design Consultants, Subcontractors, anyone employed directly or indirectly by any of them or anyone for whose acts any of them may be liable.

See DBIA Standard Form of General Conditions Between Owner & Design Builder § 7.4.1. At least one court has opined that

> the words "indemnify" and "hold harmless" are not synonymous. "One is offensive and the other is defensive—even though both contemplate third party liability situations. 'Indemnify' is an offensive right—a sword—allowing an indemnitee to seek indemnification. 'Hold harmless' is defensive: The right *not to be bothered* by the other party itself seeking indemnification.

See Queen Villas Homeowners Ass'n v. TCB Property Management, 56 Cal. Rptr. 3d 528, 534 (Cal App. 4th 2007) (emphasis in original). Other authorities note that courts make no distinction between the two terms. 3 PHILLIP L. BRUNER & PAT-RICK J. O'CONNOR, JR., BRUNER AND O'CONNOR ON CONSTRUCTION LAW § 10:25 (2002) (citing *Pinney v. Tarpley,* 686 S.W.2d 574 (Tenn. Ct. App. 1984)).

The duty to defend is separate and independent from the duty to indemnify. *George L. Smith II Georgia World Congress Center Authority v. Miller Brewery Co.,* 566 S.E.2d 361 (Ga. Ct. App. 2002). But when used in an indemnification clause, the term "defend" broadens the obligation from reimbursement to requiring a defense of the indemnitee. The duty to defend under such clauses arises before determinations of liability are made. *Stephens & Sons, Inc. v. Municipality of Anchorage,* 629 P.2d 71 (Alaska 1981); *see also Urban Investment & Development Co. v. Turner Construction Co.,* 616 N.E.2d 829 (Mass. App. 1993). The duty to defend is determined by facts known at the time of the tender of defense. The duty to indemnify arises when the party seeking indemnification prevails upon all facts that fall within coverage. *See* 3 PHILLIP L. BRUNER & PATRICK J. O'CONNOR, JR., BRUNER AND O'CONNOR ON CONSTRUCTION LAW § 10.49 (2002).

Indemnification Clause. In general, an indemnity clause "covers the risk of harm sustained by third persons that might be caused by either the indemnitor or the indemnitee. It shifts the financial burden for the ultimate payment of damages from the indemnitee to the indemnitor." *See Indianapolis City Market Corp. v. MAV, Inc.* 915 N.E.2d 1013 (Ind. App. 2009) (citing *Morris v. McDonald's Corp.,* 650 N.E.2d 1219, 1222 (Ind. Ct. App. 1995)). In other words, one person or organization agrees to secure another against loss or damage resulting from specified occurrences, acts, errors, or omissions. CARINA Y. OHARA ET AL., FUNDAMENTALS OF CONSTRUCTION LAW 342 (ABA 2001). Indemnity provisions fall into three primary forms: broad, intermediate, and limited. SAMUEL W. WENDT, THE CONSTRUCTION CONTRACTS BOOK 333 (ABA 2004). The broad or "fault free" form provides indemnification arising out of the indemnitor's work or presence or where the indemnitee is indemnified against its sole fault. The intermediate form indemnifies where the loss is due in part to the negligence or fault of the indemnitor. Under the limited version, any negligence by the indemnitee bars indemnification even if the indemnitor caused or contributed to the liability. *Id.* at 333–34; 3 PHILLIP L. BRUNER & PATRICK J. O'CONNOR, JR., BRUNER AND O'CONNOR ON CONSTRUCTION LAW § 10.2 (2002).

Validity of indemnity clauses, particularly the broader forms, varies by state. Some variations are prohibited as violations of public policy. *See* A.H. Gwyn, *Anti-Indemnity Statutes,* CONSTRUCTION LAW., April 1992, at 30.

Kentucky, for example, voids construction contract provisions purporting to indemnify or hold harmless a contractor from its own negligence. KY. REV. STAT. ANN. § 371.180(2) (2009). Other states do not void indemnification clauses, but strictly construe them. For example, Indiana courts must find that the intent to indemnify the indemnitee for its own negligence must be stated in clear and unequivocal terms. *See Indianapolis City Market Corp. v. MAV, Inc.*, 915 N.E.2d 1013 (Ind. App. 2009) (citing *Sequa Coatings Corp. v. Northern Indiana Commuter Transportation District*, 796 N.E.2d 1216, 1222 (Ind. Ct. App. 2003)).

Indemnity. The term "indemnity" is used in two general senses: First, in the sense of giving security; and second, in the sense of compensation for actual damage. *See St. Paul Fire & Marine Insurance Co. v. Elkay Mfg. Co.*, Nos. Civ.A. 98-11-262 WCC, Civ.A. 98-11-144 WCC, 2003 WL 139775 (Del. Super. Ct. Jan. 17, 2003). It is the repayment to one party by the party who caused the loss of such amounts as the first party was compelled to pay. *See United Structural Systems, Ltd. v. ERI Falls, Inc.*, No. 2004-CA-002103-MR, 2005 WL 3116056 (Ky. Ct. App. Nov. 23, 2005) (citing *Liberty Mutual Insurance Co. v. Louisville & Nashville Railroad Co.*, 455 S.W.2d 537, 541 (Ky. 1970)).

Indemnity provides a means for shifting risk between contracting parties for claims made by third persons not a party to the construction contract. FRED WILSHUSEN ET AL., CONSTRUCTION CHECKLISTS 118 (ABA 2008). Sources of indemnity may include contract provisions or statutory provisions. *Id.* at 120–21. Indemnity may also be implied in law (tort indemnity) or implied in fact (contractual indemnity). *See Peoples' Democratic Republic of Yemen v. Goodpasture, Inc.*, 782 F.2d 346, 351 (2d Cir. 1986).

Independent Contractor. Employers frequently hire individuals to assist on a project, but the individuals perform work independent of an actual employment relationship. "An independent contractor has been defined as any person who, in the pursuit of an independent business, undertakes to do a specific piece of work for other persons, using his own means and methods, without submitting himself to their control in respect to all its details." *Hathcock v. Acme Truck Lines, Inc.*, 262 F.3d 522, 527 (5th Cir. 2001). Further, "an independent contractor is one who works according to his own methods without direct supervision or control by the employer except as to the overall result." *Id.*

> The commonly recognized tests of such a relationship are, although not necessarily concurrent or each in itself controlling: (1) The existence of a contract for the performance by

a person of a certain piece or kind of work at a fixed price; (2) the independent nature of his business or of his distinct calling; (3) his employment of assistants with the right to supervise their activities; (4) his obligation to furnish necessary tools, supplies, and materials; (5) his right to control the progress of the work, except as to final results; (6) the time for which the workman is employed; (7) the method of payment, whether by time or by job; (8) whether the work is part of the regular business of the employer.

Beatty v. Halpin, 267 F.2d 561, 564 (8th Cir. 1959).

Employers may desire using an independent contractor to avoid liability for potential torts committed at the jobsite.

As a general rule, when a person (a contractee) lets out work to another and reserves no control over the work or workmen, the relation of contractee and independent contractor exists, and not that of master and servant, and the contractee is not liable for the negligence or improper execution of the work by the independent contractor.

Hunter v. Buckle, Inc., 488 F. Supp. 2d 1157, 1167 (D. Kan. 2007).

Infrastructure. A modern society utilizes road systems, utilities including water and electricity, phone lines, broadband cables, and other basic operations in order to function efficiently. Such services are commonly recognized as infrastructure. Infrastructure is "the underlying foundation or basic framework (as of a system of organization)." *nCUBE Corp. v. SeaChange International, Inc.*, 313 F. Supp. 2d 361, 370 (D. Del 2004) (quoting WEBSTER'S THIRD NEW INTERNATIONAL DICTIONARY OF THE ENGLISH LANGUAGE, UNABRIDGED 1161 (1993)). Elsewhere, "general infrastructure" is defined as "infrastructure that is created for the broad societal welfare of a country, region, state or municipality." *Bethlehem Steel Corp. v. United States*, 26 C.I.T. 1003, 1009 (Ct. Int'l Trade 2002) (quoting 19 C.F.R. § 351.511(d)).

Initial Decision Maker (IDM). A designee may be appointed to make an initial decision regarding a dispute with the understanding that a second body or entity will review and either agree or disagree with the first decision. The initial decision-maker is a body, such as an agency, or person appointed to make the initial decision in disputes. *See Alliance Communications Cooperative, Inc. v. WWC License, L.L.C.*, Civ. No. 05-4181 2007 U.S. Dist. LEXIS 24566 (D.S.D. Mar. 29, 2007). For example, an administrative agency that must come to a final decision is the initial decision-maker. *Williamson County Regional Planning Commission v. Hamilton Bank*, 473 U.S. 172, 193 (1985)); *see also Kincade v. Sparkman*, 117 F.3d 949, 953 (6th Cir. 1997) (lower court is identified as initial decision-maker).

The 2007 AIA documents address the duties of an initial decision-maker. The general conditions form provides that "[t]he Architect will serve as the Initial Decision Maker, unless otherwise indicated in the Agreement." AIA Document A201-2007, General Conditions of the Contract for Construction, § 15.2.1 (2007). "[A]n initial decision shall be required as a condition precedent to mediation of any Claim arising prior to the date final payment is due." *Id.* The document continues, "The Initial Decision Maker will render an initial decision approving or rejecting the Claim, or indicating that the Initial Decision Maker is unable to resolve the claim." AIA Document A201-2007, General Conditions of the Contract for Construction, § 15.2.5 (2007). Further, the initial decision-maker's determination shall be in writing and state the reasons for the decision. *Id.* "The initial decision shall be final and binding on the parties but subject to mediation and, if the parties fail to resolve their dispute through mediation, to binding dispute resolution." *Id.*

Insolvency. One who is no longer able to meet financial obligations is insolvent. "[I]t may generally be said that insolvency, when applied to a person, firm, or corporation engaged in trade, means inability to pay debts as they become due in the usual course of business." *United States v. Oklahoma*, 261 U.S. 253, 262 (1923) (relying on *Oklahoma Moline Plow Co. v. Smith*, 139 P. 285, 287 (1914). Elsewhere, the Court has stated, "[t]he true definition of insolvency is the failure and consequent suspension of business." *McDonald v. Dewey*, 202 U.S. 510, 518 (1906). A contractor who does "not have sufficient cash on hand to pay for the labor and materials to complete its then existing contracts" is insolvent. *First State Bank v. Reorganized School District*, 495 S.W.2d 471, 479 (Mo. Ct. App. 1973).

Inspection. Allowing participants access to a construction project to ascertain the quality, authenticity, or conditions of the project is a well-recognized concept and is commonly referred to as "inspection" in the construction industry context. Traditional construction contracts have extensive provisions covering observations and inspections by design professionals and the contractor's obligation to uncover work for inspection. AIA and the Engineers Joint Contract Documents (EJCDC) give to the owner the right of access to conduct its own inspections.

For example, "The Contractor shall provide the Owner and Architect access to the Work in preparation and progress wherever located." AIA Document A201-2007, General Conditions of the Contract for Construction, § 3.16 (2007). "Tests, inspections and approvals of portions of the Work shall be made as required by the Contract Documents and by applicable laws, statutes, ordinances, codes, rules and regulations or lawful orders of public authorities." AIA Document A201-2007, General Conditions of the Contract for Construction, § 13.5.1 (2007). The Contractor is obligated to make arrangements for such tests and inspections "with an independent testing laboratory or entity acceptable to the Owner. . . . The Contractor shall give the Architect timely notice of when and where tests and inspections are to be made so that the Architect may be present for such procedures." *Id.* When the Contractor considers the project to be substantially complete, "the Contractor shall prepare and submit to the Architect a comprehensive list of items to be completed or corrected prior to final payment." AIA Document A201-2007, General Conditions of the Contract for Construction, § 9.8.2 (2007). "Upon receipt of the Contractor's list, the Architect will make an inspection to determine whether the Work or designated portion thereof is substantially complete." *Id.* § 9.8.3.

Further, the owner can require that prematurely covered work be uncovered for inspection, require a special inspection or testing of work, and reject defective work upon inspection. STEVEN G. M. STEIN, CONSTRUCTION LAW 2009 ¶ 3.09[3][d][ii] (Matthew Bender 2006).

Insured. An individual or entity commonly purchases insurance for protection against unforeseen risks. In the event a risk that has been insured against occurs, the policyholder is entitled to insurance coverage if conditions expressly set forth in the policy are satisfied. "[T]he word 'insured,' when used in an insurance policy, includes any person covered by an applicable insurance policy." *Olivine Corp. v. United Capitol Insurance Co.*, 52 P.3d 494, 498 (Wash. 2002). "This is consistent with the dictionary definition of 'insured': The person who obtains or is otherwise covered by insurance on his health, life or property. The 'insured' in a policy is not limited to the insured named in the policy, but applies to anyone who is insured" by terms set forth in the policy. *Id.*

Integrated Project Delivery (IPD). Integrated Project Delivery (IPD) is reflective of the collection and organization of resources required for the completion of a construction project that increases the likelihood of a project's success.

Integrated Project Delivery is a project delivery method that integrates people, systems, business structures and practices into a process that collaboratively harnesses the talents and insights of all participants to optimize the project results, increase value to the owner, reduce waste and maximize efficiency through all phases of design, fabrication, and construction.

AIACC Integrated Project Delivery Steering Committee, *Integrated Project Delivery: Frequently Asked Questions* (AIA California Council 2008), *available at* http://www.ipd-ca.net/PDFs/AIACC_1108FAQ.pdf. "Commonalities of practice and procedure have evolved into teaming arrangements for the organization and design of construction work. These teaming arrangements are also known as project delivery systems." STEVEN G. M. STEIN, CONSTRUCTION LAW 2009 ¶ 21.03 (Matthew Bender 2006). Primary team members for an integrated project delivery "include the Architect, general contractor, and key subcontractors." Lean Construction Institute, Glossary of Terms (2010), *available* at http://www.leanconstruction.org/glossary.htm.

Interference. A typical construction project involves several participants, each attempting to accomplish tasks assigned to it under the construction contract. Under the pressure of timely completion of the project, conflicts may arise. Conscious interference with another participant's work may have serious consequences. "Interference" is defined as "Hampering, hindering, or intermeddling with progress of a project." *See* BLACK'S LAW DICTIONARY 730 (5th ed. 1979). "[T]here is an implied term in every construction contract that the owner or the person for whom the work is being done will not hinder or delay the contractor." *Lester N. Johnson Co. v. City of Spokane*, 588 P.2d 1214, 1217 (Wash. Ct. App. 1979). "[A]ctive interference requires a finding that defendant committed some affirmative, willful act in bad faith which unreasonably interfered with the contractor's compliance with the terms of the construction contract." *United States Steel Corp. v. Missouri Pacific Railroad*, 668 F.2d 435, 439 (8th Cir.), *cert. denied*, 459 U.S. 836 (1982). The owner's interference with a contractor's work may defeat the owner's claim for damages due to the contractor's failure to complete the project on time. *Id.* at 441.

International Center for Dispute Resolution (ICDR). Established in 1996, the International Center for Dispute Resolution is the international division of the American Arbitration Association. ICDR offers alternative dispute resolution administration services, provides neutral panels for mediation and arbitration and sets forth the procedures for conducting same. ICDR has offices in Dublin, Ireland and Mexico City, Mexico. ICDR rules and procedures are *available at* www.adr.org.

International Code Council (ICC). Established in 1994, the International Code Council is a nonprofit membership association that advocates a single set of coordinated national model construction codes focusing on building safety and fire prevention. The organization was founded by the Building Officials and Code Administrators International, Inc. (BOCA), the International Conference of Building Officials (ICBO), and the Southern Building Code Congress International, Inc. (SBCCI). The ICC develops codes used to construct houses and other residences, commercial buildings, and schools. ICC codes have been adopted by states, counties, and municipalities. ICC also provides members with technical opinions on codes and standards, accreditation, and training. ICC's website is at www.iccsafe.org.

International Federation of Consulting Engineers (FIDIC). An international group of consulting engineers has been active for nearly 100 years, providing such valuable services as creating uniform contracts. The International Federation of Consulting Engineers (Fédération internationale des ingénieurs-conseils—FIDIC) was formed in 1913 by national associations of independent consulting engineers from France, Belgium, and Switzerland. Peter C. Halls et al., *Contract Forms and Project Delivery Systems on International Projects, in* INTERNATIONAL CONSTRUCTION LAW: A GUIDE FOR CROSS-BORDER TRANSACTIONS AND LEGAL DISPUTES (ABA 2009). FIDIC has since grown dramatically, and as of 2010 had 84 national member associations representing over one million consulting engineering professionals. *Id.* FIDIC seeks to promote a strong international consulting engineering industry in support of the continuing globalization of design and construction of international projects. A major contribution of the FIDIC has been to create a set of standard form contracts for international projects, the FIDIC Rainbow. *Id.* The primary contracts of the FIDIC Rainbow are based on the design-bid-build, the design-build, and the engineer-procure-construct contract delivery approaches. *Id.*

Invitation for Bids v. Request for Proposal. An owner or other party seeking to commence construction of a project solicits bids from contractors typically through either an invitation for bids or a request for proposal.

An invitation for bids includes the following:

> project name and location; names and addresses of owner and architect; brief general description of the project; type of

contract (single or multiple); date, time, and place for receiving bids; whether opening of bids will be public or private; location and requirements for obtaining bidding documents; type and amount of deposit for return of documents; locations where bidding documents are available for inspection; conditions for submitting proposals; type and amount of bid security; owner's right to accept or reject bids; governing laws and regulations; name and address of issuing party and date issued.

STEVEN G. M. STEIN, CONSTRUCTION LAW ¶ 5A.06[5] (Matthew Bender 2006). An invitation for bids is less restrictive than a request for proposal. *Id.* "Responses to invitations for bids (sealed bidding) are offers called 'bids' or 'sealed bids.'" *Information Sciences Corp. v. United States,* 73 Fed. Cl. 70, 87 (Fed. Cl. 2006) (quoting 48 C.F.R. § 2.101).

Whether a request for proposal is an offer or a proposal for an offer may depend on the jurisdiction. Some courts hold that the request for proposal "must represent an offer to provide the exact thing called for in the request for proposals, so that acceptance of the proposal will bind the contractor in accordance with the material terms and conditions of the request for proposal." *See Centech Group, Inc. v. United States,* 554 F.3d 1029, 1038 (3d Cir. 2009). In some jurisdictions, however, "responses to requests for proposals (negotiations) are offers called proposals." *Alaska Central Express, Inc. v. United States,* 50 F.3d Cl. 510, 515 (Fed. Cl. 2001) (quoting 48 C.F.R. § 2.101).

J

JAMS (Judicial Arbitration and Mediation Services, Inc.). Founded in 1979, JAMS is an acronym for Judicial Arbitration and Mediation Services, Inc., and is one of the largest private alternative dispute resolution providers in the world. JAMS specializes in mediating and arbitrating complex, multiparty, business/commercial cases in all areas of the law, including construction, construction defects, and engineering and construction. The full current name is "JAMS, The Resolution Experts"; their website is at http://www.jamsadr.com.

Jobsite Overhead/Field Overhead. Methods for identifying overhead on a construction project may follow one of two avenues. "Jobsite overhead consists of those items that are required specifically for the project, but cannot be reasonably allocated to any specific work item within the project." WILLIAM SCHWARTZKOPF & JOHN J. McNAMARA, CALCULATING CONSTRUCTION DAMAGES § 7.01 (Aspen 2d ed. 2001). Normal jobsite overhead includes costs that increase as a result of the passage of time on a project. *Id.* § 7.02.

Field overhead, on the other hand, is described as "administrative costs to run a project, such things as [a] superintendent, quality control, vehicles associated with those people, clerical staff, [and] office supplies." *Ace Constructors, Inc. v. United States*, 70 Fed. Cl. 253, 279 (2006).

"Overhead costs are frequently segregated within the job costing system from field overhead costs." SCHWARTZKOPF & McNAMARA, *supra*, § 7.02. If an item usually included in jobsite overhead can be clearly segregated, a court or board may list it as a distinct item of damages. *See, e.g., Fehlaber Corp. v. State*, 419 N.Y.S. 2d 773, 776 (App. Div. 1979). Further, "field overhead is generally a recoverable item in the construction industry." *Ace Constructors, Inc. v. United States*, 70 Fed. Cl. 253, 279 (2006).

Joint and Several Liability. A form of liability when two or more parties are responsible mutually as well as individually for performance and resulting damages is referred to as "joint and several" liability. Stated another way, the liable parties are liable together and undivided (i.e., "jointly"); however, at the same time, each of the parties is also liable separately and distinctly (i.e., "severally"). BLACK'S LAW DICTIONARY 933 (8th ed. 2004). "Thus, each liable party is individually responsible for the entire obligation, but a paying party may have a right of contribution and indemnity from nonpaying parties." *Id.*

In practical terms, if multiple defendants are found jointly and severally liable, the plaintiff may collect the entire amount awarded from just one of the defendants, regardless of that defendant's share of culpability (even, for example, where the defendant was responsible for only a minor amount of the damages); the plaintiff also may collect different amounts from some or all of the defendants, again regardless of a particular defendant's share of culpability. *Commonwealth v. Boston Edison Co.*, 821 N.E.2d 16, 21 n. 4 (Mass. 2005); *Gulf Insurance Co. v. Cottone*, 148 P.3d 814, 820 (N.M. Ct. App. 2006). Almost all states, however, have statutes governing the application of joint and several liability to damages. *See, e.g., Allstate Insurance Co. v. Palterovich*, 653 F. Supp. 2d 1306, 1334 (noting that "under Florida law, joint and several liability exists where two or more wrongdoers negligently contribute to the injury of another by their several acts, which operate concurrently, so that in effect the damages are rendered inseparable" (citation omitted)).

Joint Check Agreement. Payment for services or supplies used on a construction project may be made to more than one party. Consequently, "joint check agreements are a commonly used payment method in the construction industry." *See Allied Building Products Corp. v. United Pacific Insurance Co.*, 549 A.2d 1163, 1169 (Md. Ct. Spec. App. 1988). For example, "[i]n order to induce a supplier to deal with a subcontractor whose credit is questionable, the general contractor may agree to pay the subcontractor with checks payable to the joint order of the subcontractor and supplier." *Id.* Further,

> [i]n a joint check arrangement, payment for services rendered in the construction industry is . . . made by a check payable jointly to the subcontractor who performed such services and his materialman. Each payee must endorse the check before it may be cashed. Since the check pays for both labor and materials it is the usual practice that the subcontractor takes part of the proceeds and the materialman retains the balance.

Rockland Credit Finance, LLC v. Fenestration Architectural Products, LLC, P.B. No. 06-3065 2008 R.I. Super. LEXIS 40 (2008).

Joint Venture. A joint venture is similar to a partnership, but the joint venture is a relationship created for one specific project or undertaking rather than a continuous relationship. BLACK'S LAW DICTIONARY 856 (8th ed. 2004); *see also Jordan v. Paul Financial, LLC*, 644 F. Supp. 2d 1156, 1174 (N.D. Cal. 2009) ("A joint venture is an undertaking by two or more persons jointly to carry out a single business enterprise for profit. Like partners, joint venturers are fiduciaries with a duty of disclosure and liability to account for profits."). To form a joint venture,

> there must be (1) a community of interest in the performance of the common purpose, (2) a joint proprietary interest in the subject matter, (3) a mutual right to control, (4) a right to share in the profits, and (5) unless there is an agreement to the contrary, a duty to share in any losses which may be sustained.

Ellsworth Paulsen Construction Co. v. 51-SPR-L.L.C., 183 P.3d 248, 252 (Utah 2008).

A "joint venture arrangement is fairly common in construction contracting." 2 PHILIP L. BRUNER & PATRICK J. O'CONNOR, JR., BRUNER AND O'CONNOR

ON CONSTRUCTION LAW § 7:58 (2002). The members of a joint venture collectively may possess all the skills needed to perform the project; for example, an architect and a general contractor may form a joint venture for a design/build project. *See* ROSS J. ALTMAN, PROJECT DELIVERY SYSTEMS 80 (ABA 2009).

Three key issues regarding joint ventures are formation, liability, and taxation. Depending on state law, a joint venture may be formed orally or even by conduct; each joint venturer may be liable for the actions of the other joint venturers or, in the alternative, according to their share of the venture; and taxation most often is similar to that of a partnership. BRUNER & O'CONNOR, *supra*, § 7:58.

Jury Verdict Award. A "verdict" refers to the formal findings or decisions made by a jury on the factual issues of a case. BLACK'S LAW DICTIONARY 1592 (8th ed. 2004). A "jury verdict award" occurs when the jury renders its decision and gives (i.e., "awards") damages to one of the parties in the dispute.

L

Labor Burden. This term refers to an employer's cost for its employees beyond wages or salaries for such items as employment taxes and fringe benefits. Examples of costs that may be included in a burden rate are federal and state payroll taxes; workers' compensation expenses; 401(k) or other retirement contributions; vacation, sick, and holiday pay; medical and other insurance costs; and bonuses.

The burden rate must be calculated in order to determine the cost of the work, a component of which includes labor costs. The parties to the contract often agree on one of three ways to calculate labor burden rate: (1) actual costs of the taxes and benefits; (2) percentage of aggregate wages/salaries; or (3) scheduled burden rates for different classes of workers. *See* WILLIAM ALLENSWORTH ET AL., CONSTRUCTION LAW 228 (ABA 2009); *see also* 1 CONSTRUCTION CONTRACTS DESKBOOK, 22:111 (BLI Thomson Reuters West Supp. 2008).

Laborer. Generally, a "laborer" is a person who makes his or her living by physical labor. BLACK'S LAW DICTIONARY 890 (8th ed. 2004). On a construction project, laborers are those workers who perform the actual construction work.

Laborers generally include the trades and working foremen. *See* 1 CONSTRUCTION CONTRACTS DESKBOOK, 22:111 (BLI Thomson Reuters West Supp. 2008).

Latent Ambiguity. An ambiguity is latent when it "does not readily appear in the language of a document, but instead arises from a collateral matter when the document's terms are applied or executed." BLACK'S LAW DICTIONARY 88 (8th ed. 2004). Latent ambiguity can be understood in terms of the parol evidence rule, which prohibits the introduction of extrinsic evidence if the contract language is clear and unambiguous. However, "latent ambiguity" provides an exception to the rule, allowing the introduction of parol evidence if the contract language was unambiguous, but a set of facts comes to light rendering the formerly clear language now ambiguous. *See* BRUCE MERWIN, CONTRACTING FOR CONSTRUCTION PROJECTS 114–18 (ABA 2009). "The classic example of a latent ambiguity cited by a variety of authorities is a contract that calls for goods to be delivered to the "green house on Pecan Street" when there are, in fact, two or more green houses on Pecan Street." *Texas v. American Tobacco Co.*, 463 F.3d 399, 409 (5th Cir. 2006) (citation omitted). In this example, parol evidence could be admissible to determine to which green house the parties intended the goods to be delivered.

Latent Defect v. Patent Defect. Generally, a "latent" defect is hidden, whereas a "patent" defect is visible. Construction defects are treated differently depending on whether they are latent or patent. The statute of limitations periods generally are longer for latent defects, allowing the owner more time to discover the defect. Insurers also treat defect claims differently depending upon whether they are latent or patent.

While various jurisdictions define these terms differently, most provide that in order for a defect to be considered latent (i.e., hidden), it cannot be readily apparent nor capable of discovery by reasonable inspection. *See, e.g., Maycock v. Asilomar Development, Inc.*, 88 P.3d 565, 568 (Ariz. Ct. App. 2004) (noting that the term "latent defect" has generally been defined "as a hidden or concealed defect that could not be discovered by reasonable and customary observation or inspection" (citation omitted)). Conversely, if a defect would have been discoverable upon reasonable inspection, then it is a patent (i.e., visible) defect—even if the defect is not readily apparent. Accordingly, "[d]isputes over whether defects are 'latent' or 'patent' often boil down to whether the . . . inspection was reasonable." 4A PHILIP L. BRUNER & PATRICK J. O'CONNOR, JR., BRUNER AND O'CONNOR ON CONSTRUCTION LAW § 13:63 (2009).

Factors considered in determining the reasonableness of an inspection include the number of items to be inspected, the cost and complexity of testing, and representations required by the contractor regarding the quality of the work. *Id.* If the defect is discoverable by testing specified in the contract, then it generally is not latent. *Id.*

Lender/Construction Lender. A construction lender can be a mortgagee, beneficiary under a deed of trust, or any other party that advances funds for the purpose of funding the construction, alteration, repair, or improvement of real property. ARIZ. REV. STAT. ANN. § 33-992(A)(1) (2001); CAL. CIV. CODE § 3087 (West 2009); UTAH CODE ANN. § 13-8-5(1)(b) (West 2001). Typically, the construction lender will fund a significant portion of the construction costs. However, construction loans are not long-term loans; the construction lender will likely require the borrower to pay off the loan shortly after completion of the project. In order to discharge the construction loan, the owner will typically obtain a permanent loan secured by a mortgage on the completed project. CARINA Y. OHARA ET AL., FUNDAMENTALS OF CONSTRUCTION LAW (ABA 2001); ROSS J. ALTMAN, PARTICIPANTS IN THE DESIGN AND CONSTRUCTION PROCESS 25–26 (ABA 2009).

Letter of Credit (LOC or LC). A letter of credit is an instrument issued by a financial institution (usually a bank) that serves as an irrevocable guarantee of payment to a designated beneficiary. For example, if a bank issues a letter of credit on behalf of a buyer of goods, it will be obligated to pay the seller if the buyer fails to make payment or otherwise defaults under its contract with the seller. 50 AM. JUR. 2d *Letters of Credit* § 2 (2009); *see also U.S. Material Supply, Inc. v. Korea Exch. Bank,* 417 F. Supp. 2d 652, 655 (D.N.J. 2006) ("A letter of credit is a promise by the 'issuer' (commonly a bank) to the 'beneficiary' (usually a seller of goods) to extend credit on behalf of the beneficiary's customer (usually a buyer of goods)." (citation omitted)).

A letter of credit is the result of a series of contracts, "a contract between the issuer and its customer; a second contract between the issuer and the beneficiary which is the actual letter of credit; and a third contract between the account customer and the beneficiary which is the underlying agreement." *Venizelos, S.A. v. Chase Manhattan Bank,* 425 F.2d 461, 464–65 (2d Cir. 1970).

"The essence of a letter of credit is the promise by the issuer to pay money, and the key to its uniqueness, commercial vitality, and recognized value is that the promise is independent of the underlying contracts." *Pringle-Associated Mortgage Corp. v. Southern National Bank,* 571 F.2d 871, 874 (5th Cir. 1978).

In the construction context, letters of credit are sometimes used as an alternative to a surety bond. This often occurs on international projects where the parties are unfamiliar with one another or on privately funded projects where owners prefer to avoid the expense associated with securing a surety bond. ROSS J. ALTMAN, PARTICIPANTS IN THE DESIGN AND CONSTRUCTION PROCESS 28 (ABA 2009). Letters of credit are often preferred by lenders because of their liquidity.

Liability Insurer. A liability insurer is a person or entity who agrees, by contract, to assume the risk of loss resulting from one party's liability to a third party. In the construction context, it is common for both owners and contractors to secure liability insurance. Liability insurance protects the owner and/or general contractor from liability arising from its actions or those of its contractors and subcontractors. Claims covered by liability insurance policies include, but are not limited to, workers' compensation or disability benefit claims; damages for bodily injury or occupational sickness; and property damage claims. BLACK'S LAW DICTIONARY 817, 823 (8th ed. 2004); AIA Document A201-2007, General Conditions of the Contract for Construction, § 11 (2007); 4 PHILIP L. BRUNER & PATRICK J. O'CONNOR, JR., BRUNER AND O'CONNOR ON CONSTRUCTION LAW § 11:2 (2010); BRUCE H. SCHOUMACHER, MECHANIC'S LIENS 532–33 (ABA 2009).

Lien Waiver. A lien waiver is "[a] sworn statement from the contractor, subcontractor, or supplier that acknowledges receipt of payment and waives or releases claims for work performed through a stated date or up to a stated amount." DAVID A. SENTER, PAYMENT 382 (ABA 2009). Often, the construction loan documents will require the general contractor or owner to compile and submit lien waivers before the lender will authorize the disbursement of loan proceeds. LORENCE H. SLUTZKY & DENNIS J. POWERS, THE OWNER'S ROLE 53 (ABA 2009).

Limitations Period. A limitations period is generally a statutory or contractually stipulated period designating the time by which a party must initiate its lawsuit or claim. Contractual provisions that attempt to diminish statutory limitations periods are disfavored by courts and will be strictly construed. In fact, some states have wholly eliminated a party's ability to contract for shorter limitations periods than provided for by statute. Other states have passed legislation that limits the extent to which a party may reduce statutory limitations periods.

R. Harper Heckman, *Drafting the "Perfect" One-Year Warranty*, Construction Law., Summer 2007, at 5, 9; Black's Law Dictionary 947 (8th ed. 2004).

Liquidated Damages. Liquidated damages refer to a sum of money that the parties to a contract stipulate will be assessed for a failure of performance (typically late completion) or the breach of a specified obligation, to be paid by the breaching party to the other party. In the construction context, owners of projects often include a provision in construction contracts that provides that the contractor will pay to the owner a specified sum for each day that the contractor delays contract completion or fails to meet other specified performance requirements. Many contracts specify that liquidated damages are often in lieu of and not in addition to actual damages for the specified breach or failure. A liquidated damages provision will be upheld "where actual damages are difficult to estimate accurately at the time the contract is entered into and the amount set is not disproportionate to the amount of damages reasonably anticipated at the time the parties entered into their contracts." 2 Philip L. Bruner & Patrick J. O'Connor, Jr., Bruner and O'Connor on Construction Law § 5:115 (2002); Restatement (First) of Contracts § 339 (2009). A liquidated damages provision that awards unreasonably large sums will be deemed a penalty and thus unenforceable on grounds of public policy. Restatement (Second) of Contracts § 356 (2009).

Liquidation Agreement/Liquidating Agreement. A form of settlement agreement in which a dispute between two parties with contractual privity is liquidated (i.e., settled) on terms delineating the rights, responsibilities, and procedures for presenting a pass-through claim to a third party and allocating the costs expended and benefits received when doing so is often referred to as a "liquidating agreement." Carl A. Calvert & Carl F. Ingwalson, Jr., *Pass Through Claims and Liquidation Agreements*, Construction Law., Oct. 1998, at 29.

Liquidation agreements are typically used when one party on a construction project has a claim against another party to which it lacks contractual privity. For example, liquidation agreements are commonly necessary when a dispute arises between a subcontractor and the owner. In this scenario, the liquidation agreement allows the subcontractor to assert its claim against the owner (via the contractor), while limiting the contractor's liability to the subcontractor if the claim is ultimately unsuccessful. In most instances, the liquidation agreement will "liquidate" the amount of the contractor's liability to the amount that the contractor can recover from the owner on behalf of the subcontractor. Carina Y. Ohara et al., Fundamentals of Construction

Law 104–05 (ABA 2001); Allen L. Overcash, Subcontractors and Suppliers 275–76 (ABA 2009).

Log (of Superintendent). A log book is a record maintained by a project participant, typically on a daily basis, that sets forth relevant project information and events. Log books frequently include details about where various project participants performed work, changes to the sequence or schedule and the reasons for any change, comments regarding any conversations, directives, telephone calls, interferences, or errors affecting the job as well as weather conditions. Although a project log book is frequently maintained by a project superintendent, other parties may also keep separate, contractor-specific logs. Robert F. Cushman et al., Proving and Pricing Construction Claims 126 (Aspen 2000); *see also* Barbara J. Jackson, Construction Management JumpStart 216 (John Wiley & Sons 2004).

Not surprisingly, parties frequently seek discovery of an opposing party's logs because the log may support their causes of action or defenses and it is a principal source of evidence to establish damages, negotiation of change orders, effects of delays, and resolution of disputes. A daily log serves to provide (1) a chronological, daily account of the number and type of workers on the project and the activities that take place; (2) a record of all visitors to the project site; (3) a description of the weather; (4) a record of the types and quantities of materials delivered; (5) a record of the types of equipment on the project site, recording both active and inactive time; (6) a record of any inspections; (7) a short description of any problems occurring on the site or unusual conditions uncovered; and (8) a listing of any discussions with the owner's consultants regarding problems, extra work items, or specific directions received from the owner or the owner's consultants. Sidney M. Levy, Construction Superintendent's Operations Manual 103–04 (McGraw-Hill Professional 2008).

"Look-Ahead" Schedule/Short-Term Schedule. "Look-ahead" schedules are rolling schedules that indicate how work will be accomplished during an upcoming short-term period, usually the next seven to ten days. Richard H. Clough et al, Construction Project Management 130 (John Wiley & Sons, Inc. 4th ed. 2000). *See also In re Electric Machinery Enterprises, Inc.*, Bankruptcy No. 8:03-bk-11047-MGW 2009 WL 2710266 at * 16 (Bankr. M.D. Fla. Aug. 28, 2009) (look-ahead schedules, also referred to as "short-term schedules" and "near-term schedules," are short-term, nondetailed bar chart schedules outlining generally where contractors are expected to be working during the period of the schedule as well as the work to be accomplished).

Every project will utilize some form of scheduling, whether it is a detailed long-term schedule or a rough, unwritten short-term schedule kept only in the mind of the contractor. Although some projects will utilize only a master schedule, look-ahead schedules allow a construction manager or superintendent to monitor construction progress on a short-term schedule.

Loss of Productivity Claim. In the construction industry context, this term refers to a type of claim made by a contractor or subcontractor that the expected production of its labor force was less than planned and reasonably expected. Such claims are generally associated with project disruptions and inefficiencies attributable to the owner or others that result in economic losses to the contractor or subcontractor. Loss of productivity claims are typically based upon the theory that individual compensable changes or time impact to a contract can have such a disruptive effect on the contractor's performance that the contractor has a compensable claim for costs in addition to the direct costs of individual change orders. *Southern Comfort Builders, Inc. v. United States*, 67 Fed. Cl. 124, 143–44 (2005) (citing *Jackson Construction Co., Inc. v. United States*, 62 Fed. Cl. 84, 103–04 (2004).

Productivity can generally be defined as "the units of work accomplished for the units of labor expended." William Schwartzkopf, Calculating Lost Labor Productivity in Construction Claims 5 (Wiley Law Publications 1995). Labor overruns occur from a variety of causes. Labor productivity claims attempt to link the claimed causes to the damages suffered measured by the amount of labor cost overrun. Schwartzkopf, *supra*, at 4–5. Some common causes of loss of productivity include increased labor/additional crews, trade stacking, overtime, adverse weather, out-of-sequence work, acceleration, contract changes, constructive changes, restricted access, and learning curves. Barry B. Bramble & Michael T. Callahan, Construction Delay Claims § 5.02 (3d ed. 2000).

M

Maintenance. Maintenance is any activity in furtherance of the ongoing upkeep of buildings, equipment, grounds, and utilities required to keep a building and its systems in a condition adequate to support its designed level of service and in the same state of being, repair, or efficiency. Cal. Gov. Code

§ 70307 (West 2009); ME. REV. STAT. ANN. tit. 23, § 562 (West 2009) (the work necessary to preserve a structure's existing structural or functional capacity and integrity to abate deterioration of its components to ensure safety of a user but not intended to increase or fully restore structural or functional capacity); *Texas Department of Transportation v. Barraza*, 157 S.W.3d 922, 928 (Tex. Ct. App. 2005) (citations omitted) (maintenance refers to the preservation of existing conditions and infrastructure); *see Esposito v. New York City Industrial Development Agency*, 1 N.Y.3d 526, 528, 770 N.Y.S.2d 682, 802 N.E.2d 1080 (N.Y. 2003) (work that involves replacing components that require replacement in the course of normal wear and tear constitutes routine maintenance); *Swieckowski v. City of Fort Collins*, 934 P.2d 1380, 1385 (Colo. 1997) (maintenance involved keeping a road in the same general state of being, repair, or efficiency as *initially constructed*) (emphasis in original).

In some cases, an owner, particularly a government owner, may be required to maintain property. *See* TEX. TRANSP. CODE ANN. § 224.031 (Vernon 2009). Often, a party injured on an owner's property alleges that the injury occurred because of the owner's failure to maintain the property. It is important in these cases to recognize that an owner is required only to maintain the property, not to upgrade, modernize, or otherwise improve the property. *See* COLO. REV. STAT. § 24-10-103(2.5) (West 2009) (maintenance does not include a duty to upgrade, modernize, modify, or improve the design or construction of a facility); *Karr v. City & County of Denver*, 677 P.2d 1384, 1386 (Colo. Ct. App. 1984) (city not required to modify or improve intersection based upon changing use).

Markup/Profit/Fee. In general, the contractor's fee/markup is a portion of the contract price that acts as an allowance for profit and home office overhead and represents the minimum acceptable return on the contracting party's investment. RICHARD H. CLOUGH ET AL., CONSTRUCTION PROJECT MANAGEMENT 49 (John Wiley & Sons 4th ed. 2000). A contractor's fee may be assessed in a number of ways. In a lump-sum contract, the contractor's profit equals the excess of the lump-sum amount less the actual cost of construction. *See, e.g., Levin v. Stratford Plaza, Inc.*, 76 A.2d 558 (Md. 1950). In contrast, cost-plus-a-percentage-of-cost or cost-plus-a-fixed-fee contracts provide for an express markup, profit, or fee. *See, e.g., Standard Oil Co. of Louisiana v. Fontenot*, 4 So. 2d 634 (La. 1941). Under a cost-plus-a-percentage-of-cost contract, a contractor is reimbursed for the costs of labor, materials, and supplies and the contractor's profit is a certain percentage of the total cost of the project. *Id.* at 671. Under a cost-plus-a-fixed-fee contract, the owner reimburses the contractor for the costs of all labor, materials, and supplies, but the contractor receives a fixed sum instead of a percentage of the total cost. *Id.* These fees, which are agreed to in advance, constitute the contractor's profit for the performance of the contract. *Id.* Additionally, a contractor's fee may vary, contractually, depending upon whether the work is extracontractual. For instance, a contract may set forth a cost-plus-10-percent fee on the original contract sum, but impose a higher cost-plus-15-percent fee on any change orders. Alternatively, a fee may depend upon the specific type of work performed, e.g., cost-plus-10-percent for general construction work but cost-plus-15-percent for any specialized postconstruction cleanup.

Because the return on investment is directly related to any risk assumed, as a party accepts additional contractual risk, the markup/percentage/fee increases. RICHARD H. CLOUGH ET AL., *supra*, at 49. Factors that may influence the exact amount of the markup/percentage/fee include, among others, (1) the size, complexity, and location of the project; (2) provisions of the contract documents; (3) an evaluation of the risk and difficulties inherent in the work; (4) the competition of other parties bidding for the same work; (5) the bidding party's desire for the work; and (6) the identity of the owner. *Id.*

Materialmen. Historically, lien statutes referred to mechanics and materialmen, granting these parties a lien for the labor and materials furnished in furtherance of an improvement to real property. *See, e.g.,* MISS. CODE ANN. §§ 85-7-131 et seq. Specifically, a materialman is a "person who furnishes materials or supplies to be used or consumed in any work of improvement." CAL. CIV. CODE § 3090 (West 2009); *see also* FLA. STAT. ANN. § 713.01(20) (West 2009). The determination of whether a party is classified as a materialman is important when asserting construction liens and Miller Act and related bond claims.

For example, on a Miller Act bond claim it is important to distinguish between a subcontractor and a materialman, as the Supreme Court has interpreted the Miller Act to allow a materialman to recover under the bond only where a supplier furnishes material to the prime contractor or a true subcontractor of the prime contractor, not to another supplier. *See MacEvoy v. United States,* 322 U.S. 102 (1944). In distinguishing a materialman from a subcontractor, courts apply a balancing test with certain factors tending to support a finding that a party is a materialman. For example, courts classified a party as a materialman where (1) the parties used a purchase order; (2) the materials came from preexisting inventory; (3) the item supplied was relatively simple in nature; (4) the contract was a small percentage of the total construction cost;

and (5) sales tax was included in the contract price. *See United States v. Aetna Casualty & Surety Co.*, 981 F.2d 448, 451 452 (9th Cir. 1992) (citations omitted).

Similarly, the determination of whether a party may be classified as a contractor or a materialman may be important to the assertion and enforcement of a mechanic's lien. For instance, California law requires a lien claimant to record a claim of lien within 30 days after the recordation of a notice of completion or 90 days after completion of the work, if a notice of completion is not recorded. CAL. CIV. CODE § 3116 (West 2009). Although an original contractor may also record a claim of lien within 90 days after completion of the work if a notice of completion is recorded, California law grants an original contractor 60 days in which to record a claim of lien if a notice of completion is filed. CAL. CIV. CODE § 3115 (West 2009). The California Court of Appeals noted that

> a materialman who merely furnishes materials for a building must not be confounded with the contractor who furnishes both materials and labor for and who constructs the building; nor with the laborer who furnishes his individual labor only upon the building. Nor must the common and statutory meaning of the word "materialman" be lost sight of when the person who furnishes the materials also, and by the same contract, furnishes or performs labor upon and in the construction of the building for which he furnishes the materials. In such cases the persons who furnish materials cease to be materialmen and become original contractors or subcontractors as the facts of the case may be.

Vaughn Materials Co. v. Security Pacific National Bank, 216 Cal. Rptr. 605 (Cal. Ct. App. 1985) (citations omitted). Therefore, where a party merely furnishes materials, even directly to an owner, the party remains a materialman and not a contractor.

Means and Methods. "Means and methods" refers to the approach to or manner of construction, including amount of labor, material, and equipment necessary to implement the selected technique adopted by the contractor to perform work. In general, a contractor's "means and methods" refers to the course of construction undertaken by the contractor. WILLIAM R. MINCKS ET AL., CONSTRUCTION JOBSITE MANAGEMENT 358 (Cengage Learning 2d ed. 2004). In many cases, construction contracts and design agreements explicitly provide that the means and methods of construction to be undertaken by the contractor as part of its scope of work are the sole responsibility of the contractor, and not the architect or design professional or the owner. For instance, the AIA A201-2007 provides: "The Contractor shall be solely responsible for, and have control over, construction means, methods, techniques, sequences and procedures and for coordinating all portions of the Work under the Contract . . . ." AIA A201-2007, General Conditions of the Contract for Construction, § 3.3.1 (2007). If the owner or architect requires the contractor to perform the work in a certain way, any increased cost over the contractor's estimated cost to perform based on its planned means and methods may constitute extra work and give rise to a claim for money damages. MARILYN KLINGER ET AL., *The Construction Project: Phases, People, Terms, Paperwork, Processes* 98 (American Bar Association, Tort Trial and Insurance Practice Section 2006).

Measured Mile Approach. The "measured mile" approach is a methodology undertaken to prove the amount of impact to a contractor's productivity. This approach is the most favored technique for pricing lost efficiency claims considering the additional effort required, as a result of delays and disruptions, to produce the same level of output. *See* JON M. WICKWIRE ET AL., CONSTRUCTION SCHEDULING: PREPARATION, LIABILITY AND CLAIMS 3.15[B] (Aspen 2d ed. 2003). This approach compares the construction progress during a "problem" period on the job with progress during a similar unimpacted time period. *Alstom Power, Inc. v. RMF Industrial Contracting, Inc.*, Nos. 2:03cv627, 2:03cv1050 2006 WL 3839235 at *2 (W.D. Pa. 2006). The measured mile is simply a section of the work, similar or identical to that which it is claimed has suffered the disruption, that has been undertaken and recorded under the contract conditions, i.e., without the effect of the alleged disrupting events. R. PETER DAVISON, EVALUATING CONTRACT CLAIMS 162 (Blackwell Publishing, Ltd. 2003). The period of time in which a contractor performs at its anticipated or normal productivity is also referred to as the "baseline." *In re Electric Machinery Enterprises, Inc.*, Bankruptcy No. 8:03-bk-11047-MGW 2009 WL 2710266 at *37 (Bankr. M.D. Fla. August 28, 2009).

For example, in constructing a multistory office building, a contractor may use a similar story as a baseline if construction proceeds on that floor without any interruptions. If a baseline cannot be established, a contractor may compare productivity rates over a longer period of time to reflect normal production rates. *See* WICKWIRE ET AL. at 12.16. In circumstances where the baseline or a normal productivity rate cannot be established, a contractor may consider using production rates on other projects, provided the other project (1) contains work that is substantially similar to the impacted work; (2) had similar weather conditions; and (3) utilized a similarly situated set of skilled craftsmen. *Id.*

Mechanic's Lien. A mechanic's lien is an encumbrance on real property granted by statute to secure a priority or preference of payment for the performance of labor or the furnishing of materials to buildings or other improvements. Mechanic's liens are enforced against the particular property in the manner, and under the limitations, set forth by statute. SAMUEL L. PHILLIPS, A TREATISE ON THE LAW OF MECHANICS' LIENS ON REAL AND PERSONAL PROPERTY 15 (Little Brown & Co. 2d ed. 1883); *see also Wyatt, Inc. v. Citizens Bank of Pennsylvania*, 976 A.2d 557 (Pa. 2008) (citing *Schwartz v. Whelan*, 145 A. 525 (Pa. 1929) ("a statutorily created lien for the purpose of securing priority for payment for work performed or materials provided in erecting or repairing a building.")).

Because liens are creatures of statute, in most cases the statutes are strictly construed. *Master Mechanical, Inc. v. Shoal Construction, Inc.*, No. 08L-12-055 (JTV) (Del. Super. May 29, 2009) (The law in Delaware is well settled that the mechanics' lien statute requires strict compliance from those seeking a lien. The idea behind strict construction of mechanics' liens complaints and intolerance for deficiencies in them is that the mechanics' lien statute is in derogation of the common law. The validity of a mechanics' lien depends upon an affirmative demonstration that each statutory prerequisite for the creation of such an encumbrance has been followed); *Dracon Construction v. Facility Construction Management*, 828 So. 2d 1069 (Fla. Dist. Ct. App. 2002) (a lienor must strictly comply with the statutory provisions to protect its lien); *Accent Store Design, Inc. v. Marathon House, Inc.*, 674 A.2d 1223 (R.I. 1996) (a statute that establishes rights not recognized by common law is subject to strict construction).

But many states only construe the statute strictly in regard to notice and filing requirements. *Regency Investments, Inc. v. Inlander Ltd.*, 855 A.2d 75, 79 (Pa. Super. Ct. 2004) (the doctrine of substantial compliance does not apply when the timeliness of serving notice is at issue). After a lien is established, most courts construe the statute liberally, in favor of the lien claimant. *See Winkler Construction Co. v. Jerome*, 734 A.2d 212 (Md. 1999) (the need for a liberal construction is particularly important with respect to subcontractors who, though benefiting the owner and enhancing the value of the owner's property, have no direct contractual relationship with the owner and therefore cannot otherwise subject the owner's property or assets to the payment of their claims); *Haz-Mat Response, Inc. v. Certified Waste Services Ltd.*, 910 P.2d 839 (Kan. 1996) (while the mechanic's lien statute requires strict compliance with the procedure prescribed in the statute in order to perfect a mechanic's lien, after the lien attaches, the statute is construed liberally); *BCI Corp. v. Charlebois Construction Co.*, 673 S.W.2d 774 (Mo. 1984) (the mechanic lien statute is remedial in nature and must be liberally construed in favor of the lien claimant); *Dolder v. Griffin*, 323 N.W.2d 773 (Minn. 1982) (questions involving the creation of a lien are subject to strict construction while issues as to the preservation of a lien that already exists may receive a more liberal construction).

Some states enacted statutes that require a liberal construction. *See* N.Y. LIEN LAW § 23 (McKinney 2009) "(a) This chapter is to be construed and applied liberally to secure the beneficial results, intents, and purposes of the chapter. (b) Substantial compliance with this chapter is sufficient for the validity of liens arising under this chapter and to give jurisdiction to the court to enforce the liens." TENN. CODE ANN. § 66-11-148 (2009) (lien statutes shall be construed and applied liberally to secure the beneficial results, intents, and purposes of the statute; substantial compliance with the statute is sufficient for the validity of liens and to give jurisdiction to the court to enforce the liens). But these statutes generally only codify the common-law rule that requires a strict construction where a question involves the creation of a lien, but then provides for a liberal construction after the lien is established.

The time in which a lien claimant must serve notice upon the owner and file or record a notice in a public office, if either is required, varies greatly among the states. For instance, Rhode Island requires a claimant to file a notice of intention to claim a lien within 200 days after the claimant does the work or furnishes materials. *See* R.I. GEN. LAWS §§ 34-28-1 et seq. (2009). The claimant must then file a notice of lis pendens and file a petition to enforce the lien within 40 days after the claimant files its notice of intent. *Id.* In contrast, if a notice of completion is filed, Alaska requires a lien claimant to file a notice of claim within 15 days from such filing. ALASKA STAT. §§ 34.35.005 et seq. (Michie 2009). However, a statute may also require notice for some claimants but not others. *See, e.g.,* TENN. CODE ANN. §§ 66-11-101 et seq. (2009) (no notice required for prime contractor but remote contractors must serve notices of nonpayment and notice of lien). Because the notice and filing requirements vary by state and even internally within a state, it is imperative to ensure that a lien claimant serves any required notice and files all notices within the applicable periods of time.

Med-Arb. Med-arb is a hybrid alternative dispute resolution process that combines mediation and arbitration and allows one neutral to perform the mediation and arbitration functions, first acting as a mediator and later assuming the role of an arbitrator as to any issues that are not resolved through mediation. *See* GEORGE W. ADAMS, MEDIATING JUSTICE: LEGAL DISPUTE NEGOTIATIONS 326 (CCH Canadian, Ltd. 2003). In some instances, a mediated agreement reached during a med-arb proceeding may be entered as an arbitration award. *See Wright v. Brockett*, 571 N.Y.S.2d 660, 663 (Sup. Ct. 1991). Because of the confidential nature of mediation, the high degree of deference enjoyed by an arbitrator, and the probability that mediation and arbitration will both be utilized in a mediation-arbitration proceeding before all disputes are resolved, it is essential that the parties agree to certain ground rules. *Bowden v. Weickert*, No. S-02-017 2003 WL 21419175 at *6 (Ohio Ct. App. June 20, 2003). For instance, the parties must (1) be aware that the mediator will also serve as an arbitrator should the mediation fail; (2) agree as to how any remaining disputed issues will be submitted to the arbitrator; and (3) set forth whether the parties agree to waive the confidentiality requirements imposed by any applicable laws. *Id. See also Town of Clinton v. Geological Services Corp.*, No. 04-0462A 2006 WL 3246464 (Mass. Super. Nov. 8, 2006).

Mediation. Mediation is a voluntary process, often mandated by contract, that is intended to assist the parties to a dispute in finding resolution. It is

> a process whereby a neutral third person called a mediator acts to encourage and facilitate the resolution of a dispute between two or more parties. Mediation is an informal and nonadversarial process with the objective of helping the disputing parties reach a mutually acceptable and voluntary agreement. In mediation, decision-making authority rests with the parties. The role of the mediator includes, but is not limited to, assisting the parties in identifying issues, fostering joint problem solving, and exploring settlement alternatives.

FLA. STAT. ANN. § 44.1011(2) (West 2009); *see also* ALA. CODE ANN. § 6-6-20 (2009); CAL. CIV. CODE § 850 (West 2009).

Although mediation is traditionally believed to be a consensual process, today many courts require the parties to engage in mediation before allowing the parties to try their disputes before the court. 6 PHILIP L. BRUNER & PATRICK J. O'CONNOR, JR., BRUNER AND O'CONNOR ON CONSTRUCTION LAW § 20:153 (2002). Similarly, several states have enacted mediation laws that govern local practice, including provisions relating to the enforceability of settlements. *Id. See, e.g.*, MINN. STAT. § 572.31–572.40 (2009). Local court rules may prevent the enforcement of an oral settlement reached in mediation. Bruner & O'Connor, *supra*, § 20:153. *See Beazer East, Inc. v. Mead Corp.*, 412 F.3d 429 (3d Cir. 2005), *cert. denied*, 126 S. Ct. 1040 (2006) (local federal appellate rules make it impossible to enforce oral settlement reached at mediation).

In addition, many contracts, especially in the construction industry, require parties to mediate. This requirement is frequently a condition precedent to other dispute resolution procedures. For instance, the AIA A201-2007 provides: "[c]laims, disputes, or other matters in controversy arising out of or related to the Contract, except those waived . . . shall be subject to mediation as a condition precedent to binding dispute resolution." AIA A201-2007, General Conditions of the Contract for Construction, § 15.3 (2007).

Meeting Minutes. Every construction project will include at least one project meeting, whether it is an initial meeting between a home improvement contractor and the homeowner or between a large general contractor and a major corporation for the construction of a hospital. Regardless of the size of a project, it is imperative to keep a record of what transpired as an official written record of the meeting. Meeting minutes frequently include information such as (1) the date of the meeting; (2) the name of the person preparing the minutes; (3) a listing of those parties in attendance; and (4) the items discussed along with a description of each topic. *See* Sidney Levy, Project Management in Construction (McGraw-Hill Professional 5th ed. 2006). The meeting minutes should also identify which parties are responsible for taking any necessary actions and the dates by which those actions must be completed, and the date of the next meeting as well as any business to be addressed in that meeting. Stephen Emmitt et al., Construction Communication 164 (Wiley-Blackwell 2003).

Meeting minutes are considered "official business records" and may be introduced as evidence in a court proceeding. Levy at 98 (McGraw-Hill Professional 5th ed. 2006). Information contained in the meeting minutes may prove to be the most reliable evidence of what transpired in a meeting, as minutes are completed soon after the meeting, when memories are fresh. Robert F. Cushman & James J. Meyers, Construction Law Handbook 23.05[C] (Aspen 1999). Some contracts require each party to receive and review a copy of the meeting minutes and note any discrepancies in writing within a given time period. *See* John M. Wickwire et al, Construction Scheduling: Preparation, Liability and Claims 6.03 (Aspen 2d ed. 2003). Thus, if a party disputes the content of the meeting minutes during the dispute resolution process, the meeting minutes may be used as a waiver of any dispute, or potentially, evidence of a prior admission. But meeting minutes of a preconstruction meeting may not be used to dispute terms contained in the contract when the parties executed the contract following the preconstruction meeting. *See Keeney Construction v. James Talcott Construction Co.*, 45 P.3d 19 (Mont. 2002) (meeting minutes not admissible to show an earlier completion date than that set forth in the parties' express written contract).

Mini-Trial. Formally recognized in the late 1970s, a mini-trial is a hybrid alternative dispute resolution process that structures private negotiation by combining elements of negotiations, mediation, and arbitration. *See* VIVIAN RAMSEY ET AL., CONSTRUCTION LAW HANDBOOK 882–83 (Thomas Telford 2007). Despite its name, a mini-trial is ordinarily a process that involves a structured negotiation of a settlement. Also known as an executive tribunal, a mini-trial allows the parties and their decision-makers, often in the presence of a neutral adviser, to formulate a voluntary settlement after hearing presentations on the merits of each side of the dispute. 4 AM. JUR. 2d *Alternative Dispute Resolution* § 8 (2009). *See also* COLO. REV. STAT. ANN. § 13-22-302(4.3) (West 2009); WIS. STAT. ANN. § 802.12(1)(f) (West 2009).

Because a mini-trial is completely voluntary, it is not binding upon the parties. BRIAN G. CORGAN ET AL., CONSTRUCTION DISPUTES: PRACTICE GUIDE WITH FORMS 14.06[A] (Aspen 2d ed. 2002). Similarly, because a mini-trial is flexible, the parties may tailor the process to suit their particular situation, project, or dispute. *See* VIVIAN RAMSEY ET AL., *supra*, at 882–83. The process is best suited for mixed legal and factual issues; thus, cases that deal primarily with legal issues or credibility determinations are not well-suited for a mini-trial. BRIAN G. CORGAN ET AL., *supra*, at 14.06[A].

Mini-trials are creatures of contract and are utilized in various forms for resolving disputes on construction contracts. For example, the U.S. Army Corps of Engineers' first mini-trial concerned an acceleration claim pending before the Armed Services Board of Contract Appeals. Utilizing the mini-trial, the parties settled a $630,000 claim for $380,000 in only three days. The Corps' second mini-trial lasted a combined four days, but resolved a $55,600,000 claim for changed conditions relating to the construction of the Tennessee Tombigbee Waterway for $17,200,000. *See* PETER R. HIBBERD ET AL, ADR AND ADJUDICATION IN CONSTRUCTION DISPUTES 119 (Wiley-Blackwell 1999). Thus, a mini-trial may be used to resolve any dispute, regardless of the amount in controversy.

Mitigation of Damages. It is a generally accepted principle of law that one who is injured by the wrongful acts of another, whether as a result of a tortious act or a breach of contract, is bound to exercise that degree of reasonable care and diligence that an ordinarily prudent person would use under similar circumstances to avoid loss and thus minimize (i.e., mitigate) the resulting damage. Whether a party has mitigated its damages is a factual question. *See Shelton v. Clements*, 834 So. 2d 775 (Ala. Ct. App. 2002) (internal citations omitted). If an owner abandons a project or otherwise stops work for an extended period of time, for example, mitigation may require the contractor to return rental equipment, lay off or reassign personnel, or cancel supply orders. However, if the duration of a delay is to be short-term or uncertain, lesser mitigation efforts may be required. The failure of an injured party to mitigate damages may result in a court either reducing the amount of that party's claim or even disallowing any damages. *See Graybar Electrical Co. v. Stratton of Florida, Inc.*, 509 So. 2d 1133 (Fla. Dist. Ct. App. 1987). "A party may not recover for any part of his loss that was caused or increased by his failure to act reasonably." *Kuruvilla v. Red Bay Hospital*, 497 So. 2d 829 (Ala. Civ. App. 1986).

Multi-Prime Contracting. In a traditional contracting framework, an owner will hire a general contractor who, in turn, contracts with various subcontractors responsible for discrete portions of the work. However, in some circumstances an owner may desire to act as its own general contractor. In such event, the owner contracts directly with separate trade contractors responsible for discrete portions of the work. This less used contracting framework is referred to as multi-prime contracting. Selection of the multi-prime approach is sometimes made in order to avoid a general contractor's markup or profit. *See* 2 PHILIP L. BRUNER & PATRICK J. O'CONNOR, JR., BRUNER AND O'CONNOR ON CONSTRUCTION LAW § 6.14 (2002). In other cases, particularly with respect to public projects, this approach has been mandated by law. N.Y. STATE FIN. LAW § 135; N.J. STAT. ANN. § 52:32-2; OHIO REV. CODE ANN. § 153.03; PA. STAT. ANN. tit. 71, § 1618; N.C. GEN. STAT. § 143-128; WIS. STAT. ANN. § 66.29.

By contracting directly with each trade contractor, an owner is burdened with all the duties and responsibilities of the traditional general contractor, including coordination and scheduling of the trade contractor's work. An owner choosing to use the multi-prime framework of contracting should be well informed in the process and possess sufficient time, skill, and sophistication to properly manage the project. *See* CARINA Y. OHARA ET AL., FUNDAMENTALS OF CONSTRUCTION LAW 181 (ABA 2001).

Mutual Mistake. Mutual mistake most often arises in one of two scenarios: (1) where there has been a meeting of the minds of the parties, but the agreement in its written form does not express what was actually intended by the parties, or (2) where there has been no true meeting of the minds because of a misunderstanding of a material fact. In most jurisdictions, either party may avoid or rescind a contract based on a mutual mistake about the same material fact or seek reformation of the contract by a court of equity. As an example of the doctrine of mutual mistake in the construction context, a Florida court allowed a homeowner to rescind its contract with its builder, finding that there was a mutual mistake of fact where both were mistaken in their belief that the soil on which the owner's house was to be constructed had been properly demucked and filled with clean fill by another contractor. *See Native Homes, Inc. v. Stamm*, 721 So. 2d 809 (Fla. Dist. Ct. App. 1998). Also, "[a] court of equity has the power to reform a written instrument where, due to a mutual mistake, the instrument as drawn does not accurately express the true intention or agreement of the parties to the instrument." *See Brandsmart of West Palm Beach, Inc. v. DR Lakes, Inc.*, 901 So. 2d 1004 (Fla. Dist. Ct. App. 2005) (internal citations omitted.).

The Supreme Court of New Mexico allowed a paving contractor to obtain reformation of a contract with an owner to correct a mutual mistake that resulted in double deduction of the costs for certain paving work deleted by a change order after the parties discovered that the same work had already been deducted in the price of the original contract. *Ballard v. Chavez*, 868 P.2d 646 (N.M. 1994).

N

Named Insured. Under most typical insurance policies, the "named insured" is the person or organization designated the insured party on the declarations page of the policy. That person or organization will generally be the entity that has purchased the coverage and in whose name the policy is written. Most commercial general liability (CGL) policies provide certain other parties an insured (but not named insured) status and are usually identified under a section in the policy entitled "Who Is an Insured." The insured status of each of these automatic insureds is usually tied to that person's or organization's relationship to the policy's named insured. Examples would be the spouse of an individual named insured; partners and joint venturers in a named insured partnership or joint venture; members and managers of a named insured limited liability company; and officers, directors, and stockholders of a named insured corporation or organization. A typical automobile policy will include residents of the insured's household as automatic insureds. 8 LEE R. RUSS & THOMAS F. SEGALLA, COUCH ON INSURANCE § 114:147 (West Group 3d ed. 1995). However, there are differences in the rights and responsibilities of an insured and a named insured that may vary according to particular policy terms and policy interpretations in different jurisdictions. 1 PATRICK J. WIELINSKI ET AL., CONTRACTUAL RISK TRANSFER XI.C.2–3, (International Risk Management Institute, Inc. 2008); 1 PATRICK J. WIELINSKI ET AL., COMMERCIAL LIABILITY INSURANCE V.C.2. (International Risk Management Institute, Inc. 2008).

Named insureds and automatic insureds should not be confused with additional insureds. Under most construction contracts, a party may desire, or be contractually obligated, to extend its insurance coverage to other individuals or entities. Owners often require general contractors to name the owner as an additional insured under the contractor's liability policies. General contractors usually require that they be named as additional insureds under each subcontractor's policy. Coverage for such additional insureds may be accomplished pursuant to a specific endorsement expressly naming the individual or entity as an additional insured on the policy, or by a blanket additional insured endorsement that provides coverage for a limited category of individuals or entities without having to be expressly identified. 9 LEE R. RUSS & THOMAS F. SEGALLA, COUCH ON INSURANCE § 126:7 (West Group 3d ed. 1995).

National Society of Professional Engineers (NSPE). Founded in 1934, NSPE is a national trade organization composed of licensed professional engineers (PEs) and those on the path to licensure (engineer interns/engineer in training or EITs) who show the highest level of dedication to their profession. NSPE, in partnership with the State Societies, is committed to addressing the professional concerns of its members across all engineering disciplines, through education, licensure advocacy, leadership training, multidisciplinary networking, and outreach. In 1975, NSPE established a joint venture with the American Council of Engineering Companies (ACEC), the American Society of Civil Engineers—Construction Institute (ASCE-CI) and the Associated General Contractors of America (AGC) known as the Engineers Joint Contract Documents Committee (EJCDC). EJCDC was formed to develop and update fair and objective standard documents for use between all parties involved in engineering design and construction projects. The EJCDC documents represent a major portion of the professional groups engaged in the practice of providing engineering and construction services for the constructed project, and the documents are a frequent source of reference and use in the construction industry.

Negligence. One who fails to exercise the standard of care that a reasonably prudent person would ordinarily have exercised under similar circumstances is considered to be negligent. Negligence may be active or passive in nature, and may consist of acts of commission or omission or both. In other words, negligence may consist of doing or performing an act that one should not have performed, and it may also consist of leaving undone that which ought to have been done. *See Baltimore & Potomac Railroad Co. v. Jones*, 95 U.S. 439 (1877); *Hoelter v. Mohawk Services, Inc.*, 365 A.2d 1064 (Conn. 1975); *Spielman v. New York, New Haven & Hartford Railroad Co.*, 147 F. Supp. 451 (E.D.N.Y. 1956); *Ferguson v. Gurley*, 125 S.E.2d 218 (Ga. Ct. App. 1962); BLACK'S LAW DICTIONARY 846 (7th ed. 1999). Simple negligence is the failure to exercise reasonable care. Gross negligence is the failure to use slight care. *See Concrete Construction, Inc. of Lake Worth v. Petterson*, 216 So. 2d 221 (Fla. 1968). Gross negligence is not generally considered synonymous with willful and wanton conduct that involves the absence of all care and may expose the offending party to exemplary or punitive damages. *BLI Construction Co. v. Debari*, 217 S.E.2d 426 (Ga. Ct. App. 1975).

Contractors have an implied duty to perform their work skillfully, carefully, diligently, and in a workmanlike manner. *Howell v. Ayers*, 202 S.E.2d 189 (Ga. Ct. App. 1973). Similarly, design professionals have "an obligation to exercise a reasonable degree of care, skill and ability such as is ordinarily exercised under similar conditions and like circumstances by persons employed in the same or similar profession." *Mauldin v. Sheffer*, 150 S.E.2d 150 (Ga. Ct. App. 1966). A breach of these implied duties is considered negligence and may expose the contractor or design professional to damages arising from the negligent act or omission.

Negligent Misrepresentation. One who supplies information during the course of his business, profession, or employment, or in any transaction in which he has a pecuniary interest, owes a duty of reasonable care to parties who rely upon the information if that person was aware of the use to which the information was to be put and intended that it be so used; to do otherwise is considered negligent misrepresentation. *Robert & Co. Associates v. Rhodes-Haverty Partnership*, 300 S.E.2d 503 (Ga. 1983). In many states, proven "negligent misrepresentation" is an exception to the economic loss rule that would otherwise bar recovery of purely economic losses from a party with whom a claimant does not have privity of contract. Common elements of negligent misrepresentation are (1) misrepresentation of material fact, (2) absence of reasonable grounds for believing that such representation is true, (3) intent of inducing another's reliance on the misrepresentation, (4) justifiable reliance upon the misrepresentation by the damaged party, and (5) damages. *See United States v. Neustadt*, 366 U.S. 696 (1961); *Breckenridge Creste Apartments, Ltd. v. Citicorp Mortgage, Inc.*, 826 F. Supp. 460 (N.D. Ga. 1993); *Glenn K. Jackson Inc. v. Roe*, 273 F.3d 1192 (9th Cir. 2001); *Hydro Investors, Inc. v. Trafalgar Power Inc.*, 227 F.3d 8 (2d Cir. 2000). Contractors frequently assert claims for negligent misrepresentation against various design professionals regarding the preparation and dissemination of project information. A contractor might assert a claim for negligent misrepresentation against a civil engineer if the contractor relied on the engineer's geotechnical reports in preparing a bid and incurred additional costs when the information proved incorrect. *See Ramsey Construction Co. v. Apache Tribe of Mescalero Reservation*, 673 F.2d 315 (10th Cir. 1982). Contractors have also successfully sued a project engineer because of errors in the plans and specifications that caused the contractor to be delayed in performance of its work. *Hardaway Co. v. Parsons Brincherhoff, Quade & Douglas, Inc.*, 479 S.E.2d 727 (Ga. App. 1997).

No Damage-for-Delay Clause. A no-damage-for-delay clause attempts to contractually bar recovery by a contractor or subcontractor for extra costs incurred due to a project delay for which the injured party is not responsible. A properly worded no-damage-for-delay clause may limit the delayed party's claim solely to an extension of time and preclude the recovery of monetary damages. Provided the clause is unambiguous, a majority of jurisdictions hold that no-damage-for-delay provisions are valid and enforceable with few exceptions, as in Ohio where such clauses have been legislatively determined contrary to public policy and thus unenforceable. *See* OHIO REV. CODE ANN. § 4113.62).

Several jurisdictions have their own rules for interpreting no-damage-for-delay clauses, but the most common exceptions to enforcing these clauses are where delays are caused by (1) the protected party's fraud, misrepresentation, or bad faith; (2) the protected party's active interference with the contract; (3) unreasonable delay justifying abandonment; (4) the gross negligence of the protected party, or (5) delays that are uncontemplated. *See Trataros Construction, Inc., v. NYCHA*, 34 A.D.3d 451 (N.Y. App. Div. 2d Dept. 2006); *Blake Construction Co. v. Upper Occoquan Sewage Authority*, 587 S.E.2d 711 (Va. 2003); *Green International, Inc.. v. Solis*, 951 S.W.2d 384 (1997). Some jurisdictions, such as Maryland

and South Carolina, take a literal enforcement approach, holding that such an exculpatory clause is enforceable, even if the delay is uncontemplated by the parties. (*See State Highway Administration v. Greiner Engineering Sciences, Inc.*, 577 A.2d 363 (Md. Ct. Spec. App. 1990); *United States v. Metric Construction, Inc.*, 480 S.E.2d 447 (S.C. 1997)). Case law in the relevant jurisdiction should always be reviewed prior to relying on a no-damage-for-delay clause.

Noncompensable Delay. Although a delay may be excusable, it is not necessarily compensable. IRV RICHTER ET AL., HANDBOOK OF CONSTRUCTION LAW & CLAIMS 179 (Reston Publishing Co. 1982). Noncompensable delay is an "excusable delay" to the critical path in that it is outside the "control" of the party delayed, but at the same time it is not within the "control" of the other contracting party. Simply stated, it is not the fault of either contracting party. Damages allowed for noncompensable delays are typically limited to an extension of time without monetary damages. Hence, the name "noncompensable" delay. Noncompensable delays are one subcategory of excusable delay, the other being compensable delays.

Examples of noncompensable delays would include "abnormal weather, unforeseeable strikes, acts of God, etc." 5 PHILIP L. BRUNER & PATRICK J. O'CONNOR, JR., BRUNER AND O'CONNOR ON CONSTRUCTION LAW §§ 15:29, 15:50 (2002). However, a noncompensable delay may become compensable if it arises as a result of another compensable delay. For example, adverse weather conditions encountered because of an owner's wrongful refusal to shut down have been ruled compensable. *Bignold v. King County*, 399 P.2d 611 (Wash. 1965); *See also Luria Bros. & Co. v. United States*, 369 F.2d 701 (Ct. Cl. 1966).

Notice of Claim. Most contracts in the construction context require contractors (or subcontractors as applicable) to provide to the owner (or contractor in the case of subcontracts) timely and written notice of events that could give rise to a claim or of an intent to assert a claim for a contract adjustment or extension of time. 2 PHILIP L. BRUNER & PATRICK J. O'CONNOR, JR., BRUNER AND O'CONNOR ON CONSTRUCTION LAW § 7:140 (2002). As an example, article 15 of the AIA's General Conditions for Construction (A201) requires that "[C]laims by either party must be initiated within 21 days after occurrence of the event giving rise to such Claim or within 21 days after the claimant first recognizes the condition giving rise to the claim, whichever is later." AIA Document A201-2007, § 15.1.2 (2007). Most subcontracts also have certain notice of claim requirements as conditions precedent to asserting claims against the prime contractor.

In addition to specific contract requirements, one should always adhere to the ancient equitable principle of "notice and opportunity to cure." A breach cannot be said to be material if it is curable, notice to cure is given, and prompt steps are taken to cure or to offer assurances of cure. 5 BRUNER & O'CONNOR, *supra*, § 1815 (2002).

Notice of Commencement. Generally, the use of the term "notice of commencement" refers to a document filed prior to or at the time construction commences by the owner or prime contractor with the Clerk of Court in the county where the project is located for the purpose of notifying subcontractors, suppliers, and other third parties that construction work has begun on specific property and to provide certain information regarding the property. The document usually contains a legal description of the property being improved and the names of the owner, the contractor, the lender, and any surety along with other information beneficial to all contractors, subcontractors, and others performing work or supplying materials to the project. The contents of a notice, the time in which it must be filed, and the furnishing and/or posting of such notice varies from state to state, requiring a careful review of the lien laws in the state where the project is located. Typical requirements and contents can be found in OHIO REV. CODE. ANN. § 1311.04 and GA. CODE ANN. § 44-14-361.5(b).

Some states make no provision for a notice of commencement. Other states differ as to whether a notice of commencement is mandatory or just an extra protection that owners or contractors can use to trigger other requirements for those parties not in privity of contract with the owner or general contractor to preserve lien rights. In many states, a notice of commencement when timely filed by an owner or prime contractor may protect the owner and prime contractor from lien and payment bond claims from persons not in privity of contract with that owner or contractor, unless certain written notices are timely provided by those persons without privity. In other instances, failure to properly file a notice of commencement might expose a party to liabilities to which it would not have been exposed had a notice of commencement been properly filed. (*See RN Building Materials, Inc. v. C.R. Huffer Roofing & Sheetmetal, Inc.*, 683 N.E.2d 884 (Ohio Com. Pl. 1997) (holding that failure to properly file a notice of commencement excuses opposing party's failure to file a notice of furnishing, thereby exposing first party to liabilities).)

Notice to Contractor. The law in most jurisdictions contains notice to contractor requirements relating to both claims of lien and claims under a contractor's payment bond. A notice to contractor (a/k/a notice of furnishing) is a written notice typically sent by any person having a right to a lien (or bond claim) who does not have privity of contract with the contractor and is providing labor, services, or materials for the improvement of property. Usually prepared and submitted in response to a notice of commencement, the notice to contractor alerts the contractor of the fact that the party sending the notice to contractor is performing or providing labor, services, and/or materials in furtherance of the subject property or project. The contents of the notice to contractor vary by jurisdiction and many jurisdictions mandate the use of specific forms utilizing specific language. These notice to contractor provisions are generally mandatory conditions precedent to filing a claim of lien or a payment bond claim. *See General Electric Co. v. North Point Ministries, Inc.*, 657 S.E.2d 297 (Ga. Ct. App. 2006) (holding that notice to contractor necessary to preserve materialman's lien filed against property after subcontractor failed to pay supplier); *United States v. York Electrical Construction Co.*, 184 F. Supp. 520 (holding that a prime contractor's actual notice of subcontractor's claim does not dispense with the necessity of a written notice to contractor as required by statute to perfect a payment bond claim). Applicable laws regarding claims of lien and surety bond claims should always be carefully reviewed for any required notice to contractor.

Notice to Proceed. A notice to proceed is a written notice given to a contractor (or subcontractor as appropriate) directing it to begin or commence performance of specified work. A notice to proceed is but one method of establishing the date of commencement of a construction project. Although there are other methods of establishing the start date (e.g., the date the contract is executed, a date established by the terms of the contract, or the date of governmental approval in public projects), the notice to proceed is critically important because it alerts all parties involved in a project of the earliest date work can begin. The notice to proceed also marks the point from which delays may be measured. The contractor is expected neither to commence work prior to receipt of the notice nor to delay commencement of the work thereafter. An owner's untimely issuance of a notice to proceed—either too early or too late—may disrupt or delay the contractor's critical path and, thus, result in a compensable delay claim by the contractor. *U.S. Steel Corp. v. Missouri Pacific Railroad Co.*, 668 F.2d 435 (8th Cir. 1982); *Ross Engineering Co. v. United States*, 92 Ct. Cl. 253 (1940); 5 PHILIP L. BRUNER & PATRICK J. O'CONNOR, JR., BRUNER AND O'CONNOR ON CONSTRUCTION LAW § 15:52 (2002).

O

Occupational Safety and Health Administration (OSHA). OSHA is an agency of the U.S. Department of Labor that was created by the Williams-Steiger Occupational Safety and Health Act of 1970 (OSH Act), 29 U.S.C.A. §§ 651 et seq., to prevent work-related injuries, illnesses, and occupational fatality by issuing and enforcing standards for workplace safety and health. Construction industry standards are set forth in 29 C.F.R. part 1926. Failure to follow OSHA requirements can result in fines and other civil and criminal penalties. *See Bechtel Power Corp. v. Secretary of Labor*, 548 F.2d 248 (8th Cir. 1977). OSHA inspectors have the right to inspect any construction site during business hours and other reasonable times; question owners, employers, employees, and operators; and issue subpoenas. 29 C.F.R. § 657. OSHA does not create a private right of action, but whistle-blower protections limit an employer's ability to discriminate against an employee for filing an OSHA complaint. 29 U.S.C.A. § 666(e). OSHA citations can be damaging evidence in related civil litigation stemming from a workplace injury, possibly demonstrating negligence per se or breach of a duty of care. 4A PHILIP L. BRUNER & PATRICK J. O'CONNOR, JR., BRUNER AND O'CONNOR ON CONSTRUCTION LAW § 13:15 (2009); *Walton v. Potlatch Corp.*, 781 P.2d 229 (Idaho 1989); *Bellamy v. Federal Express Corp.*, 749 S.W.2d 31 (Tenn. 1988); *Donovan v. General Motors*, 762 F.2d 701 (8th Cir. 1985).

OSHA federal regulations cover most private sector workplaces, but states are free to develop their own approved plans as long as they cover public sector employees and provide equivalent protection to that provided under federal regulations. Twenty-two states and territories operate plans covering both the public and private sectors and five—Connecticut, Illinois, New Jersey, New York, and the U.S. Virgin Islands—operate public employee–only plans. In those five jurisdictions, private sector employment remains under federal OSHA jurisdiction.

In recent years, general contractors have been held responsible for the employees of their subcontractors. *See Secretary of Labor v. Bridge Builders, Inc.*, O.S.H.R.C. Docket No. 83-328 1984 WL 158950 (O.S.H.R.C. 1984); *Secretary of Labor v. Seppala & Aho Construction, Inc.*, O.S.H.R.C. Docket No. 91-0270 1991 WL 318835 (O.S.H.R.C. A.L.J. 1991); *Secretary of Labor v. Sparrow Construction*, O.S.H.R.C. Docket No. 92-3009 1993 WL 369062 (O.S.H.R.C. A.L.J. 1993); *contra Brennan v. Gilles & Cotting, Inc.*, 504 F.2d 1255 (4th Cir. 1974); *Southeast Contractors, Inc. v. Dunlop*, 512 F.2d 675 (5th Cir. 1975). Additionally, some state regulations impose strict liability upon owners and contractors for the omissions of their subcontractors. *See Allen v. Cloutier Construction Corp.*, 376 N.E.2d 1276, 1280 (1978); 5 Bruner & O'Connor, *supra*, § 16:3 (2002). However, off-site operations have been deemed beyond the purview of OSHA. 2 Bruner & O'Connor, *supra*, § 5:197 (2002) (citing *Brock v. Cardinal Industries, Inc.*, 828 F.2d 373 (6th Cir. 1987)).

Over-Inspection. An owner's use of different or more stringent inspection standards or tests than is required by the contract, or an owner's insistence that a contractor perform at a higher standard than is recognized in the industry absent a contractual provision so requiring, is characterized as over-inspection. Over-inspections violate the owner's implied duty of cooperation and noninterference. *See Astro Dynamics, Inc.*, ASBCA No. 28381, 88-3 BCA 20,832 (1988) (government's use of different and more stringent inspection standards than required by the contract amounts to a constructive change and entitles the contractor to recover its increased costs of performance); *Process Equipment Co.*, NASABCA No. 166-3, 67-1 BCA 6,142 (1967) (rejection of a contractor's work on the basis of different and more stringent inspection standards than those required by the contract is improper); *D.E.W. Inc.*, ASBCA No. 37232, 93-1 BCA 25,444 (1993) (government cannot require the contractor to perform at a higher standard than is recognized in the industry). Where an owner has engaged in over-inspection, the owner will generally be responsible for the contractor's increased costs to comply. *See W.F. Kilbride Construction, Inc.*, ASBCA No. N62467-73-C-6235 76-1 BCA 11,726 (1976). Similarly, when a contractor is subjected to confusing and vacillating inspection procedures, any delays the contractor experiences as a result will generally be considered excusable delay. *See Appeal of United States Instrument Co.*, WDBCA 940, 3 CFF 814 (1945). Generally, the owner bears the burden to establish that work it rejects failed to conform to the contract requirements. *See Orbas & Associates*, ASBCA No. 32922 et al., 87-3 BCA 20,051 (1987); *Southwest Welding & Manufacturing Co. v. United States*, 188 Ct. Cl. 925, 413 F.2d 1167 (1969).

Owner-Controlled Insurance Program (OCIP). An OCIP is a single insurance policy purchased and controlled by the owner of a construction project that provides coverage for the other participants in the project. Depending upon the policy language, coverage generally extends to the owner, contractor, and subcontractors with contract values over a certain amount, and may extend to design professionals. *See Safeway Environmental Corp. v. American Safety Insurance Co.*, No. 08 Civ. 6977(WHP) 2010 WL 331693, *2 (S.D.N.Y. Jan. 28, 2010) (OCIP that covers "all contractors and subcontractors on the projects for damages and defense costs arising out of personal injury, property damage, and wrongful death claims"). The coverage can include general liability, builder's risk, workers' compensation, design errors and omissions, excess coverage, umbrella coverage, and other special coverages. *See Bacon v. Liberty Mutual Insurance Co.*, 575 F.3d 781 (8th Cir. 2009) (OCIP provided contractors with coverage for commercial liability and workers' compensation benefits). Generally, coverage is limited to operations at the project site during construction and will not include coverage for off-site operations, such as transportation and warranty work. Owners obtain owner-controlled insurance programs in order to reduce the costs associated with each contractor or subcontractor obtaining a separate insurance policy for the project. *See Osowski v. AMEC Construction Management, Inc.*, 887 N.Y.S.2d 11, 12 n.1 (App. Div. 1st Dept. 2009) ("OCIPs eliminate the costs of overlapping coverage and delays caused by coverage or other disputes between the parties involved in a project"); *Safeway*, 2010 WL 331693 at *2 (explaining that because the OCIP covered all contractors, the construction company "was relieved from obtaining its own insurance" for the project). The contractors or subcontractors who benefit from the policy typically give the owner credit for the insurance coverage in the bid deduct process. *See Safeway*, 2010 WL 331693 at *2 (the owner required the construction company to give it a credit for the insurance premiums the company otherwise would have paid absent the OCIP policy); *In re Electric Machinery Enterprises, Inc.*, 416 B.R. 801 (Fla. 2009) (describing OCIPs as "resulting in a better insurance rate"). Additionally, resolution of claims may be easier when a single carrier insures all of the participants in a project. *See Osowski*, 887 N.Y.S.2d at 12 n.1 ("OCIPs were developed to make the insurance programs used primarily for construction projects more equitable, uniform and efficient"). However, problems can arise when the coverage offered by the owner-controlled insurance program is insufficient to replace the contractor's existing insurance coverage. *See Howrey LLP, Owner Controlled Insurance Programs (OCIPS): Why Owners Like Them and Why Contractors May Not*, Construction Weblinks, July 14, 2003, http://www.constructionweblinks.com/Resources/Industry_Reports_Newsletters/July14_2003/ocip.htm; *Entergy Gulf States, Inc. v. Summers*, 282 S.W.3d 433 (Tex. 2009).

P

Parol Evidence. Extrinsic evidence that contradicts, explains, or expands the terms of a written contract is considered parol evidence. The parol evidence rule, which is a rule of contract interpretation rather than a rule of evidence, governs when parol evidence can be used to aid in contract interpretation. The parol evidence rule provides that when two parties have made a contract and have expressed it in a writing to which they have assented as the complete and accurate integration of that contract, evidence of antecedent understandings and negotiations will not be admitted for the purpose of varying or contradicting the writing. 3 ARTHUR L. CORBIN, CORBIN ON CONTRACTS § 573 (Matthew Bender 1960 & Supp. 2002). The parol evidence rule will not bar the admission of prior agreements or negotiations unless the parties' written contract is intended to be the final expression of their agreement. The parol evidence rule does not bar admission of subsequent agreements, only those agreements that are made prior to the execution of the parties' integrated contract. Similarly, evidence of a collateral agreement, one that would naturally and normally be included in a separate writing, will not be barred. Parol evidence is not prohibited for purposes of determining whether a written contract is the parties' complete, integrated agreement. See Citizens Progress Co. v. James O. Held & Co., 438 N.E.2d 1016 (Ind. Ct. App. 1982) (oral testimony considered in deciding whether there was an integrated writing); State ex rel. Cipriano v. Triad Mechanical, Inc., 925 P.2d 918 (Or. 1996) (discussing when a writing should be considered a complete integration of the parties' contract).

Many courts recognize exceptions to the parol evidence rule. For example, parol evidence is often admissible to prove (1) that a writing is or is not integrated; (2) that an integrated writing is or is not complete; (3) that the parties intended words in a writing, whether integrated or not, to have either an ordinary or special meaning; (4) that a writing, even if unambiguous and complete, is unenforceable because of illegality, fraud, mistake, unconscionability, or duress; (5) that consideration was not actually paid; (6) the identity of the parties; (7) to resolve an ambiguity; or (8) that equitable relief, such as rescission, reformation, or specific performance, should be granted. See 1 PHILIP L. BRUNER & PATRICK J. O'CONNOR, JR., BRUNER AND O'CONNOR ON CONSTRUCTION LAW § 3:18 (2002) (citing RESTATEMENT (SECOND) CONTRACTS § 214).

The change order process can implicate the parol evidence rule when contractors and subcontractors execute change orders that contain broad release language and the contractor or subcontractor later seeks to recover additional monies for the work covered by the change order. Where the change order and release language is unambiguous, parol evidence will not be admissible to vary or contradict the terms of the writing. BRUNER & O'CONNOR, supra, § 3:20 at 403; Vulcan Painters, Inc. v. MCI Constructors, Inc., 41 F.3d 1457 (11th Cir.

1995); *Peeples Construction Co. v. Escoe Green, Inc.*, 522 So. 2d 493 (Fla. Dist. Ct. App. 1988). "The parol evidence rule also applies to settlement agreements." BRUNER & O'CONNOR, *supra*, § 3:20 at 403–04; *King Fisher Marine Service, Inc. v. United States*, 16 Cl. Ct. 231 (1989).

Partnering/Partnering Agreement. "A partnering agreement has been characterized as a set of strategic actions which embody the mutual objectives of a number of firms achieved by co-operative decision-making aimed at using feedback to continuously improve their joint performance." BENNET & JAYES, THE SEVEN PILLARS OF PARTNERING (Thomas Telford Publishing Ltd., London 1998); 2 PHILIP L. BRUNER & PATRICK J. O'CONNOR, JR., BRUNER AND O'CONNOR ON CONSTRUCTION LAW § 6:17 at 521 (2002). "Partnering is a proactive management process that integrates and optimizes the value-added services of each party to best achieve the business objectives of all parties within the relationship." CONSTR. INDUS. INST., RESEARCH REPORT 102-11, THE PARTNERSHIP PROCESS—ITS BENEFITS, IMPLEMENTATION AND MEASUREMENT 1–2 (1996). There are two types of partnering relationships: strategic alliances and project-specific partnering. "Strategic alliances are long-term commitments between two or more organizations for the purpose of achieving specific business objectives through maximizing the effectiveness of each participant's resources." *Id.* Project-specific partnering "is a commitment between two or more organizations for the purpose of achieving specific project objectives by maximizing the effectiveness of each participant's contribution." *Id.*

Partnering workshops are typically conducted subsequent to the award of the contract, to provide a forum in which participants discuss objectives and the process by which to achieve them. BRUNER & O'CONNOR § 6:17 at 522. A critical product of the partnering workshop is the creation of a written document called the "partnering charter," which sets forth the participants' goals. *Id.* Partnering charters are ordinarily not intended as legally binding commitments, nor are they typically identified as one of the contract documents. *Id.*

Pass-through Agreement (Liquidation Agreement). A type of settlement agreement wherein the contracting parties settle the dispute between them by agreeing to pass through some or all of the claims to a third party is referred to as a pass-through agreement. 3 PHILIP L. BRUNER & PATRICK J. O'CONNOR, JR., BRUNER AND O'CONNOR ON CONSTRUCTION LAW § 8:51 (2002). These agreements are generally entered into between the general contractor and one or more subcontractors and typically arise where a subcontractor asserts a claim for additional compensation and believes the owner or its agents should be responsible. *Id.* at

124–25. Typically, under these agreements the general contractor will acknowledge liability to the subcontractor in exchange for the subcontractor's agreement to only seek recovery to the extent the general contractor receives additional compensation from the owner. *Id.* at 125. These agreements help avoid duplicative litigation by permitting the subcontractor to prosecute its claim directly against the owner. *Id.* However, these agreements will not arise by inference. *Id.*

Typically, these agreements are negotiated after a claim has arisen, but they can be included in the subcontract for exculpatory purposes. *Id.* at 125–26. Exculpatory clauses contained in subcontracts can interfere with the subcontractor's ability to recover from either the general contractor or the owner. *See Severin v. United States*, 99 Ct. Cl. 435 (1943) (because subcontract contained a clause disclaiming general contractor's liability for losses caused by the owner, neither the general contractor nor the subcontractor could recover against the government-owner). Additionally, if a subcontractor signs an unconditional release against a general contractor, both the subcontractor and the general contractor may be unable to recover any amount beyond the settlement from the owner. *See Appeal of H.E. Johnson Co.*, 98-2 B.C.A. (CCH) ¶ 29868, 1998 WL 354199 (A.S.B.C.A. 1998) (general contractor could not recover for amount beyond settlement amount with subcontractor because there was no legal obligation to pay the subcontractor).

Patent Ambiguity. A patent ambiguity is an ambiguity that is apparent on the face of a legal instrument, such as where a contract contains two inconsistent provisions, in contrast to a latent ambiguity, which occurs where the wording of an instrument seems clear on its face but may actually refer to two different subject matters. The distinction between patent and latent ambiguities is most often emphasized during discussions of the parol evidence rule, which limits the introduction of extrinsic evidence to explain the meaning of contract terms under certain circumstances. Some courts have held that "parol evidence will not be considered to explain a patent ambiguity, that is, to supply the understanding that the parties could have reasonably been expected to reach where the language of an agreement reflects no understanding." *Galloway Corp. v. S.B. Ballard Construction Co.*, 464 S.E.2d 349 (Va. 1995). However, most courts admit parol evidence to explain contract terms if the contract is ambiguous, without regard to whether the ambiguity was patent or latent. *See Joseph Projects Diversified, Inc. v. B.W. Birk & Associates, Inc.*, 827 S.W.2d 264, 265 (Mo. Ct. App. 1992) (holding parol evidence to explain patent ambiguity was admissible); 1 PHILIP L. BRUNER & PATRICK J. O'CONNOR, JR., BRUNER AND O'CONNOR ON CONSTRUCTION LAW § 3:8, at 365 n.13 (2002).

The distinction between patent and latent ambiguities can also affect a bidder's or a contractor's duty to seek clarification of obvious discrepancies in bid or contract documents prior to bidding. *Id.* at 362. Under the patent ambiguity doctrine, where a patent ambiguity exists in the contract language, a bidder or a contractor "has a duty to inquire of the owner regarding the true meaning of the contract documents." 2 BRUNER & O'CONNOR, *supra*, § 6:29 at 547; *Appeal of Crowder & Son Construction Co.*, 1963 B.C.A. (CCH) ¶ 3744, 1963 WL 1057 (A.S.B.C.A. 1964). This is an exception to the general rule that ambiguities in contract language will be construed against the drafter. *See Interstate General Government Contractors, Inc. v. Stone*, 980 F.2d 1433 (Fed. Cir. 1992) (contract ambiguities construed against government-drafter); 1 BRUNER & O'CONNOR, *supra*, § 3:28; 2 BRUNER & O'CONNOR, *supra*, § 6:29. However, as a defense to the patent ambiguity doctrine, bidders or contractors may be able to invoke the superior knowledge doctrine, which holds that where the balance of knowledge is clearly on the government's side, "it can no more betray a contractor into a ruinous course of action by silence than by the written or spoken word." *Helene Curtis Industries, Inc. v. United States*, 312 F.2d 774, 778 (Ct. Cl. 1963); 2 BRUNER & O'CONNOR, *supra*, § 6:30. In other words, "[w]here the contractor is able to establish that the government has superior knowledge, it may be able to avoid the consequences of an obligation to seek clarification." *Id.* at 552.

Pay-if-Paid Clause v. Pay-When-Paid Clause. Pay-if-paid and pay-when-paid clauses are contractual clauses designed to transfer the credit risk of an owner's nonpayment or delayed payment down through the contracting tiers. A pay-if-paid clause obligates the contractor to pay its subcontractors only if it receives payment from the owner and attempts to protect the contractor in the event of the owner's nonpayment or other default. In contrast, a pay-when-paid clause limits the contractor's obligation to pay its subcontractors to only after it receives payment from the owner. While less restrictive than a pay-if-paid clause, pay-when-paid clauses may still entitle subcontractors to payment from the contractor in spite of owner's lack of payment. *See Architectural Systems, Inc. v. Gilbane Building Co.*, 760 F. Supp. 79, 82 (D. Md. 1991) (following owner's insolvency, general contractor was not bound to pay subcontractor where subcontractor's contract included "pay-if-paid" provision); *Galloway Corp. v. S.B. Ballard Construction Co.*, 464 S.E.2d 349 (Va. 1995) (pay-when-paid provision was absolute with respect to some subcontractors, eliminating general contractor's obligation to pay them, but not with respect to other subcontractors); most courts interpret the "pay-when-paid" clause as a timing provision and not a basis for nonpayment. *See Thos J. Dyer Co. v. Bishop International Engineering Co.*, 303 F.2d 655, 661 (6th Cir. 1962); 3 PHILIP L. BRUNER & PATRICK J. O'CONNOR, JR., BRUNER AND O'CONNOR ON CONSTRUCTION LAW § 8:47 (2002).

Despite the language of these clauses, many courts interpret them as timing provisions, not as a basis for nonpayment. *See Thos. J. Dyer Co.*, 303 F.2d at 661 (clause construed as a reasonable provision to postpone payment after the work was completed during which time the general contractor would be afforded the opportunity to procure the funds to pay the subcontractor); *Wm. R. Clarke Corp. v. Safeco Insurance Co.*, 938 P.2d 372 (1997) (pay-if-paid clause void as against public policy).

Payment Bond (Labor and Material Payment Bond). A payment bond is a surety's commitment to pay certain subcontractors and materialmen for labor or material supplied to the bonded project in the event that the contractor fails to make payment. Payment bonds are required on federal public works projects under the Miller Act, 40 U.S.C.A. § 3131–3134, and state and local public works projects under state-adopted legislation often referred to as the "Little Miller Acts." Payment bonds are surety bonds issued typically at the behest of a contractor at the owner's insistence or the requirements of statute, to guarantee payment of subcontractors and materialmen. They are an obligation similar to, but by no means the same as, insurance, by which an owner or contractor pays a surety a premium, in return for a guarantee by the surety of prompt payment to subcontractors, if the contractor does not pay the subcontractors. A surety's obligation to make payment on a payment bond is conditioned upon (1) the claimant's substantial performance of its obligations to provide notice of the claim and commence suit in conformance with the terms of the bond; (2) the claimant's proof of entitlement to recovery within the coverage of the bond; and (3) the absence of contract or statutory defenses that would preclude entitlement to or reduce recovery. 3 PHILIP L. BRUNER & PATRICK J. O'CONNOR, JR., BRUNER AND O'CONNOR ON CONSTRUCTION LAW § 8:152 (2002).

Although principles of suretyship typically allow sureties to assert all of the defenses of their principals, courts sometimes stray from this principle with respect to payment bonds where the principal-contractor has a valid defense based upon a pay-if-paid clause. *Id.* § 8:50 at 121; *see Moore Bros. Co. v. Brown & Root, Inc.*, 207 F.3d 717, 723 (4th Cir. 2000) (holding that surety needed to incorporate conditional payment provision into the bond in order to avoid payment). This interpretation is counterintuitive because surety law is clear that sureties are only obligated to pay to the extent that their principal is obligated to pay. BRUNER & O'CONNOR, *supra*, § 8:50; *St. Paul Fire & Marine*

139

Insurance Co. v. Georgia Interstate Electric Co., 370 S.E.2d 829 (Ga. Ct. App. 1988) (payment bond does not need to incorporate subcontract for the surety's liability to be limited to the liability of its principal). Issues often arise as to how remote a claimant's connection can be with a contractor or subcontractor while still being entitled to coverage under a payment bond. The results of this analysis vary greatly depending on the specific factual circumstances and the language of the bond or requirements of a statute. *See United States ex rel. Daniel H. Hill v. American Surety Co.*, 200 U.S. 197 (1906); *Clifford F. MacEvoy Co. v. United States ex rel. Calvin Tomkins Co.*, 322 U.S. 102 (1944); *LaGrand Steel Products Co. v. A.S.C. Constructors, Inc.*, 702 P.2d 855 (Idaho Ct. App. 1985); BRUNER & O'CONNOR, *supra*, § 8:163.

Peer Review. The evaluation of work performance by other people in the same field in order to maintain or enhance the quality of the work or performance in that field, to ensure that the work meets specific criteria, or to provide suggestions for improvement is referred to as a peer review. *See* S.B. Kaplanogu & D. Arditi, *Pre-Project Peer Reviews in GMP/Lump Sum Contracts*, 16 ENGINEERING, CONSTRUCTION AND ARCHITECTURAL MGMT 175 (2009); S.D. CODIFIED LAWS § 36-4-43 (defining peer review activities in the health care context as "the procedure by which peer review committees monitor, evaluate, and recommend actions to improve the delivery and quality of services within their respective facilities, agencies, and professions").

Pending Change Order/Change Notice/Contemplated Change Order. A pending change order is a writing issued by an owner to a contractor or by a contractor to a subcontractor describing a proposed change in the parties' preexisting contract or subcontract and requesting a quotation for that proposed change. Once the parties agree on a price and timing for the proposed changes, the parties will typically execute a final change order memorializing the changes that the contractor or subcontractor has agreed to perform, and this change order will operate as a legally enforceable modification of the parties' original contract or subcontract. *See Hawa Construction, LLC v. Pollock*, Civil Action No. 09-1728(RMC) 2009 WL 4884018 (D.D.C. Dec. 18, 2009); *Midwest Curtainwalls, Inc. v. Pinnacle 701, L.L.C.*, No. 92269 2009 WL 2332049 (Ohio Ct. App. 2009) (awarding amounts stated in pending change orders, despite that a change order was never signed, because contractor performed the work after receiving verbal instructions); *Industrial Window Corp. v. Fed. Insurance Co.*, 609 F. Supp. 2d 329 (S.D.N.Y. 2009) (granting summary judgment in part in favor of owner because although a pending change order was submitted, the contractor failed to comply with the change order procedures set forth in the contract).

Performance Bond. A performance bond guarantees an owner that the project will be completed despite contractor default. Performance bonds are required on federal public works projects under the Miller Act, 40 U.S.C.A. § 3131–3134 and state and local public works projects under state-adopted legislation often referred to as "Little Miller Acts." Performance bonds are surety bonds issued at the behest of a contractor at the owner's insistence or pursuant to the requirements of statute, to guarantee satisfactory completion of a project by the contractor. A performance bond may be issued for completion of a building contract or to protect the owner against the risk that the contractor will fail to construct the building according to the contract specifications. If the contractor fails to meet his obligations, often due to the contractor's insolvency, performance bonds typically provide that the owner will receive compensation for any monetary loss, up to the penal amount of the bond, or specific performance of the contract. Payment under performance bonds is typically triggered upon (1) the obligee's substantial performance of its obligations under the bonded contract; (2) the principal's material breach of the bonded contract sufficient to warrant termination; and (3) the obligee's proper notice to the principal and surety of the material breach and termination of the bonded contract. 4A PHILIP L. BRUNER & PATRICK J. O'CONNOR, JR., BRUNER AND O'CONNOR ON CONSTRUCTION LAW § 12:13 (2009). Performance bonds typically contain defeasance language, which renders the bond void upon successful completion of the project by the contractor. *Id.* § 12:14.

Performance bonds come in many varieties, including (1) traditional performance bonds, such as the AIA's performance bond; (2) indemnity bonds, such as the Federal Standard Form 25 performance bond; (3) completion bonds; and (4) manuscript bonds. *Id.* § 12:14. Depending on the language of the bond, the surety can be responsible for performance of the contract and payment for labor and materials furnished in furtherance of the bonded contract, protection of the land against the filing of mechanic's liens, indemnification of the obligee against loss caused by the contractor's failure to perform, or completion of the bonded contract unconditionally. *Id.* at 76. In the event that a surety has to pay under a performance bond, the surety is typically entitled to reimbursement from the contractor. 4 BRUNER & O'CONNOR , *supra*, § 11:29 (2010). Contractors do not secure performance bonds to protect themselves, but rather to assuage owners. *Id.*

Performance Specifications. In the construction context, performance specifications are a set of performance-related requirements to be satisfied by the contractor or subcontractor. Performance specifications set forth an objective or standard to be achieved requiring the contractor to exercise its ingenuity and means and methods in achieving the standard of performance, in selecting the means, and in assuming a corresponding responsibility for that selection. This is in contrast to a design specification, which sets forth in precise detail the materials to be employed and the manner in which the work is to be performed, from which the contractor is not privileged to deviate but is required to follow as one would follow a road map. *See Aleutian Constructors v. United States*, 24 Cl. Ct. 372, 378 (1991) (citing *J.L. Simmons Co. v. United States*, 412 F.2d 1360, 1362 (Ct. Cl. 1969)); *see also Blake Construction Co. v. United States*, 987 F.2d 743 (Fed. Cir. 1993), *reh'g denied, in banc suggestion declined* (Apr. 13, 1993).

Plain-Meaning Rule. The plain-meaning rule holds that if a writing, or a provision in a writing, appears to be unambiguous on its face, its meaning must be determined from the writing itself without resort to extrinsic evidence. In the context of contract interpretation, the plain-meaning rule dictates that where a term is not defined in the contract, the court will presume that the parties intended the term to have its plain, ordinary meaning. *See Auto-Owners Insurance Co. v. Harvey*, 842 N.E.2d 1279, 1283 (Ind. 2006) (if a contract is clear and unambiguous, its language is given its plain meaning). However, many courts deviate from the plain-meaning rule to allow admission of evidence regarding a particular industry's use of a term, or evidence of the parties' understanding of a particular term. In the statutory construction context, the plain-meaning rule dictates that undefined words in a statute be interpreted using their plain, ordinary meaning. There are exceptions to the statutory plain-meaning rule, such as where a literal reading of the language would lead to an absurd result. *See Church of the Holy Trinity v. United States*, 143 U.S. 457 (1892). The plain-meaning rule is applied in conjunction with the basic principle that, where possible, all statutes should be read to give effect to the intent of the legislature. *See State v. Hartman*, 602 N.E.2d 1011, 1013 (Ind. 1992). The plain-meaning rule will generally not operate to exclude from consideration material bearing on legislative intent. *See Johnson v. State*, 304 N.E.2d 555, 558 n.2 (Ind. Ct. App. 1973) (the plain-meaning rule is not to be used to thwart or distort the legislative intent by excluding from consideration enlightening material from the legislative files).

Precedence of Documents. This contract clause establishes a hierarchy of the contract documents so that in the event of a conflict between such documents, the document that is higher up in the hierarchy that is established by this clause will prevail. This clause will affect the overall interpretation of the contract because the hierarchy of contract documents that is set forth will resolve apparent or actual conflicts of the language in the contract as opposed to letting such conflicts remain unresolved. *See also* 1 PHILIP L. BRUNER & PATRICK J. O'CONNOR, JR., BRUNER AND O'CONNOR ON CONSTRUCTION LAW § 3:40 (2002) (the concept of a construction contract clause or provision "stating that to the extent conflicts arise between the various contract documents they will be resolved by giving preference to one document over another."); *cf.* S. GREGORY JOY & EUGENE J. HEADY, ALTERNATIVE CLAUSES TO STANDARD CONSTRUCTION CONTRACTS 118, Aspen (3d ed. 2010) ("The AIA generally does not favor use of hierarchy [of the contract documents] because the contract documents are intended to be complementary and to form a single, unified contract when read together.").

If no such clause is found in the contract, it is possible that the apparent or actual conflict in the contract language may lead to the argument that the contract is ambiguous and open to various interpretations. However, in the case of a conflict between the terms of a subcontract and a prime contract, some courts have held that, even if fully incorporated into a subcontract, the general provisions of a prime contract do not overcome the specific provisions of the subcontract. *Dugan & Meyers Construction Co. v. Worthington Pump Corp.*, 746 F.2d 1166 (6th Cir. 1984), *cert. denied*, 471 U.S. 1135 (1985); *McKinney Drilling Co. v. Collins Co.*, 517 F. Supp. 320 (N.D. Ala. 1981), *aff'd*, 701 F.2d 1132 (11th Cir. 1983); and *Johnson, Inc. v. Basic Construction Co.*, 429 F.2d 764, 772 (D.C. Cir. 1970).

Prime Contract/General Contract. A prime contract (or general contract) is a contract between the owner (or an authorized agent of the owner) of a construction project and the general or prime contractor, and typically consists of several contract documents, including a written agreement between the owner and the general contractor, the general and special conditions to that agreement, the plans and specifications for the project, and any subsequent amendments to the written agreement or any change orders modifying the scope of work defined in the agreement. *See* CARINA Y. OHARA ET AL, FUNDAMENTALS OF CONSTRUCTION LAW 95 (ABA 2001). The general practice is that an owner will enter into a single prime contract with a general contractor who, in turn, hires the necessary specialty trade subcontractors to perform the work.

See also Capricorn Power Co. v. Siemens Westinghouse Power Corp., 324 F. Supp. 2d 731, 751 (W.D. Pa. 2004) ("The nature of the prime contract is such that when executed the owner and contractor have established rights as between themselves and the contractor may or may not subcontract those portions of the work to be performed under the prime contract."); *and see* TEX. PROP. CODE ANN. § 53.001(6) (sometimes referred to as "original contract," which means a contractor has a construction contract directly with the owner of a project). However, and in contrast, in some projects an owner may enter into multiple prime contracts with different contractors either on its own accord or because required by law in certain jurisdictions.

Prime Contractor/General Contractor. Sometimes referred to as the general or main contractor, a prime contractor is a person or entity who supervises or performs work or labor or who furnishes material, services, equipment, or machinery in furtherance of any improvement, provided that the person is in direct privity of contract with an owner of the improvement, or the owner's agent. TENN. CODE ANN. § 66-11-101(12) (2009); *see also* NEV. REV. STAT. § 108.22164 (2009). On construction projects utilizing the multiple prime contracting method, an owner may retain several "main" contractors. The important distinction between main/prime contractors and subcontractors is that subcontractors do not contract directly with the owner.

Privatization. This term refers to the participation by the private sector with the government "in financing, developing, building, and operating infrastructure projects that have traditionally been financed and operated by governments." STEPHEN G.M. STEIN, STEIN ON CONSTRUCTION LAW 22–24 (Matthew Bender 1986). The General Accounting Office defines the term as "any process aimed at shifting functions and responsibilities, in whole or in part, from the government to the private sector." U.S. GEN. ACCOUNTING OFFICE, TERMS RELATED TO PRIVATIZATION ACTIVITIES AND PROCESSES, GAO/GGD-97-121 (1997). Privatization is sometimes referred to as "a joint venture, [when] a contractual arrangement is formed between public and private sector partners that can include a variety of activities that involve the private sector in the development, financing, ownership, and operation of a public facility or service." *Id.* Privatization is the concept behind the recent trend of the so-called public private partnership or PPP, which "can broadly be defined as follows: in order to bid for a contract proposed by a government, a private group of interest (consortium) creates a legal entity . . . with a mission to build, maintain, and operate the assets." Andre de Palma et al., *Towards a Principal-Agent Based Typology of Risks in Public-Private Partnerships*, International Monetary Fund 5 (IMF Working Paper No.WP/09/177 2009).

Procurement. In the construction industry, "procurement" can be broadly defined as the acquisition of project resources for the realization of a constructed facility or project. STEPHEN M. ROWLINSON & PETER MCDERMOTT, PROCUREMENT SYSTEMS: A GUIDE TO BEST PRACTICE IN CONSTRUCTION 34, Routledge (1999). In other words, procurement involves the selection of bidders for each portion of the work of a construction project "who are qualified, competitive, interested in [performing] the [w]ork, and capable of doing the [w]ork within the project time requirements." CONSTRUCTION MANAGEMENT ASSOCIATION OF AMERICA (CMAA), INC., STANDARD CONSTRUCTION MANAGEMENT SERVICES AND PRACTICES 27, CMAA (2d ed. 1993). The ultimate goal of the procurement endeavor is to secure the successful bidders under contract and direct them to commence the work. *Id.* at 59. *See also R&D Dynamics Corp. v. United States*, 80 Fed. Cl. 715, 718 (2007) (citing 41 U.S.C. § 403(2)) (Congress broadly defines "procurement" as encompassing "all stages of the process of acquiring property or services, beginning with the process for determining a need for property or services and ending with contract completion and closeout.").

Professional Liability Insurance (Errors & Omissions). Professional liability insurance provides coverage to design professionals for their alleged negligent acts or omissions arising from their rendering of professional services; it is also "[k]nown as malpractice insurance, errors and omissions insurance, or 'E&O' insurance [and] is insurance that attempts to exclude coverage of all types of liability except for liability that arises from the professional practice of architecture or engineering." JAMES E. ACRET & LISA J. PERROCHET, ARCHITECTS AND ENGINEERS § 13:6, 13–19, Thompson West (4th ed. 2009). In other words, it is a type of insurance "that protects the insured against liability for committing an error or omission in performance of professional duties." International Risk Management Institute, Inc. (IRMI), Glossary of Insurance & Risk Management Terms, http://www.irmi.com/online/insurance-glossary/terms/e/errors-and-omissions-eo-insurance.aspx. "A professional errors and omissions insurance policy provides limited coverage, usually as a supplement to a general comprehensive liability (CGL) policy, for conduct undertaken in performing or rendering professional acts or services." *Medical Records Associates, Inc. v. American Empire Surplus Lines Insurance Co.*, 142 F.3d 512, 513 (1st Cir. 1998).

Program Management. A project owner may hire a professional with the requisite "knowledge of the construction cost of materials, methods, and labor, and expertise in scheduling, coordination, and supervision to act as the owner's agent." In this form of program management, the owner's agent will oversee the project from beginning to end. KENNETH M. CUSHMAN, CONSTRUCTION LITIGATION 329, Aspen (1981). Program management is also described as a management program for the "entire project . . . [and this professional] is engaged before the architect, and [his] responsibilities encompass the management of the design as well as construction" of the project. STEPHEN G.M. STEIN, STEIN ON CONSTRUCTION LAW 3.01[4][b] at 3–31 (Matthew Bender 1986). "[T]he practice of professional construction management applied to a capital improvement program of one or more projects from inception to completion." Construction Management Association of America, FAQs, at http://cmaanet.org/faq#program.

Progress Payment. In the context of commercial construction projects, whether privately or publicly owned, contractors are typically paid based on the progress of work that is completed during a set interval, such as a month. These "progress" payments are distinguishable from a contractor's "final" payment and the final payment usually consists of the contractor's retainage, which is a percentage of each progress payment that has been withheld by the project owner either by law or by contract. In order to get paid a progress payment, contractors generally must submit a pay request or pay application to the owner with detailed backup documentation, including a schedule of values and invoices, that shows what work was performed by the contractor during the interval at issue and for which payment is requested. Sometimes in residential construction projects, a partial payment by the owner to the contractor is made at agreed-upon "milestones of completion" during the construction project. CARINA Y. OHARA ET AL., FUNDAMENTALS OF CONSTRUCTION LAW 346 (ABA 2001). Also, construction contracts may provide for these partial payments to be made on a periodic basis, such as monthly. STEPHEN G.M. STEIN, STEIN ON CONSTRUCTION LAW 7.01[1] (Matthew Bender 1986).

Project Engineer. Generally, a project engineer is an individual with engineering training or an engineering firm. The project engineer traditionally has responsibilities in both the design and construction phases of a construction project and is often a subcontractor to the architect of record on the project "which designs certain project elements such as mechanical, electrical or structural systems." See CARINA Y. OHARA ET AL., FUNDAMENTALS OF CONSTRUCTION LAW 346 (ABA 2001). See also U.S. DEP'T OF LABOR, DICTIONARY OF OCCUPATIONAL TITLES § 019.167-014

(4th ed. 1991) ("Directs, coordinates, and exercises functional authority for planning, organization, control, integration, and completion of engineering project within area of assigned responsibility."). However, sometimes this term refers to a construction professional who is not a licensed professional engineer but rather a project manager who has construction experience in engineering issues related to his particular trade (such as mechanical or plumbing).

Project Labor Agreement (PLA). A PLA is generally a prebid contract between a construction project owner and a labor union (or unions) establishing the union as the collective bargaining representative for all persons who are to perform work on a project. *Buffalo Laborers' Welfare Fund v. MCS Remedial Services, Inc.*, No. 06-CV-101C 2008 U.S. Dist. LEXIS 25484, *6 (citing *Matter of New York State Chapter, Inc., v. New York State Thruway Authority*, 666 N.E.2d 185 (N.Y. 1996). PLAs are used on both public and private projects. They are project-specific agreements, such as a contract to build a particular structure, in which the local unions enter into a collective bargaining agreement with an owner, developer, or contractor, and then the owner, developer, or contractor selects local unions to accomplish the various types of work needed for that project. *District Council No. 9 v. Empire State Regional Council of Carpenters*, 589 F. Supp. 2d 184, 188 (E.D.N.Y. 2008). On February 6, 2009, President Obama issued an executive order encouraging the use of PLAs on federal projects of $25 million or more. Exec. Order No. 13,502 (Feb. 6, 2009). *See also* definition of "Project Labor Agreement" in the National Labor Relations Act, 29 U.S.C. 158(f).

Project Manager. Generally, both prime contractors and specialty trade contractors employ a project manager, a person or entity who is intended to ensure the timely and proper completion of the work, and who often helps to secure timely payment of the specialty contractors, subcontractors, or prime contractors by coordinating the work and managing the paper flow and other components of the project. *See* CARINA Y. OHARA ET AL., FUNDAMENTALS OF CONSTRUCTION LAW 347 (ABA 2001). A project manager may be located on-site at the construction project, or may work out of the contractor's home office and provide support to colleagues who are working in the field.

Project Manager at-Risk. A person or entity that provides construction management services under a contract with the owner/client for a fixed-price contract with the traditional general contractor's risk for the cost and timeliness of construction and the corresponding entrepreneurial profit motive is referred to as a "project manager at-risk." KENNETH M. CUSHMAN, CONSTRUCTION

Litigation 321, Aspen (1981). In other words, a project manager at-risk "assumes the obligations to construct the project for a stipulated sum or guaranteed maximum price . . . [and] holds the trade contracts, and is at risk for performance, deficiencies, construction delays, and cost overruns." John I. Spangler & William M. Hill, *The Evolving Liability of Construction Managers*, Construction Law., Jan. 1999, at 30.

Project Manager Not at-Risk. A project manager not at-risk is "solely the agent for the owner working for a fee for its professional service, taking no entrepreneurial risk or profit." Unlike a project manager at-risk, the project manager not at-risk does not obligate itself to the owner to build the project and enter into contracts with specialty trade subcontractors in order to accomplish such completion of the project. Kenneth M. Cushman, Construction Litigation 329–30, Aspen (1981). The project manager not at-risk takes "responsibility for [its] own acts, errors and omissions, *but not* for the timeliness, quality, or cost of the work, which remains the responsibility of the trade contractors who have a direct contractual relationship with the owner." Stephen G.M. Stein, Stein on Construction Law 5B-94, Matthew Bender (1986) (emphasis added).

Project Neutral. Prior to the start of a construction project, the owner, prime contractor, and architect of record may agree to designate in their respective contracts with each other a neutral third party to serve as both an arbitrator and a mediator throughout the duration of the entire project, and this neutral party will mediate and/or arbitrate any disputes that arise on the project. Such designation of a project neutral "provides [the parties] the advantage of contemporaneous alternative dispute resolution." *See* Carina Y. Ohara et al., Fundamentals of Construction Law 347 (ABA 2001); *see also* Justin Sweet, Sweet on Construction Law 474, ABA Forum on the Construction Industry (1997) ("[T]he Project Neutral is really a team of experts . . . [that] finds the facts, evaluates the claims, and provides recommendations to the parties.").

Prompt Payment. Many jurisdictions, including the federal government and some states, have enacted "prompt payment" statutes that require payment be made on construction contracts within a designated period of time. The Prompt Payment Act enacted by the federal government (31 U.S.C. §§ 3901 et seq.) requires that within certain times federal agencies make payment to prime contractors and prime contractors make payment to subcontractors and suppliers. "So-called 'prompt-payment statutes' require payment of construction invoices within a statutorily mandated period of time." Daniel E. Toomey

& Gregory Brown, *The Incredible Shrinking "American Rule": Navigating the Changing Rules Governing Attorney's Fee Awards in Today's Construction Litigation*, Construction Law., Spring 2007, at 34, 35.

Proprietary Specification. A proprietary specification is generally a specification that is so narrow or so specific that there is a sole source for the described product. "According to the Federal Acquisition Regulations (FARs) and case law, a 'proprietary specification' is one identified by brand name, or by details that describe a particular brand name product." *American Renovation & Construction Co. v. United States*, 45 Fed. Cl. 44, 46 (1999) (citing FAR 6.302(b)(1)(ii)). "In ordinary government procurement, that means a product made by only one manufacturer. Government policy discourages use of proprietary specifications because by definition it inhibits competition." *Id.* (citing 10 U.S.C. § 2304 and 41 U.S.C. § 253.)

Public-Private Partnership (PPP). A public-private partnership is a contractual arrangement formed between public- and private-sector partners. These arrangements typically involve a government agency contracting with a private partner to renovate, construct, operate, maintain, and/or manage a facility or system, in whole or in part, that provides a public service. *LaSalle Partners v. United States*, 48 Fed. Cl. 797, 810 (2001) (citing U.S. Gen. Accounting Office, Public-Private Partnerships: Terms Related to Building and Facility Partnerships, GAO/GGD-99-71 (1999)). Depending upon the contractual arrangement, the use of the term "public-private partnership" may simply describe a manner of doing business and may not create a legally binding partnership. *Id.* at n.15.

Public Works. Public works are generally construction projects that are paid for with public funds and constructed by the government for the benefit of the public. For example, under one state statute the term "public works" "includes, but is not limited to, roads, highways, buildings, structures and improvements of all types, the construction, reconstruction, major renovation or painting of which is carried on or contracted for by any public agency to serve the public interest but does not include the reconstruction or renovation of privately owned property which is leased by a public agency." *State ex rel. Gardner v. City of Salem*, 05C18435; A135218, 2009 WL 3107713, *4–5 (Or. Ct. App. 2009) (citing Or. Rev. Stat. § 279.348(3)).

Under a different state's statutes, public works is defined as "the erection, construction, alteration, repair or improvement of any building, road, street, public utility or other public facility owned by the public entity." *Collins & Hermann, Inc. v. TM2 Construction Co.*, 263 S.W.3d 793, 797 (Mo. Ct. App. 2008) (citing Mo. REV. STAT. § 107.170.1(3)). Public works projects are generally subject to procedures set forth by statutes or ordinances such as bonding requirements and competitive bidding.

Punch List. A punch list is generally a list of minor work that remains to be performed after a contractor or subcontractor has reached substantial completion. "Punch list work, in the parlance of the construction industry, is work called for by the original contract (or subcontract) which the contractor (or subcontractor) has not satisfactorily completed." *Aniero Concrete Co. v. New York City Construction Authority*, 308 F. Supp. 2d 164, 192 (S.D.N.Y. 2003). Not uncommonly when it believes the project is substantially complete, the contractor submits to the architect a list of items to be completed prior to final payment. The architect then inspects the project and ultimately prepares a punch list of incomplete or incorrect work items the contractor must correct and complete to achieve final completion. WILLIAM ALLENSWORTH ET AL., CONSTRUCTION LAW 388 (ABA 2009).

Punitive Damages. Punitive damages are damages that may be awarded by a court for the purpose of deterring a defendant from continuing or repeating its harmful conduct. Generally, punitive damages are "[d]amages awarded in addition to actual damages when the defendant acted with recklessness, malice, or deceit." BLACK'S LAW DICTIONARY 418 (8th ed. 2004).

Punitive damages "are aimed not at compensation but principally at retribution and deterring harmful conduct." *See Exxon Shipping Co. v. Baker*, 128 S. Ct. 2605, 2621 (2006). The prevailing rule in American courts also limits punitive damages to cases where a defendant's conduct is outrageous, owing to gross negligence, willful, wanton, and reckless indifference for the rights of others, or even more deplorable behavior. *Id.* Many states have a cap on the amount of punitive damages that can be awarded and some require proof of an independent tort in order to recover punitive damages.

Purchase Order. A purchase order is generally a written offer to purchase goods or services subject to the terms and conditions set forth in the purchase order. A purchase order is "an offer which may then be accepted or rejected by a seller." *Roanoke Cement Co., L.L.C. v. Falk Corp.*, 413 F.3d 431, 433 (4th Cir. 2005) (citing *J.B. Moore Electrical Contractor, Inc. v. Westinghouse Electrical Supply Co.*, 273 S.E.2d 553, 556 (Va. 1981)).

With respect to government contracting, a purchase order

is an offer by the government to the supplier to buy certain supplies or services upon specified conditions. A contract is established when the supplier accepts the order, by furnishing the
supplies or services ordered or by proceeding with the work
to the point of substantial performance prior to the due date.

Zhengxing v. United States, 71 Fed. Cl. 732, n.21 (2006) (citing *Friedman Enterprises*, ASBCA No. 54886, 05-2 BCA ¶ 32,991 (June 3, 2005)).

Q

Quantum Meruit. Quantum meruit is an equitable claim that is often treated
synonymously with unjust enrichment. "The expression 'quantum meruit'
means 'as much as he deserves.'" *Associated Wrecking & Salvage Co. v. Wiek-
horst Bros. Excavating & Equipment Co.*, 424 N.W.2d 343, 348 (Neb. 1988) (citing
BLACK'S LAW DICTIONARY 1119 (5th ed. 1979)). "The general principle of quantum meruit is a contract implied in law theory of recovery based on the equitable doctrine that one will not be allowed to profit or enrich oneself unjustly
at the expense of another." *Id.*

Quantum meruit is typically employed to fashion a remedy in the absence
of an express, enforceable contract between two parties, but in circumstances in
which a court will find that a contract is implied by law. WILLIAM ALLENSWORTH
ET AL., CONSTRUCTION LAW 676 (ABA 2009). "The elements of [a quantum meruit]
claim are the performance of services in good faith, the acceptance of the services
by the party for whom they were rendered, the expectation of compensation for
those services, and a statement of the reasonable value of the services . . . ." *Pulver
Roofing Co. v. SBLM Architects, P.C.*, 65 A.D.3d 826, 827 (N.Y. App. Div. 2009).

R

Receiver. A receiver is generally a third party who oversees an asset that is the
subject of a dispute. Furthermore, a receiver is defined as a "disinterested person appointed by a court, or by a corporation or other person, for the protection or collection of property that is the subject of diverse claims." *University*

System of Maryland v. Mooney, 966 A.2d 418, 430 (Md. 2009) (citing BLACK'S LAW DICTIONARY 1296 (8th ed.2004)).

> As a general matter, a "receiver" is an indifferent person between parties appointed to receive rents, issues, or profits of land, or other things in question pending suit, where it does not seem reasonable that either party should do it. In other words, a receiver is an officer of the court subject only to its direction and control and he is a mere custodian and agent whose functions are limited to the care of the property committed to its charge; he owes its allegiance to the court and not to the one who sought his appointment.

65 AM. JUR. 2D *Receivers* § 1 (2009).

A receiver can be appointed by a court, or creditors, to run a company. When the receiver is appointed, the company is said to be in receivership. A receiver can be empowered by the court to, among other things, collect and dispose of assets a party placed in receivership, subject to orders of the court. The receiver is compensated for his efforts.

> There is a very clear distinction between the appointment of a receiver for certain assets of a corporation and the appointment of a receiver for the corporation itself. A receiver may still be, and often is, appointed to perform the original role of custodian of specific property to insure its preservation while litigation concerning its ownership and proper disposition is being conducted. Such a receiver may be referred to as a 'passive' receiver. Where, however, a receiver is sought for the corporation itself, the receiver's role is likely to be broader and more active. A receiver in such a case is more likely to be the agent through which the court provides the ultimate relief sought in the action: the collection of assets illegally diverted to officers or shareholders, the equitable distribution of the corporate assets in insolvency, the overhaul of the corporate management, and in some cases, the restoration of the corporation to economic health.

WILLIAM MEADE FLETCHER, FLETCHER CYCLOPEDIA OF THE LAW OF CORPORATIONS § 7665, Thompson West (Cum. Supp. 2008–2009) (internal footnotes omitted).

Receivership. A receivership is "[t]he state or condition of being in the control of a receiver." BLACK'S LAW DICTIONARY 1297 (8th ed. 2004).

"A general receivership of a corporation contemplates the ultimate sale of the property, the payment of debts in full or pro rata and the distribution of the balance to those held by the appointing court to be entitled to the same." *Liberte Capital Group, LLC v. Capwill*, 148 F. App'x 426, 433 (6th Cir. 2005) (citing 3 RALPH E. CLARK, A TREATISE ON THE LAW AND PRACTICE OF RECEIVERS § 711 (3d ed. 1959).

Red Book. The term "Red Book" may have more than one common meaning; however, the most common reference appears to be to a publication by the American Association of State Highway and Transportation Officials (AAS-HTO), formerly known as the American Association of State Highway Officials (AASHO). The publication *A Policy on Geometric Design of Urban Highways and Arterial Streets*, which was published in 1957 and updated in 1973, is often referred to as the Red Book. *See* 14 AM. JUR. *Proof of Facts* 3d 527 (2009); *see also McKay v. Boyd Construction Co.*, 571 So. 2d 916, 918 (Miss. 1990) (noting that the project specifications "came from the Red Books published by the American Association of State Highway Officials.").

Reimbursable. Reimbursable costs are those costs that involve payment from one party to another for that party's actual costs incurred. "Reimbursable costs typically are clearly defined with great care, and are distinguished expressly from non-reimbursable costs." 1 PHILIP L. BRUNER & PATRICK J. O'CONNOR, JR., BRUNER AND O'CONNOR ON CONSTRUCTION LAW § 2:18, 74 (2002) (citing FAR 31.105 and 31.205, 48 C.F.R. § 31.105, and AIA. Document A201-1997, General Conditions of the Contract for Construction, Article 7.3.6 (2007)).

Reimbursable costs can be direct costs, such as the costs that have been incurred for the purpose of the project (for example, labor and material consumed on the project), or indirect costs, such as administrative costs and general overhead costs. In several standard form contracts, certain costs are defined as reimbursable while others are defined as nonreimbursable.

Request for Equitable Adjustment (REA). In federal governmental contracts under the Federal Acquisition Regulation (FAR), the government has the right to unilaterally change the terms of a construction contract. Since these changes often involve a change in scope of work on the project, the contractor is entitled to file a Request for Equitable Adjustment (REA) to the contract price and/or schedule when governmental changes will impact the cost of performance and/or project schedules. The REA can originate from the contractor or the federal government when these changes arise. Equitable adjustment is the equivalent of quantum meruit or quantum valebant at common law because it entitles the contractor to recover its reasonable costs incurred from the changes in scope of the underlying contract. W. NOEL KEYES, GOVERNMENT CONTRACTS UNDER THE FEDERAL ACQUISITION REGULATION § 43.14, West (3d ed. 2009). Contractors are generally entitled to equitable adjustments of a contract price for (1) added work; (2) substituted materials; and (3) deleted work, based on the "altered position in which the contractor finds himself," rather than on the "value received by the Government." *Bruce Construction Corp. v. United States*, 324 F.2d 516 (Ct. Cl. 1963). *See also* SAM DAVIDSON, WHITE PAPER: INTRODUCTION TO THE EQUITABLE ADJUSTMENT (2005), *available at* http://www.gaffeycpa.com/WhitePaper/Intro_to_Equitable_Adjustment.pdf; 6 PHILIP L. BRUNER & PATRICK J. O'CONNOR, JR., BRUNER AND O'CONNOR ON CONSTRUCTION LAW §§ 19:49–19:51 (2002).

Request for Information (RFI). An RFI is a formal avenue by which a contractor, architect, owner, or other party in a construction project can request clarification and further information from another party involved in the construction project. RFIs usually involve requests from the contractor to the architect to clarify the requirements of the plans and specifications and are often submitted with requests to approve minor deviations from the contract requirements that do not involve any time or cost adjustments. RFIs are often a precursor to a change order or construction change directive. *See* STEVEN G.M. STEIN, CONSTRUCTION LAW § 8.01[1][p] (LexisNexis Matthew Bender 2009); CARINA Y. OHARA ET AL., FUNDAMENTALS OF CONSTRUCTION LAW 348 (ABA 2001); AIA Document G716-2004, Request for Information (2004).

Resident Officer in Charge of Construction (ROICC). In the military and construction industry, the ROICC is an officer of the U.S. military that has been designated by the contracting officer to oversee the field administration of construction contracts for a particular military station or facility.

Retainage/Retention. In the construction industry, owners and general contractors run the risk of a contractor or subcontractor accepting payment and not completing the project as required. To mitigate this risk, a contractee often withholds a portion of requested amounts from progress payments that are earned by the contractor or subcontractor during the construction project. Retainage/retention is "a percentage of the contract amount owed to the contractor or subcontractors but held back (i.e., retained) by the owner to ensure complete performance of the work, especially of punchlist items." CARINA Y. OHARA ET AL., FUNDAMENTALS OF CONSTRUCTION LAW 348 (ABA 2001). Retainage is an effective way to reduce the contractee's risk that its contractor will fail to fully perform its contractual obligations. 3 PHILIP L. BRUNER & PATRICK J. O'CONNOR, JR., BRUNER AND O'CONNOR ON CONSTRUCTION LAW § 8:18 (2002). Typical construction contracts that involve retainage allow the contractee to withhold approximately 5 to 10 percent of the amount owed to the contractor, but retainage can be arranged in many ways. Retainage is usually determined by the terms of the construction contract, but can also be established by statute. STEVEN G.M. STEIN, CONSTRUCTION LAW § 7.04[1][a] (LexisNexis Matthew Bender 2009).

S

Schedule: Project Schedule/Progress Schedule/Master Schedule. A construction project schedule is a baseline for ensuring that a project is completed in a timely and cost-efficient manner. The schedule is "the timetable for project completion [which] may contain milestone dates, against which progress of the project is compared." CARINA Y. OHARA ET AL., FUNDAMENTALS OF CONSTRUCTION LAW 348 (ABA 2001). The schedule is intended to reflect the means and methods of construction by the contractor based on the owner's required completion date. Project master schedules can be organized in many forms, including critical-path method scheduling, to implement the sequential ordering of work to maximize productivity and minimize costs. To implement the master schedule, before beginning work each contractor involved in the project may be asked to provide a progress schedule, which outlines the schedule for that particular contractor's portion of the overall project. STEVEN G.M. STEIN, CONSTRUCTION LAW § 3.02[4][b][i] (LexisNexis Matthew Bender 2009); AIA Document A201-2007, General Conditions of the Contract for Construction (2007). These progress schedules are then incorporated into the overall master plan for the project.

Schedule of Values. A schedule of values is a listing of the various portions of the work with monetary amounts assigned to each. Industry standard construction contracts require the contractor to submit a schedule of values to the architect at the beginning of the project "allocating the entire contract sum to the various portions of the work and prepared in such form and supported by such data to substantiate its accuracy as the architect may require." AIA Document A201-2007, General Conditions of the Contract for Construction, ¶ 9.2 (2007). The schedule of values is used by the architect to evaluate the contractor's applications for progress payments during the project and to calculate the value of work performed. The schedule of values usually includes itemized quantities and prices for labor, materials, and other costs that are subdivided into each portion of the work to be performed under the contract, and often includes an appropriate amount of overhead and profit for each portion. *See also* 2 PHILIP L. BRUNER & PATRICK J. O'CONNOR, JR., BRUNER AND O'CONNOR ON CONSTRUCTION LAW § 5:164 (2002); EJCDC Document No. 1910-8, Standard General Conditions of the Construction Contract, ¶ 2.6.3 (1990).

Schedule Updates. Since many variables can and do impact the project schedule, and construction projects are rarely completed as planned, there are often many updates to the project schedule throughout the project that are recommended and often required by contract. Schedule updates should reflect progress as well as changes to the construction schedule that occur during the construction phase of the project. Schedule updates are often necessitated by weather, unforeseen ground conditions, owner design changes, trade coordination issues, and a variety of other issues. If any event occurs during the construction phase that would impact the overall master schedule, the general contractor and/or the architect must update the construction schedule to ensure that subsequent events in the construction schedule are not delayed. *See* 5 PHILIP L. BRUNER & PATRICK J. O'CONNOR, JR., BRUNER AND O'CONNOR ON CONSTRUCTION LAW § 15:10 (2002); CARINA Y. OHARA ET AL., FUNDAMENTALS OF CONSTRUCTION LAW 225 (ABA 2001).

Schematic Design Documents. Schematic design documents are preliminary designs generated by the architect and engineer or design-builder that illustrate the size and configuration of the building, its elevation, and its relationship to other components in the project, including the overall site plan. The schematic design documents usually include the building floor plans; the roof plan; conceptual building sections and elevations; structural and aesthetic elements of the design; mechanical, electrical, and plumbing; and the site plan based on the owner's budget and usage requirements. During the schematic design phase of the project, the architect and engineer also create a project schedule and budget to implement the schematic design. *See* CARINA Y. OHARA ET AL., FUNDAMENTALS OF CONSTRUCTION LAW 63–64 (ABA 2001).

Scope of Work/Work. The term "scope of work" is intended to define the work to be performed on a project and is contractually defined as "the construction and services required by the contract documents, whether completed or partially completed, and includes all other labor, materials, equipment and services provided or to be provided by the contractor to fulfill the contractor's obligations." AIA Document A201-2007, General Conditions of the Contract for Construction, ¶ 1.1.3 (2007). The scope of work provision in a contract determines the extent of the work the contractor is required to perform under the contract and often includes references to the plans and specifications and/or the owner–general contractor agreement. Work performed by the contractor that is outside the scope of work of the contract may be in the form of a change order and may require contract price adjustments and time extensions. *See also* CARINA Y. OHARA ET AL., FUNDAMENTALS OF CONSTRUCTION LAW 123–24 (ABA 2001).

Sealed Bidding. Most public and many private construction projects are procured by the sealed bidding process. Sealed bidding or competitive sealed bidding is a process used by owners to solicit and procure contracts in which contractors submit bids in sealed envelopes based on plans and specifications that are published by the owner. For most public contracts, the bid envelopes are opened and read publicly after the deadline for submission. The contract is then awarded to the "lowest responsive and responsible bidder," meaning that the bid must adhere to the plans and specifications for the project and the owner must deem the contractor responsible enough to fulfill its obligations under the contract. Competitive sealed bidding can be used for both public and private contracts, and has become the preferred method of public contract formation. Most federal contracts are procured by competitive sealed bidding as regulated by the Federal Acquisition Regulations. 48 C.F.R. pt. 14; CARINA Y. OHARA ET AL., FUNDAMENTALS OF CONSTRUCTION LAW 87 (ABA 2001); 1 PHILIP L. BRUNER & PATRICK J. O'CONNOR, JR., BRUNER AND O'CONNOR ON CONSTRUCTION LAW § 2:222–223 (2009); STEVEN G.M. STEIN, CONSTRUCTION LAW § 2.02[1]–[2], [6]–[7] (LexisNexis Matthew Bender 2009).

Shop Drawings, Samples, Product Data. Shop drawings, samples, and product data are used in construction contracts to explain the project's technical and functional specifications in more detail, often through the use of examples. Shop drawings are "designs prepared by contractors, subcontractors and suppliers to illustrate how a particular aspect of the design will actually be constructed, fabricated or installed." STEVEN G.M. STEIN, CONSTRUCTION LAW § 8.01[1][b] (LexisNexis Matthew Bender 2009). Shop drawings typically illustrate the installation in much greater detail than the plans and specifications. Product data are "illustrations, standard schedules, performance charts, instructions, brochures, diagrams and other information furnished by the contractor to illustrate materials or equipment for some portion of the work." AIA Document A201-2007, General Conditions of the Contract for Construction, ¶ 3.12.2 (2007). Samples are "physical examples that illustrate materials, equipment or workmanship and establish standards by which the work will be judged." AIA Document A201-2007, General Conditions of the Contract for Construction, ¶ 3.12.3 (2007).

Shop drawings, product data, and samples are used to demonstrate the manner in which the contractor proposes to conform to the project design and specifications. The contractor is usually obligated to prepare the shop drawings, product data, and samples or approve the shop drawings, product data, and samples prepared by a subcontractor, manufacturer, or supplier before submitting them to the designer for review against the design drawings. After the designer approves the shop drawings, product data, and samples submitted by the contractor, the contractor is obligated to perform work in conformity therewith. See STEIN, supra, § 8.01[1][p]; AIA Document A201-2007, General Conditions of the Contract for Construction, ¶¶ 3.12.4–10 (2007)

Shopping Bids. Owners and contractors sometimes attempt to manipulate the bidding process during the procurement phase of a project to obtain more economically beneficial contracts. Shopping bids or bid shopping generally refers to an attempt by a general contractor to underbid a competing subcontractor by reopening the subcontractor bidding process and soliciting other subcontractors' bids either before or after the general contractor's bid has been accepted by the owner. Tektron, Inc. v. Builders Bid Service of Utah, Inc., 676 F.2d 1352 (10th Cir. 1982); CARINA Y. OHARA ET AL., FUNDAMENTALS OF CONSTRUCTION LAW 117 (ABA 2001). Since a subcontractor is not allowed to revoke its bid after the general contractor incorporates that bid into the general contractor's bid to the owner, the general contractor has leverage to obtain a lower bid for the subcontractor's scope of work. This leverage can lead the general contractor to pressure the subcontractor to lower its bid or to solicit additional bids from other subcontractors. Many subcontractors, politicians, and academics believe that bid shopping is detrimental to the construction industry. See Eric Degn & Kevin R. Miller,

Bid Shopping, J. Construction Educ., Spring 2003, 47–55. Therefore, Congress recently introduced bills to prevent bid shopping on federal contracts. *See* The Construction Quality Assurance Act of 2007, H.R. 3854, 110th Cong. (2007).

Silver Book. In the context of the construction industry, the Silver Book is a standard form EPC (engineer-procure-construct) contract published by the International Federation of Consulting Engineers (FIDIC), an international association of consulting engineers based in Lausanne, Switzerland. Also known as "Conditions of Contract for EPC/Turnkey Projects (1999 ed.)," the Silver Book is

> [i]ntended for use on process or power plant, factories or infrastructure projects done on a turnkey basis in which the contractor takes total responsibility for the design and construction of the project with little involvement from the owner, providing a fully equipped facility ready for operation (at the "turn of the key").

Robert F. Cushman et al., Design-Build Contracting Handbook § 4.06 (Aspen 2d ed. 2001). *See also* Richard K. Allen & Stanley A. Martin, Construction Law Handbook § 41.03 (Aspen 2d ed. 2008).

Site Meeting. As used in the context of the construction industry, the term "site meeting," while not susceptible of one precise definition, generally describes a physical meeting regarding the project that occurs at the project site and involves the representatives of the various project participants (owner, design professional, contractor, subcontractor, etc.). The "site" is generally regarded as the real property on which a project is constructed, and the term has been defined as "Lands or areas indicated in the Contract Documents for a Specific Project as being furnished by Owner upon which the Work is to be performed, rights-of-way and easements for access thereto, and such other lands furnished by Owner which are designated for use of a Contractor." EJCDC Document No. E-505, Standard Form of Agreement Between Owner & Engineer for Professional Services, Task Order Edition, at 14 (2004 ed.).

Site meetings may occur at any stage of the project between or among the various project participants and for a variety of purposes. They may take place at regular intervals, such as weekly project meetings during which participants discuss the current status of the project and proposed adjustments to project activities and the project schedule, or they may be singular in nature, as a result of a unique event or development.

Site Review. Because the term "site review" is commonly used in various contexts in the construction arena, it is not susceptible of one precise definition. Contractors who wish to bid on complex projects are, for example, typically required to review and become familiar with the site of the project prior to submission of their bid. Further, owners, architects, engineers, and/or contracting officers typically conduct an on-site review prior to any regularly scheduled progress meeting in order to inspect the progress of the work and to make note of items for discussion among project participants. A site review may also take place during project termination (typically to determine the percentage of project activity completed) or upon substantial completion (typically to prepare a punch list or to inspect punch list items before final payment).

Socioeconomic Programs/Requirements. Socioeconomic programs are sometimes instituted by governments that procure or fund construction activities. Under such programs, the government directs procurement officials to look beyond traditional award criteria, such as price and proven responsibility, in order to further the policy of including otherwise overlooked, and perhaps less competitive, business sectors. While price and likely quality of work are important considerations when awarding construction contracts, socioeconomic requirements ensure that additional concerns related to furtherance of government policies are also taken into account.

As described in one text, socioeconomic programs and their related contracting requirements are "incorporated into the procurement process to foster the achievement of national goals . . . [such as] fostering small business, overcoming regional unemployment, assisting minority workers, giving preference to domestic and other special sources, ensuring fair treatment of employees, maintaining integrity and fair competitive practices, and protecting the environment." RALPH C. NASH ET AL., THE GOVERNMENT CONTRACTS REFERENCE BOOK 533 (CCH Inc. 3d ed. 2007).

Specifications. In a construction context, specifications are those portions of the contract or subcontract, typically prepared by the project design professional, that describe, in narrative form as opposed to the pictorial form of drawings, the specific, technical contract requirements.

One text defines specifications as "[a] description of the technical requirements for a material, product, or service that includes the criteria for determining whether these requirements are met. Specifications may be prepared to cover a group of products, services, or materials, or a single product, service, or material." RALPH C. NASH ET AL., THE GOVERNMENT CONTRACTS REFERENCE BOOK 542 (CCH Inc. 3d ed. 2007). *See also* AIA Document A201-2007, General Conditions of the Contract for Construction, § 1.1.6 (2007) ("The Specifications are that portion of the Contract Documents consisting of the written require- ments for materials, equipment, systems, standards, and workmanship for the Work, and performance of related services.").

Statute of Limitations. A statute of limitations is a law or written statute set- ting forth the time period for bringing legal action against another party, with the time period typically accruing from the date the injury occurred or was discovered. The time periods for bringing actions vary from state to state, and even among types of claims. For example, the time period for bringing a suit based on negligence may be two years but may be six years for claims for breach of contract in the same state.

According to Black's Law Dictionary, a statute of limitations is "[a] law that bars claims after a specified period; specif[ically], a statute of establishing a time limit for suing in a civil case, based on the date when the claim accrued (as when the injury occurred or was discovered)." BLACK'S LAW DICTIONARY 1546 (9th ed. 2009). The purpose of a statute of limitations is "to require dili- gent prosecution of known claims, thereby providing finality and predictabil- ity in legal affairs and ensuring that claims will be resolved while evidence is reasonably available and fresh." *Id.*

Statutes of limitations function no differently in the context of construc- tion law than in any other area of law.

Statute of Repose. A statute of repose is a law, typically asserted as an affir- mative defense, under which a party's rights are lost by the mere passage of time.

A statute of repose will bar "any suit that is brought after a specified time since the defendant acted (such as by designing or manufacturing a product), even if this period ends before the plaintiff has suffered a resulting injury." BLACK'S LAW DICTIONARY 1546 (9th ed. 2009).

A statute of repose cannot be tolled. Unlike a statute of limitations, which prevents a party from *judicially pursing* a valid legal claim, a statute of repose *completely extinguishes* the right of action. In other words, while a statute of limitations affects a party's rights procedurally, a statute of repose substan- tively affects a party's otherwise valid claim.

As further explained in the case of *Shadburne-Vinton v. Dalkon Shield Claim- ants Trust*:

In contrast to statutes of limitation, statutes of repose serve primarily to relieve potential defendants from anxiety over liability for acts committed long ago. Statutes of repose make the filing of suit within a specified time a substantive part of plaintiff's cause of action. . . . In other words, *where a statute of repose has been enacted, the time for filing suit is engrafted onto a substantive right created by law.* The distinction between statutes of limitation and statutes of repose corresponds to the distinction between procedural and substantive laws. Statutes of repose are meant to be a substantive definition of rights as distinguished from a procedural limitation on the remedy used to enforce rights.

60 F.3d 1071, 1079 (4th Cir. 1995) (internal quotations omitted).

Statutory Bond. A statutory bond is one whose terms are mandated or contemplated by a statute. *In re Mayville Feed & Grain, Inc.*, 96 B.R. 755, 765 (E.D. Mich. 1989) (citing *Commissioner of Insurance v. Central West Casualty Co.*, 3 N.W.2d 830 (1942)).

A contractor that is awarded a public construction project is typically required, by a statute specific to the jurisdiction of the awarding authority, to provide performance and payment bonds in compliance with that statute. Although statutory bonds vary by jurisdiction, generally speaking, the relevant statute will often require that certain provisions be included in the bond and that certain other provisions not be included. As described in *In re Mayville Feed & Grain, Inc.*, "In [a statutory] bond, the existing law becomes a part of the bond, omitted conditions required by law are read into the bond and conditions contrary to the law are read out of it." *Id.*

Stipulated Price Contract. See definition of "Fixed-Price Contract/Lump-Sum Contract."

Stop Notice. A stop notice is a mechanism to secure payment for persons or entities supplying labor, material, or equipment to a project.

The purpose of a stop notice is to notify an owner (generally, a public owner, but in some states, a private owner) of the nonpayment to the person or entity providing the notice. CARINA Y. OHARA ET AL., FUNDAMENTALS OF CONSTRUCTION LAW 348–49 (ABA 2001). The effect of the notice is to require the owner to withhold further payments to the person or entity that has been withholding payment from the person or entity providing the stop notice until such time as the owner receives assurance that the unpaid party has been paid. *Id.* Failure of the owner to do so may result in the owner having to pay twice. *Id.*

Typically, a stop notice is "[a] written notice in a form required by statute." *Id.*

Stored Materials. Stored materials are those materials necessary to complete a construction project that have been purchased either in bulk or well before the time when they are to be consumed or otherwise incorporated into the project and, as such, must be safely stored until the time of their use.

Project stored materials issues, beyond material quality or contract compliance, sometimes arise. For example, where a contractor or project is terminated prior to incorporation of the materials or where the materials are stolen, lost, or damaged, disputes may arise regarding ownership of and responsibility for the stored materials. As noted by one construction law text, in such situations "there must be a means by which the risk of loss is allocated between the parties." 2 Philip L. Bruner & Patrick J. O'Connor, Jr., Bruner and O'Connor on Construction Law § 5:168 (2002). Although risk of loss historically followed title, the Uniform Commercial Code (UCC) instituted a change by tying the risk of loss to the parties' contract. *Id.* The UCC also provides that

> [i]n the absence of any contractual provision pertaining to the issue, risk of loss passes from the seller to the buyer (generally from a manufacturer or supplier to a subcontractor) either when the goods are delivered to a common carrier (in the case where no particular destination is identified) or when the goods are duly tendered to the buyer so as to enable it to take delivery.

Id.

Structured Negotiations. Structured negotiations, sometimes called "step negotiations," refers to a process of dispute resolution often found in construction contracts, especially in owner-contractor agreements. There are many variations on how to provide for this process, but they all rely upon setting time frames for negotiations and then moving the dispute to higher and higher levels of authority within the owner's and the contractor's organizations, if the problem is not resolved before an established deadline. 6 Philip L.

BRUNER & PATRICK J. O'CONNOR, JR., BRUNER AND O'CONNOR ON CONSTRUC-
TION LAW § 20:150 (2002). A dispute that is not settled quickly and at a primary
level (such as between an owner's representative and the contractor's project
manager) would then be handed over to more senior personnel (such as an
owner's vice-president for facilities and the contractor's regional manager).
Each level of authority to negotiate would be designated in the contract's dispute resolution sections, along with a time limit for such negotiations. *See* 4
ALBERT H. DIB, FORMS AND AGREEMENTS FOR ARCHITECTS, ENGINEERS AND
CONTRACTORS § 38:15 (Thomson Reuters 2009).

The process often leads to mediation or arbitration, as an endpoint of
negotiations, but neither of these forms of alternative dispute resolution is a
necessary part of the process.

Subcontract. An agreement to provide a portion of the labor, materials, or
equipment required for performance of a prime contract, a subcontract is typically executed between a general contractor and a lower-tier contractor or supplier. *See Grigsby v. Lexington & Eastern Railway Co.*, 153 S.W. 232 (Ky. 1913);
Executive House Building, Inc. v. Demarest, 248 So. 2d 405 (La. Ct. App. 4th Cir.
1971). The subcontract may be referred to as a second-tier agreement, and,
properly used, describes only agreements involving an individual or entity
that already has contracted to perform work for a third party, the ultimate cli-
ent of the project. Subcontracts often are distinguished from supply contracts
or purchase orders in that subcontracts typically involve some actual work on
the project, rather than simply a purchase of equipment or materials off-site
and ultimately transported to and used or consumed at the project itself. Subcontracts also are distinguished from sub-subcontracts, which refer to third-
tier or lower agreements to provide still smaller scopes of labor, materials, or
equipment than encompassed within the subcontract (and all of which represent fractions of the work involved in the prime contract).

Subcontractor. A subcontractor is an individual or business that agrees to
perform a portion of the work (such as to supply labor, provide materials, or
operate equipment) on a project for another party, which has contracted to perform the entire work. *See Winter v. Smith*, 914 S.W.2d 527 (Tenn. Ct. App. 1995).
The scope of the subcontractor's agreement is a subset of the prime contract
between the general contractor or construction manager and an owner or its
surrogate. Subcontractors typically are distinguished from sub-subcontractors
because the former occupy the tier immediately below the general contractor,
and the latter are individuals or entities agreeing to provide a fraction of the

scope of work in the subcontractor's agreement. *See* 2 PHILIP L. BRUNER & PATRICK J. O'CONNOR, JR., BRUNER AND O'CONNOR ON CONSTRUCTION LAW §§ 5:122–123 (2002). Construction subcontractors also generally perform work specifically identified to the project and at the site, in contrast to construction suppliers, for instance, who generally are in the business of selling material or equipment used on various projects, and who do not work on-site. *See Executive House Building, Inc. v. Demarest*, 248 So. 2d 405 (La. Ct. App. 4th Cir. 1971). Subcontractors normally provide some construction services, in addition perhaps to materials or equipment, although strictly speaking a subcontractor's agreement could call for any scope of work. Subcontractors agree to perform a portion of the project and therefore base their scope of work on some portion of the plans and specifications. Subcontractors are not in privity with the owner, and normally have no right of direct action against the owner, except through statutory lien rights. *See Brookville Floor Coverings Unlimited v. Fleming*, 784 N.E.2d 721 (Ohio Ct. App. 2003); *Bates & Rogers Construction Corp. v. North Shore Sanitary District*, 414 N.E.2d 1274 (Ill. Ct. App. 1981). Because subcontractors often are synonymous with trade contractors, trade contractors sometimes are loosely referred to as subcontractors, even when contracting directly with an owner (such as where an owner utilizes a construction manager to sign agreements with trade contractors), when in that situation they actually are multiple prime contractors.

Submittals. The term "submittal" refers to a broad category of information, documents, tangible specimens, depictions, and mock-ups of materials, equipment, and systems that are proposed to be supplied to or utilized in a project. Submittals are transmitted by the general contractor or construction manager to the owner and/or the architect or engineer of record. Often, the general contractor or construction manager merely forwards the submittal from its subcontractor or supplier, who created it. The purpose of submittals is to demonstrate in advance of ordering, installing, or constructing the work that the particular material, equipment, system, or method of installation in question actually conforms to the plans and specifications, and therefore should (if supplied or installed as described) provide the desired and depicted end product. *See* AIA Document A201-2007, General Conditions of the Contract for Construction, § 3.12.4 (2007). Frequently, the submittal amplifies and describes in greater detail the work to be performed. Examples of submittals are shop drawings and samples.

While submittals, such as shop drawings, are expected and intended by the owner and the design professionals to conform in all respects to the plans and specifications, they may vary slightly or substantially from the actual design. Therefore, submittals are reviewed (at least in theory) by the general contractor, and the architect or engineer of record for conformance to the design documents. *See* AIA Document A201-2007, General Conditions of the Contract for Construction, § 3.12.5 (2007). Submittals may be revised and resubmitted until they are accepted.

Substantial Completion. Many construction contracts define what is necessary to attain substantial completion of the work covered by that particular contract. Substantial completion also is defined in case law and in construction industry custom and practice. By judicial interpretation and within industry usage, the phrase signifies that the work is sufficiently finished that it can be safely used for its intended purpose. *See* AIA Document A201-2007, General Conditions of the Contract for Construction, ¶ 9.8.1 (2007); *Dittmer v. Nokleberg*, 219 N.W.2d 201, 206 (N.D. 1974). Portions of major projects sometimes have separate substantial completion milestones, such as the first unit in a dual-unit power plant. Traditionally and in many standard forms of agreement, substantial completion triggers an obligation to pay over the contract retention (less money necessary for any back charges and to complete the remaining work). This stage also is usually followed by preparation of a punch list (incomplete work, rework needed) and the completion of the various items of work on that list to reach final completion. *See* Robert F. Cushman et al., Design-Build Contracting Formbook § 12.6.1 (Aspen 2006).

Substantial Performance Rule. The substantial performance rule holds that a contract has not been materially breached if the work called for under the agreement has been sufficiently performed that no significant benefit of that bargain has been impeded or prevented. Immaterial breaches, which may entitle a party harmed by them to certain contractual remedies, do not allow for termination of an agreement or suit for breach of contract. *See* AIA Document A201-2007, General Conditions of the Contract for Construction, ¶ 2.4 (2007) (authorizing the owner to carry out the work after giving proper notice to the contractor but without terminating the contract). In construction contracts, the substantial performance rule generally excuses minor deviations from the strict provisions of the plans, specifications, general or special conditions, or the contract itself. The remedy is to backcharge or deduct a sum sufficient to make good the deviation, subject to the concept of not causing economic waste (for instance, replacing one brand of pipe at great expense with another brand of the same quality and performance simply to follow the literal terms of a specification). *See Prudential Insurance Company of America v. Stratton*, 685 S.W.2d 818 (1985), *opinion supplemented*, 690 S.W.2d 750 (1985).

Substitutions. Materials, equipment, or systems called for in the plans and specifications may be varied, but construction contracts normally specify and constrain how such substitutions occur. The most common method of proper substitution is for a general contractor (or its subcontractor/supplier) to propose an alternate type of material, a different but equivalent piece of equipment, or a comparable system and clearly label it as a substitute for that which is specified. Many specifications allow for various items to be submitted without being a substitution because they call for certain specified "or equal" materials, equipment, or systems. That approach permits a submission that conforms to the qualities and characteristics of the specifications, but that is not actually a substitution because the variance was allowed by the terms of the specifications themselves. In contrast, a substitution deviates from the terms of the specifications or plans, but (usually) offers equivalent or superior performance or value. Particularly in the case of a major piece of equipment or a substantial system, substitution may require separate testing and demonstration of the capabilities of the proffered item. *See Sherwin v. United States*, 436 F.2d 992, 999 (1971).

It is not uncommon for a disappointed supplier of equipment or a system designated in the plans and specifications of a public works project to object to any substitution of an unspecified rival piece of equipment or system. On the other hand, in most projects the general contractor proposes at least some substitutions based upon price, availability, or performance and generally expects the architect or engineer of record to accept the alternative because there is good reason to deviate in this manner from the strict terms of the contract documents. *See* 2 PHILIP L. BRUNER & PATRICK J. O'CONNOR, JR., BRUNER AND O'CONNOR ON CONSTRUCTION LAW § 5:56 (2002). Unauthorized substitutions either provided contrary to submittals or without a proper submittal can occur and may be cause for replacement or backcharge by the designer and owner.

Sub-Subcontractor. A sub-subcontractor is an individual or business that agrees to perform a portion of the work (such as to supply labor, provide materials, or operate equipment) on a project for a subcontractor or for another sub-subcontractor. *See* 2 PHILIP L. BRUNER & PATRICK J. O'CONNOR, JR., BRUNER AND O'CONNOR ON CONSTRUCTION LAW § 5:123 (2002). Sub-subcontractors are not in privity with the general contractor or prime contractor, and they occupy the third tier, or lower, in the scope of their work. There is no absolute limit on the number of agreements separating a sub-subcontractor from the prime contract. Sub-subcontractors provide a fraction of a subcontract, and typically on construction projects some portion of their work is a service, not just the provision of equipment or materials. Those supplying only goods, and no services, are referred to as suppliers.

Subsurface Reports. Many projects have geologic or soils reports prepared to allow the architect or engineer of record to properly design foundations, drainage systems, and utilities (among other elements of the work). Contractors bidding work that involves excavation for such portions of the project often base their price (and plan the work and schedule) according to what is shown on the plans, specifications, and in subsurface reports (if available). *See* 1 Albert H. Dib, Forms and Agreements for Architects, Engineers and Contractors § 9:7 (Thomson Reuters 2009). The subsurface reports often append the results of borings or trenches made at various locations on the site. The logs often depict conditions encountered from the soil's surface to the lowest point of the test hole or trench. The soils engineers or geologists producing the report describe the soil and rock conditions, and take periodic samples. They typically measure the bearing capacity of the various strata, the apparent level of ground water, and the types of materials encountered (such as sand, cobbles, and bedrock). Other measurements, such as for the tendency of surface soils to expand when wet, or the location of unsuitable soils for foundations (for instance, organic matter), may be noted or measured. Subsurface reports often prescribe the types of foundations recommended for the specific site and the forms of drainage or moisture protection that may be installed below slabs or along basement walls and utility ducts.

Superintendent. An individual who oversees and directs the labor of workers on the project, and who represents the contractor or subcontractor that employs him, is a superintendent. On small projects, the most senior person on-site for the general contractor would be the job superintendent. On large projects, there may be several superintendents, directing the work of various trades or subcontractors, with one general superintendent overseeing all of them. Selection of an experienced and qualified superintendent represents an important aspect of any project; standard form contracts provide for such a position and may address what rights, if any, an owner has to object to the person designated to fill the position. *See* AIA Document A201-2007, General Conditions of the Contract for Construction, ¶ 3.9.1 (2007).

Supplementary General Conditions. Most standard form construction agreements include, or cross-reference, a set of general conditions governing many of the details of the project and of its contractual relationships. Some agreements, particularly for large jobs or public works projects, contain additional provisions that address specifications and terms designed specifically for the project. These are supplementary general conditions. Indeed, the practice of appending specific provisions to a set of standard general conditions, such as the American Institute of Architects' seminal A201 General Conditions, is a form of supplementary general conditions, even if not denominated that way. The essential nature of supplementary general conditions is that they were prepared specifically for the project in question. As such, they often modify or augment the general conditions, and any order of precedence clause (the contract provision delineating which portion of the contract documents governs over which other portions) normally would give the supplementary general conditions preference over the more generic general conditions. *See* 1 STEVEN G.M. STEIN, CONSTRUCTION LAW ¶ 3.02(2)(g) (LexisNexis 2009).

Supplier. An individual or business that agrees to provide materials or equipment to be used on a project is a supplier. A construction industry supplier generally receives a purchase order, which specifies the goods to be provided. A supplier typically does not endeavor to perform a piece of the prime contract, as such, and therefore does not contract to review the plans and specifications and then supply materials or equipment that it judges to meet the project standards. *See Theisen v. County of Los Angeles*, 5 Cal. Rptr. 161 (Cal. 1960). Rather, the general contractor, a subcontractor, or a sub-subcontractor (or an owner, who self-supplies certain items to the general contractor) issues a contract for goods that it, rather than the supplier, determines it needs to perform the work.

Supply Contract. An agreement to provide materials or equipment utilized in a project, but that is not a subcontract or prime contract, is a supply contract. The supplier may contract with one of a variety of project parties, including an owner (who might order "long lead time" equipment, which is then turned over to the general contractor for installation), a general contractor (who may issue any number of purchase orders for everything from ordinary goods, such as sand, to complex equipment representing the majority value of the work, such as turbines), a subcontractor (who installs the supplier's products and determines what brand to supply to the project to meet the plans and specifications), or a sub-subcontractor (at any tier). Supply contracts often are denominated purchase orders (typically when issued by a general contractor or subcontractor) or a procurement agreement (the terminology often preferred by owners when ordering commodities or goods for a construction project). The supply contract ordinarily is governed by the Uniform Commercial Code and concerns goods, not services. *See CarboMedics, Inc. v. ATS Medical, Inc.*, No. 06-CV-4601(PJS/JJG) 2008 U.S. Dist. LEXIS 70172 (D. Minn. Sept. 17, 2008).

Surety. A person or entity that is primarily liable for the payment of a debt or the performance of an obligation of another acts as a surety. *See, e.g., National Union Fire Insurance Co. v. David A. Bramble, Inc.*, 879 A.2d 101, 107 (Md. 2005); *Branch Banking & Trust Co. v. Creasy*, 269 S.E.2d 117 (N.C. 1980). In the context of a performance bond, the surety assures the owner or government (obligee) that if the contractor (principal) fails to perform its contractual duties, the surety will discharge the duties itself, either by performing them or paying the obligee the excess costs of performance. *See United States Fidelity & Guaranty Co. v. Feibus*, 15 F. Supp. 2d 579, 580 (M.D. Pa. 1998), *aff'd*, 185 F.3d 864 (3d Cir. 1999); *Atlantic Contracting & Material Co. v. Ulico Casualty Co.*, 844 A.2d 460, 468 (Md. 2004) (The liability of a surety is coextensive with that of the principal. The surety is primarily or jointly liable with the principal and, therefore, is immediately responsible if the principal fails to perform.). In a payment bond, the surety guarantees the contractor's duty to the obligee to pay the contractor's laborers, subcontractors, and suppliers. *See Atlantic Contracting*, 844 A.2d at 468. A surety may also provide a bid bond, or a written security guaranteeing that the bidder will sign the contract, if awarded the contract, for the stated bid amount.

A surety generally has both a right of subrogation and indemnification when its principal fails to perform its obligations. *See generally* 4A PHILIP L. BRUNER & PATRICK J. O'CONNOR, JR., BRUNER AND O'CONNOR ON CONSTRUCTION LAW §§ 12.99, 12:100 (2009). Subrogation allows the surety to "step into the shoes of" the principal and assume the principal's contractual rights, even in the absence of an express agreement between the surety and the principal allowing subrogation. *See, e.g., Prairie State Bank v. United States*, 164 U.S. 227 (1896); 17 AM. JUR. 2D *Contractors' Bonds* § 65 (2009). With respect to indemnification,

> [i]n the construction industry, it is standard practice for surety companies to require contractors for whom they write bonds to execute indemnity agreements by which principals and

their individual backers agree to indemnify sureties against any loss they may incur as a result of writing bonds on behalf of principals.

Atlantic Contracting, 844 A.2d at 468.

Surety Bond. The government and private owners may require a prime contractor to provide a surety bond either to insure performance of a construction project or to insure payment to laborers and materialmen, or both. *See, e.g.*, 40 U.S.C. § 3131–3134 (federal Miller Act bonds "for the construction, alteration, or repair of any building or public work of the United States"). A surety bond has been referred to as a "tripartite agreement among a principal obligor, his obligee, and a surety . . . intended to provide personal security for the payment of a debt or performance of an obligation." *National Union Fire Insurance Co. v. David A. Bramble, Inc.*, 879 A.2d 101, 107 (Md. 2005) (quoting *General Motors Acceptance Corp. v. Daniels*, 492 A.2d 1306, 1309 (1985)). The value of the bonds may vary depending on the jurisdiction and the type of project.

Survey. The term "survey" can address different parts of a construction project. A survey may be a measurement of a parcel of land to determine its dimensions, as well as the document on which these measurements are recorded. *See* BLACK'S LAW DICTIONARY 1445 (6th ed. 1990) ("to survey land is to ascertain corners, boundaries, and divisions, with distances and directions, and not necessarily to compute areas included within defined boundaries."). This measurement can be a two-dimensional metes and bounds (boundary) survey that identifies property lines, or a three-dimensional topographic or contour survey. By contrast, a quantity survey may provide a detailed listing of all materials, equipment, and services needed to complete a particular project.

Suspension of Work Notice of Claim. On federal fixed-price construction and architect-engineer contracts, the standard suspension of work clause, FAR 52.242-14, allows the contracting officer to issue written orders to suspend, delay, or interrupt a contract's performance, or any part of it, for such time as the contracting officer determines to be in the government's interest. Commercial contracts may allow the owner a similar right to suspend the work and may impose different notice requirements. *See, e.g.*, Engineers Joint Contract Documents Committee, Standard General Conditions of the Construction Contract 15.01, 10.5 (2002). If the contracting officer suspends the work for an unreasonable period of time, or if the contracting officer fails to take some action within the time set out in the contract and the work is effectively suspended, the contractor may seek an adjustment in the contract price for its increased performance costs and an extension in the contract time. *See* FAR 52.242-14(b).

Acts other than an express suspension order that can result in compensable delays include poor contract administration by the government, *see, e.g., CJP Contractors v. United States*, 45 Fed. Cl. 343 (1999); delays in issuing notice to proceed, *see, e.g., Ross Engineering Co. v. United States*, 92 Ct. Cl. 253 (1940) (all time beyond 12 days unreasonable when there was no reason for delay and failure to issue notice to proceed forced contractor to work in winter); delays in approving materials, *see, e.g., Altmayer v. Johnson*, 79 F.3d 1129 (Fed. Cir. 1996); *Northeast Construction Co.*, ASBCA No. 11109, 67-1 BCA ¶ 6282; failing to promptly approve shop drawings, *see, e.g., Sydney Construction Co.*, ASBCA No. 21377, 77-2 BCA ¶ 12,719 (unreasonable delay in approving shop drawings); dilatory inspections, *see, e.g., Gardner Displays Co. v. United States*, 346 F.2d 585 (Ct. Cl. 1965) ("dilatory and inconclusive" inspection); insisting on compliance with an impossible requirement, *see, e.g., Guy F. Atkinson Co.*, ENG BCA No. 4771, 88-2 BCA ¶ 20,714; and hindering access to the work site, *see, e.g., Fruehauf Corp. v. United States*, 587 F.2d 486 (Ct. Cl. 1978); *John A. Johnson & Sons, Inc. v. United States*, 180 Ct. Cl. 969 (1967); *Merritt-Chapman & Scott Corp. v. United States*, 439 F.2d 185 (Ct. Cl. 1971).

If the suspension results from an act or failure to act other than an express suspension order, the contractor must provide the contracting officer notice of the delay in writing. *See, e.g.,* FAR 52.242-14(c). Where the government has knowledge of the delays and is not prejudiced by a lack of notice, courts and boards have refused to bar a contractor's claim for compensation despite the absence of formal notice. *See Hoel-Steffen Construction Co. v. United States*, 456 F.2d 760 (Ct. Cl. 1972); *see generally* JOHN CIBINIC, JR. ET AL., ADMINISTRATION OF GOVERNMENT CONTRACTS 476–78, George Washington University (4th ed. 2006). Where the notice provision is applied, FAR 52.242-14(c) provides that the contractor may not recover suspension costs incurred more than 20 days prior to providing notice.

T

Takeover Agreement. An agreement between an owner (or the government) and a performance bond surety, by which the surety agrees to complete a contract terminated for default or cause is referred to as a takeover agreement. *See* FAR 49.404 ("Since the surety is liable for damages resulting from the contractor's default, the surety has certain rights and interests in the completion of the contract work and application of any undisbursed funds"). In other words, when "the surety chooses to step into the contractor's shoes and complete the contract . . . it will perform and (hopefully) complete under a new contract between it and the owner." *International Fidelity Insurance Co. v. County of Rockland*, 98 F. Supp. 2d 400, 423 (S.D.N.Y. 2000). That new contract, a takeover agreement, "should include specific terms addressing the future apportionment of responsibilities between the parties, [and] will control the terms of the new relationship, just as would be the case if another contractor took over the contract." *Id.* The surety generally enters into a completion contract with a new contractor, or sometimes the defaulted contractor, to complete the work. Under a government contract, "[a]ny takeover agreement must require the surety to complete the contract and the government to pay the surety's cost and expenses up to the balance of the contract price unpaid at the time of default." FAR 49.404(e). The surety is protected against setoff claims by the government, *see Aetna Casualty & Surety Co. v. United States*, 435 F.2d 1082 (5th Cir. 1970), and may have access to the Court of Federal Claims and the Boards of Contract Appeals as a result of its agreement. *See* Ralph C. Nash, Jr., *The Rights of Performance Bond Sureties: It Depends on the Circumstances*, 6 Nash & Cibinic Report ¶ 57 (Oct. 1992); Ralph C. Nash, Jr., *Dealing with Performance Bond Sureties*, 1 Nash & Cibinic Report ¶ 35 (Apr. 1987).

Teaming Agreement. Similar to a joint venture, a teaming agreement is a form of business arrangement in which two or more firms join together for a specific purpose, such as the performance of a particular contract or project. The agreement itself defines the relationship of the parties involved, and often involves a partnership arrangement, a prime-sub relationship, or any other valid means of combination for the project. The federal government has accepted teaming arrangements for government contracting on construction projects as well as other contracts. *See* FAR 9.601 (defining "Contractor team arrangement," as "an arrangement in which (1) two or more companies form a partnership or joint venture to act as a potential prime contractor; or (2) a potential prime contractor agrees with one or more other companies to have them act as its subcontractors under a specified government contract or acquisition program.").

Termination for Cause. In commercial contracts, an owner may terminate a contract for cause where the contractor substantially fails to abide by the terms of the agreement, i.e., gives the owner cause. Termination for cause may be equated to a termination for material breach. *See* 5 PHILIP L. BRUNER & PATRICK J. O'CONNOR, JR., BRUNER AND O'CONNOR ON CONSTRUCTION LAW § 18.32 (2002). "Cause" in this circumstance has been defined as the persistent failure to perform the work in accordance with the contract documents, disregard of laws or regulations, or disregard of the authority of the owner's authorized representative. *See* Engineer Joint Contract Document Committee Standard General Conditions of the Construction Contract, *supra*, Article 15.02 (A). When the owner terminates an agreement for cause, the owner may exclude the contractor from the site, take possession of material and equipment on the site, assume existing subcontracts, and finish the work on its own. *See* AIA Document A201-2007, General Conditions of the Contract for Construction, § 14.2.2 (2007). Generally, the contract provides a procedure for termination of the contract for cause, including notice to the contractor. *See Enterprise Capital v. San-Gra Corp.*, 284 F. Supp. 2d 166 (D. Mass 2000) (failure to provide seven-day notice under AIA contract material breach relieving surety from its obligation); *but see Ingrassia Construction Co.. v. Vernon Township Board of Education*, 784 A.2d 73 (N.J. Super. App. Div. 2001) (opining that failure to follow contract procedures "is not a condition precedent to the owner's exercise of its common-law right of termination subject to the normal and traditional burden of proof of material breach . . . ."). Some standard form commercial agreements also allow a contractor to terminate an agreement for cause in certain situations. *See, e.g.*, AIA Document A201-2007, *supra*, § 14.1.1.

Termination for Convenience. A termination for convenience clause allows a party to a contract to terminate a contract, wholly or in part, without regard to whether the contractor has fulfilled its obligations under the agreement. *See generally* MICHAEL T. CALLAHAN, CONSTRUCTION CHANGE ORDER CLAIMS § 12.02 (2d ed. 2009 Supp.); FAR 52.249-2. In other words, it provides a no-fault process and procedure for terminating the contract for the convenience of the owner or government. Upon receiving the notice of termination, generally the contractor must stop all work, cancel orders for materials, and take steps necessary to preserve the project. *See, e.g.*, AIA Document A201-2007, General Conditions of the Contract for Construction, § 14.4.2 (2007). The clause also articulates a contractor's remedies, if any, that may arise from a termination for convenience. Costs generally recoverable under both government and commercial contracts in the event of a termination for convenience include the cost of the terminated work to date, termination costs for subcontracts already entered into, demobilization or incidental costs of winding up the project, and either a designated or reasonable profit based on the value of the work performed. For government contracting, the government must make major deletions to the work through the termination for convenience clause rather than under the changes clause. *See J. W. Bateson Co. v. United States*, 308 F.2d 510 (5th Cir. 1962).

Termination for Default. In construction contracts, a termination for default equates to a termination for cause in commercial agreements. Many standard form commercial agreements retain the term "default" as opposed to "cause." *See, e.g.*, ConsensusDOCS 200, Standard Agreement and General Conditions Between Owner and Contractor (Where the Contract Price Is a Lump Sum), art. 11.3 (2007). In federal contracting, FAR 52.249-10 Default (Fixed-Price Construction) provides the bases for a default termination. Those bases, generally reflective of other public agencies' approach, allow a termination for default where the "Contractor refuses or fails to prosecute the work or any separable part, with the diligence that will insure its completion within the time specified in this contract including any extension, or fails to complete the work within this time . . . ." FAR 52.249-10(a). The federal termination for default clause also enumerates several bases for excusable, but not compensable, delays, which type of delay is defined as a delay that "arises from unforeseeable causes beyond the control and without the fault or negligence of the Contractor." FAR 52.249-10(b). Excusable delays under the clause include (i) acts of God or of the public enemy, (ii) acts of the government in either its sovereign or contractual capacity, (iii) acts of another contractor in the performance of a contract with the government, (iv) fires, (v) floods, (vi) epidemics, (vii) quarantine restrictions, (viii) strikes, (ix) freight embargoes, (x) unusually severe weather, or (xi) delays of subcontractors or suppliers at any tier arising from unforeseeable causes beyond the control and without the fault or negligence of both the contractor and the subcontractors or suppliers. *See* FAR 52.249-10(b).

Third-Party Beneficiary Rule. Under the third-party beneficiary rule, a third party to a contract may sue to enforce a contract or promise made for that party's benefit even though it provided no consideration under the agreement, is not named in the agreement as a contracting party, or is a "stranger" to the agreement. *Pickelsimer v. Pickelsimer*, 127 S.E.2d 557, 563 (N.C. 1962); *see also* 17A AM. JUR. 2d *Contracts* § 425 (2008). To qualify under the rule, the third party must demonstrate that the contracting parties entered into the agreement expressly for the benefit of the third party. *See, e.g., Robins Dry Dock & Repair Co. v. Flint*, 275 U.S. 303 (1927) ("Libellants that are not parties to that contract, or in any respect beneficiaries, are not entitled to sue for a breach of it even under the most liberal rules that permit third parties to sue on a contract made for their benefit. Before a stranger can avail himself of the exceptional privilege of suing for a breach of an agreement, to which he is not a party, he must, at least, show that it was intended for his direct benefit"); *Thacker v. Hubard & Appleby*, 94 S.E. 929, 932 (Va. 1918) ("It is not every promise made by one to another, from the performance of which a benefit may inure to a third, which gives a right of action to such third person, he being neither a privy to the contract nor to the consideration. The contract must be made for his benefit as its object and he must be the party intended to be benefited. Where the contract was entered into primarily for the benefit of the parties thereto, the mere fact that a third person would incidentally derive a benefit from its performance does not entitle him to sue for a breach thereof.").

In the construction context, various jurisdictions have limited the application of the rule based on the often intricate relationships between owner, contractor, subcontractor, and materialmen. *See, e.g., Port Chester Electrical Construction Corp. v. Atlas*, 40 N.Y.2d 652, 655–56 (1976) ("Difficulty may be encountered, however, in applying the intent to benefit test in construction contracts because of the multiple contractual relationships involved and because performance ultimately, if indirectly, runs to each party of the several contracts. . . . Generally it has been held that the ordinary construction contract—i.e., one which does not expressly state that the intention of the contracting parties is to benefit a third party—does not give third parties who contract with the promisee the right to enforce the latter's contract with another. Such third parties are generally considered mere incidental beneficiaries.").

Time and Material. Time and material refers to a method of compensating a contractor for work performed on the basis of the labor and material costs incurred to perform the work. These costs are generally based on predetermined hourly rates for labor and actual costs for material.

Time and Materials (T&M) Contract. A construction contract that provides compensation to the contractor on a time and materials basis may qualify as a time and materials (T&M) contract. *See generally* 1 PHILIP L. BRUNER & PATRICK J. O'CONNOR, JR., BRUNER AND O'CONNOR ON CONSTRUCTION LAW § 2:20, at 76–77 (2002). In other words, a T&M contract provides payment to the contractor based on the labor hours used at specified fixed hourly rates and the actual costs of materials used in the work. In federal contracting, a T&M contract may be used only where "it is not possible at the time of placing the contract to estimate accurately the extent or duration of the work or to anticipate costs with any reasonable degree of confidence." FAR 16.601(c); *accord Dixie South Industrial Coating, Inc. v. Mississippi Power Co.*, 872 So. 2d 769, 770 (Miss. App. 2004). Unlike cost-reimbursable contracts, a T&M contract does not ordinarily impose cost restrictions or goals on the contractor, or provide any incentive or disincentives to the contractor to control the cost of the work. *See, e.g.*, FAR 16.601(c)(1) ("A time-and-materials contract provides no positive profit incentive to the contractor for cost control or labor efficiency."). An owner or the government may also issue change orders on a T&M basis when the parties cannot accurately estimate the cost of the changed work or cannot otherwise agree on a negotiated price for the change. *See* 2 PHILIP L. BRUNER & PATRICK J. O'CONNOR, JR., BRUNER AND O'CONNOR ON CONSTRUCTION LAW § 6:83 (2002).

Time Extension. A time extension clause generally provides a remedy of extending contract performance time and provides relief to the contractor from responsibility for delayed completion under certain events. BARRY B. BRAMBLE & MICHAEL T. CALLAHAN, CONSTRUCTION DELAY CLAIMS § 2.07 (Aspen 2000). Where a contractor can demonstrate that a delay to the project results from excusable causes, it is generally entitled to an extension of time to perform the work. Delays generally fall into one of four categories: (1) excusable and compensable; (2) excusable but not compensable; (3) not excusable; and (4) concurrent. *See, e.g., Kink Bros. Mechanical Contractors, Inc.*, ASBCA No. 43788, 93-1 BCA ¶ 25,325 (1992) ("Where the delay is caused solely by the government, it is compensable; where the delay is caused solely by the [contractor], [the contractor] is responsible. . . . Where the delay is prompted by inextricably intertwined concurrent government and contractor causes, the delay is not compensable. . . ."); *see generally* BRONCA, ET AL., FEDERAL GOVERNMENT CONSTRUCTION CONTRACTS 534–39 (ABA 2d ed. 2009). To the extent a delay is not excusable, it does not qualify for a time extension. Courts and boards have generally considered concurrent delays to fall within the second category of delays—i.e., excusable but not compensable—on the theory that "[w]here both parties contribute to the delay 'neither can recover damage.'" *Blinderman Construction Co. v. United States*, 695 F.2d 552, 559 (Fed. Cir. 1982) (quoting *Coath & Goss, Inc. v. United States*, 101 Ct. Cl. 702, 714–15 (1944)).

FAR 52.249-10, Default (Fixed-Price Construction), provides the conceptual foundation for excusable delay, stating: "The Contractor's right to proceed shall not be terminated nor the Contractor charged with damages under this clause, if (1) the delay in completing the work arises from unforeseeable causes beyond the control and without the fault or negligence of the

Contractor." *See also* FAR 52.249-8 Default (Fixed-Price Supply and Service); FAR 52.249-9 Default (Fixed-Price Research and Development). Thus, where a contractor does not contribute to the causes of a project delay, the government may not assess liquidated damages and must extend the time allowed for performance of the work, "excusing" the contractor from liability for the delay. To obtain a time extension, the contractor must demonstrate that the excusable delay impacted overall project completion. *See generally* JOHN CIBINIC, JR., ET AL., ADMINISTRATION OF GOVERNMENT CONTRACTS 570–72, George Washington University (4th ed. 2006) (describing requirements that overall completion be delayed in order to receive an extension of time). *See also Sauer, Inc. v. Danzig*, 224 F.3d 1340 (Fed. Cir. 2000) ("In addition, the unforeseeable cause must delay the overall contract completion; i.e., it must affect the critical path of performance"); *KATO Corp.*, ASBCA No. 51462, 06-2 BCA ¶ 33,293 (2006) ("It is not sufficient . . . for a contractor to show that the Government delayed completion of a segment of the work. Rather, in order for the contractor to recover, it must establish that completion of the entire project was delayed by reason of the delay to the segment."); *accord* FAR 52.242-14 (Suspension of Work) ("However, no adjustment shall be made under this clause for any suspension, delay, or interruption to the extent that performance would have been so suspended, delayed, or interrupted by any other cause, including the fault or negligence of the Contractor, or for which an equitable adjustment is provided for or excluded under any other term or condition of this contract.").

Time Impact Analysis (TIA) v. Windows Analysis. The time impact analysis or TIA is a method of assessing and proving contractor claims of delay using critical path method (CPM) scheduling. *See Morganti National, Inc. v. United States*, 49 Fed. Cl. 110, 125 at n.7 (2001).

TIA is the study of how an event impacted the CPM both in terms of time and cost. In the windows approach, a "window" or period of time during which the delay at issue occurred is analyzed. To perform the schedule analysis, a monthly schedule update is utilized immediately prior to the advent of the delay at issue, and the critical path and plan completion date are determined. The actual events and delays encountered during the window of time are introduced into the schedule, and the job is updated at end of the window period, typically by using a monthly update immediately after the delay is resolved. This establishes the planned completion at the beginning and end of the window, and the total delay to the project during the window of time. All delays that occurred during the window are analyzed to see which delays impacted the critical path, as well as which delays may represent concurrent delays. The "window analysis" is chronological and cumulative and is a valuable tool for analyzing delay to the job. Jon M. Wickwire & Stuart Oakman, *Use of Critical Path Method on Contract Claims 2000*, CONSTRUCTION LAW., Oct. 1999, at 12, 15.

Tort. Tort law is about the rules for shifting losses from injured parties to injurers. DOMINICK VETRI ET AL., TORT LAW AND PRACTICE § 1.01 (2d ed. 2002). Much of formal tort law is an attempt to define what counts as a legal wrong in particular settings. Some torts are also crimes; but tort law is not concerned with the separate issue of criminal responsibility. The essence of tort is the defendant's potential for civil liability to the victim for harmful wrongdoing and correspondingly the victim's potential for compensation or other relief. Conduct that counts only as a breach of contract will lead to legal liability, but breach of contract is not considered to be a tortious wrong. Tort law is predominately common law, but may also be derived from statutes or constitutions. DAN B. DOBBS, THE LAW OF TORTS 1 (West Group 2001).

Courts generally distinguish tort liability from contract liability as between the parties to a contract, seeking to avoid the availability of both tort and contract liability for the same conduct and the same kind of harm or loss. *National Union Fire Insurance Co. of Pittsburgh, PA v. Care Flight Air Ambulance Service, Inc.*, 18 F.3d 323 (5th Cir 1994). However, when certain legal relationships exist between contracting parties, the law may impose affirmative duties that are separate and apart from the contractual promises made between those parties. *National Union*, 18 F.3d at 326.

The economic loss rule is a judicially created doctrine that sets forth the circumstances under which a tort action is prohibited if the only damages suffered are economic losses. The application of the economic loss rule generally requires contractual privity. *Indemnity Insurance Co. of North America v. American Aviation, Inc.*, 891 So. 2d 532, 536 (Fla. 2004). The doctrine operates to preclude contracting parties from pursuing tort recovery for purely economic or commercial losses associated with the contract relationship. *Plourde Sand & Gravel v. JGI Eastern, Inc.*, 154 A.2d 1250 (N.H. 2007). Some courts recognize two exceptions: (1) special relationship exception; and (2) negligent misrepresentation exception.

A growing number of states have refused to apply the "economic loss" rule to actions against design professionals when there is a "special relationship" between the design professional and the contractor. *Griffin Plumbing & Heating v. Jordan*, 320 S.E.2d 85, 88 (S.C. 1995). This is sometimes referred to as the "professional negligence" exception. *Plourde Sand & Gravel*, 154 A.2d at 1255.

Total Cost Method (Total Cost Approach). The total cost method for calculating damages suffered by a contractor based on the additional cost of performance to the contractor is calculated using the following equation: the constructor's cost of performance of the work minus the contract price equals the damages suffered. For example, if the constructor's cost of performance equals $10,000, and the contract price was $8,000, then the damages suffered by the constructor would be $2,000.

The total cost method has great appeal to contractors because it allows them to recover what they invariably feel are their damages: all costs expended in excess of the estimate. The courts have often disfavored the total cost method because of the implicit assumption that the contractor did everything right and all cost overruns must be the result of owner actions. SCHWARTZKOPF ET AL., CALCULATING CONSTRUCTION DAMAGES § 1.6, Aspen (1992).

The total cost method of computing the amount due a contractor under a cause of action against the federal government (the difference between the contractor's bid price and the actual cost of performing the contract as changed by order of the government) is not a method favored by courts and is tolerated only when no more reliable method is available, where the contractor's bid or estimate is realistic, its actual costs were reasonable, and the contractor was not responsible for the added expense of performance. Where the contractor failed to maintain accurate cost records during performance and was unable to rebut at the trial the owner's evidence that some of the increased costs were due to the contractor's fault, the contractor will not be entitled to base his recovery on the total cost method of computing damages. *WRB Corp. v. United States*, 183 Cl. Ct. 409 (1968).

The total cost method may be used only when a plaintiff can demonstrate:

1. It is impractical to prove actual losses;
2. The bid was reasonable;
3. The actual costs were reasonable; and
4. The plaintiff is not responsible for the additional costs.

Tecom, Inc. v. United States, 86 Cl. Ct. 437, 465 (2009) (citing *Servidone Construction Corp. v. United States*, 931 F.2d 860, 861–62 (Fed. Cir. 1991).

Total Time Approach. The total time approach method for establishing proof of delay and resulting damages is based on the following equation: the total time (typically measured in number of days) required by the contractor to perform minus the number of days allowed under the contract, which equals the number of additional days that the contractor should be allowed to complete or for which it seeks compensation. The total time approach is susceptible to the same criticisms as the total cost method in that it does not distinguish between days chargeable to the constructor as compared with days chargeable to the owner or third party. *Law v. United States*, 195 Ct. Cl. 370 (1971). Such proof of delay is ordinarily as unsatisfactory as the total cost method of proving damages. "A 'total time' approach is no less susceptible to inaccuracies than the total-cost theory." *WRB Corp. v. United States*, 183 Ct. Cl. 409, 427 (1968).

> Where an expert analyst simply takes the original and extended completion dates, computes therefrom the intervening time or overrun, points to a host of individual delay incidents for which defendant was allegedly responsible and which "contributed" to the overall extended time, and then leaps to the conclusion that the entire overrun time was attributable to defendant.

Law, 195 Ct. Cl. at 382. It is well settled that this "total time" theory of proving delay is insufficient to meet the contractor's burden to prove that government-caused delay actually delayed the overall completion of the project. *Mel Williamson, Inc. v. United States*, 229 Ct. Cl. 846, 852 (1982) (citing *Law*, 195 Ct. Cl. at 382). The "total time" approach to proving delay is "as unsatisfactory as the 'total cost' method of proving damages," because it assumes that the owner is responsible for all of the delay. *Law*, 195 Ct. Cl. at 382; *Morganti National, Inc. v. United States*, 49 Fed. Cl. 110 (2001).

Trade Contractor Permit. Municipalities often require workers engaged in certain critical building trades to obtain a permit to perform work within the municipality. Licensing of the building trade contractors by municipalities typically has extended to those whose work has involved the structural, electrical, sanitary, heating, ventilating, and plumbing integrity of a project. MCQUILLIN LAW OF MUNICIPAL CORPORATIONS §§ 26.109, 26.110, 26.112, 26.127 (Callaghan 1949).

Trade Permit. Trade permits are issued by municipalities to licensed tradesmen for work on a particular project. Municipalities categorize the permits according to the trade involved in the work. The categories are generally broken into electrical permits, plumbing permits, or mechanical permits. *See* Town of Portland, CT, Building Department Trade Permit Application, *available at* http://www.portlandct.org/pdf/forms/Firemarshal3.pdf.

Turnkey. In the construction context the term "turnkey" generally represents the circumstances where one party is responsible for the design and construction of the work or project, particularly where the contractor agrees to complete the work of the building and installation to the point of readiness for operation or occupancy. *Hawaiian Independent Refinery, Inc. v. United States,* 697 F.2d 1063 *cert. denied,* 464 U.S. 816 (1983) (citing to WEBSTER'S THIRD NEW INTERNATIONAL DICTIONARY (1971 ed.)). The developer "assumes all risks incident to the creation of a fully completed facility," *Securities & Exchange Commission v. Senex Corp.,* 399 F. Supp. 497, 500 n. 1 (E.D. Ky. 1975), *aff'd,* 534 F.2d 1240 (6th Cir. 1976), and must bear "the risk for all loss and damage to the work until its completion and acceptance." *Chemical & Industrial Corp. v. State Tax Commission of Utah,* 360 P.2d 819, 820 (Utah 1961).

U

Unconscionability. A defensive contractual remedy, a claim of unconscionability serves to relieve a party from an unfair contract or from an unfair portion of a contract. *Germantown Manufacturing Co. v. Rawlinson,* 491 A.2d 138, 146 (Pa. Super. 1985). Unconscionability has generally been recognized to include an absence of meaningful choice on the part of one of the parties together with contract terms that are unreasonably favorable to the other party. Whether meaningful choice is present in a particular case can be determined only by consideration of all the circumstances surrounding the transaction. In many cases the meaningfulness of the choice is negated by a gross inequality of bargaining power. *Williams v. Walker-Thomas Furniture Co.,* 350 F.2d 445, 450 (D.C. Cir. 1965). The doctrine of unconscionability consists of (1) "substantive unconscionability," i.e., unfair and unreasonable contract terms, and (2) "procedural unconscionability," i.e., individualized circumstances surrounding parties to the contract such that no voluntary meeting of the minds was possible. *Dorsey v. Contemporary Obstetrics & Gynecology, Inc.,* 680 N.E.2d 240 (Ohio App. 1996).

If a contract or term thereof is unconscionable at the time the contract is made, a court may refuse to enforce the contract, or may enforce the remainder of the contract without the unconscionable term, or may so limit the application of any unconscionable term as to avoid any unconscionable result. The determination that a contract or term is or is not unconscionable is made in the light of its setting, purpose, and effect. Relevant factors include weaknesses in the contracting process such as those involved in more specific rules as to contractual capacity, fraud, and other invalidating causes; the policy also overlaps with rules that render particular bargains or terms unenforceable on grounds of public policy. The principle is one of the prevention of oppression and unfair surprise and not of disturbance of allocation of risks because of superior bargaining power. RESTATEMENT (SECOND) OF CONTRACTS § 208 and cmts. a, b (1981).

Unexcused Delay. A delay caused by an event (1) within the "control" of the contractor or its subcontractors and suppliers, and (2) outside the "control" of the owner is considered an unexcused delay. These risk events are within the contractual undertaking of the contractor and its subcontractors and suppliers, and they are presumed to have been taken into consideration by them in establishing their contract prices. Unexcused delays may provide a claim and potential recovery to the project owner for damages incurred by the owner as a result of the unexcused delay in the form of actual damages or liquidated damages, depending on the terms of the contract between the parties. The project owner typically has other remedies available for an unexcused delay for breach of contract, including default termination.

In the case of an unexcused delay the responsible party is not entitled to any recovery. For example, if the contractor fails to meet the required completion dates because of an unexcused delay, the contractor would not be entitled to either an extension of contract time or compensation, and it will be obligated either to accelerate work to recover the schedule or to pay damages for delayed completion and possibly suffer termination of the contract (or subcontract) for default. 5 PHILLIP L. BRUNER & PATRICK J. O'CONNOR, JR., BRUNER AND O'CONNOR ON CONSTRUCTION LAW § 15:30 (2002).

Unforeseen Condition/Unforeseen Site Condition. Unforeseen conditions and unforeseen site conditions relate to the unexpected circumstances often encountered on a project. Such conditions form the basis of a claim by the contractor that it is entitled to relief on the basis that the site conditions relevant to construction, e.g., soil, water, or hazardous waste, either (1) are different than represented in the contract (*Foster Construction C. A. & Williams Bros. Co. v. United States*, 435 F.2d 873, 880 (1970)) (referred to as a Type I claim); or (2) were unknown by the parties and differed from ordinarily encountered or expected conditions (*Servidone Construction Corp. v. United States*, 19 Cl. Ct. 346, 360 (1990) (referred to as a Type II claim). A Type I claim is usually based on the alleged breach of the representations made and the terms of risk allocation within the contract. A Type II claim is considered more difficult to prove because the contractor must show that it encountered an "unknown physical [condition] at the site, of an unusual nature, differing materially from those ordinarily encountered and generally recognized as inhering in the work of the character provided for in this contract." *See generally Vann v. United States*, 420 F.2d 968, 982 (1970); *Kaiser Industries v. United States*, 340 F.2d 322, 325 (1965); *Loftis v. United States*, 76 F. Supp. 816 (1948); *Servidone Construction Corp.*, 19 Cl. Ct. at 360. Entitlement for claims arising from unforeseen site conditions is often dictated by the terms of the construction contract.

Uniform Commercial Code (UCC). The Uniform Commercial Code is a comprehensive modernization of various statutes relating to commercial transactions including sales, leases, negotiable instruments, bank deposits and collections, funds transfers, letters of credit, bulk sales, documents of title, investment securities, and secured transactions. The UCC is prepared under the joint sponsorship of the American Law Institute (ALI) and the National Conference of Commissioners on Uniform State Laws (NCCULSL); *see* www .ali.org/ali_old/com_ucc.htm. The UCC was devised as a recommended code of laws governing commercial conduct. Its substantial adoption by all 50 states except Louisiana resulted in a system of relatively uniform state laws governing frequently recurring forms of business transactions.

Article 2 of the UCC's nine articles governs transactions involving the sale of movable goods. Jurisdictions differ as to whether construction contracts, which typically involve the sale of services primarily and goods only secondarily, are covered by Article 2. ROBERT F. CUSHMAN ET AL., CONSTRUCTION DISPUTES: REPRESENTING THE CONTRACTOR § 2.02[C], Aspen (3d ed. 2001). In determining whether the UCC applies to a mixed transaction, the majority of jurisdictions utilize the "predominant factor test."

> The test for inclusion or exclusion is not whether they are mixed, but, granting that they are mixed, whether their predominant factor, their thrust, their purpose, reasonably stated, is the rendition of service, with goods incidentally involved (e.g., contract with an artist for painting) or is a transaction of sale, with labor incidentally involved (e.g., installation of a water heater in a bathroom.)

Princess Cruises, Inc. v. GE Co., 143 F.3d 828, 833 (4th Cir. 1998) (citing *Bonebrake v. Cox*, 499 F.2d 951 (8th Cir. 1974); *Tacoma Athletic Club, Inc. v. Indoor Comfort Systems, Inc.*, 902 P.2d 175 (Wash. App. 1995).

Under the predominant factor test, courts have deemed the following factors significant in determining the nature of the contract: (1) the language of the contract, (2) the nature of the business of the supplier, and (3) the intrinsic worth of the materials. *Princess Cruises, Inc.*, 143 F.3d at 833.

Unit Price Contract. In a unit price contract, the contractor's compensation is determined based upon set prices for various units of production. The contractor receives payment based upon the product of the number of units and the unit price for each type of unit. For example, in an excavating contract, there may be a set unit price for excavating each cubic yard of a certain type of material with another unit price for excavating another type of material that may be more or less difficult to handle. 2 PHILLIP L. BRUNER & PATRICK J. O'CONNOR, JR., BRUNER AND O'CONNOR ON CONSTRUCTION LAW § 6:72 (2002).

Unjust Enrichment. Unjust enrichment is an equitable principle that serves to remedy the injustice that may result where goods or services are provided to another in the absence of a written agreement. The elements of unjust enrichment are (1) a benefit obtained from another (2) not intended as a gift and not legally justifiable (3) a benefit for which the beneficiary must make restitution. *See Foster Poultry Farms, Inc. v. SunTrust Bank*, 2008 1:04-cv-5513 OWW SMS U.S. Dist. LEXIS 36595 (E.D. Cal. May 2, 2008).

In the context of unjust enrichment, a benefit is a possession or some other interest in money, land, or chattels, the performance of services beneficial to or at the request of the other, satisfaction of a debt or a duty of the other, or any addition to the other's security or advantage. A benefit is conferred not only where one adds value to the property of another, but also where one saves the other from expense or loss. RESTATEMENT (FIRST) OF RESTITUTION § 1 (1937).

The remedy for unjust enrichment is restitution.

> A person obtains restitution when he is restored to the position he formerly occupied either by the return of something which he formerly had or by the receipt of its equivalent in money. Ordinarily, the measure of restitution is the amount of enrichment received, but if the loss suffered differs from the amount of benefit received, the measure of restitution may be more or less than the loss suffered or more or less than the enrichment.

Id.

Use Plaintiff. A use plaintiff is a person or entity that brings a lawsuit in the name of its principal. *See In re Thompson*, Civil Case No. AW-09-1140 2009 LEXIS 2985 (Bankr. D. Md. Sept. 17, 2009). Typically in the context of construction law, a use plaintiff is found in claims brought pursuant to the Miller Act. The Miller Act is a body of federal law that gives an entity that has furnished labor or materials in the prosecution of work for the construction, alteration, or repair of any public building or work of the United States a right of action on the bond required of the general contractor to recover any unpaid balance due for his labor or materials. *United States ex rel Munroe-Langstroth, Inc. v. Praught*, 270 F.2d 235 (1st Cir. Me. 1959).

The Miller Act allows such an action to be brought against the bond of the general contractor even in the absence of privity of contract. *Id.* Generally, such an action is brought by the party not in privity as a use plaintiff of the United States.

V

Value Engineering. Also called value analysis, value methodology or value management, value engineering is intended to be a cost-saving measure employed on many construction projects. Value engineering

> involves reviewing the architectural and engineering plans and evaluating the life-cycle and construction costs of a project to determine whether lower costs can be achieved without compromising functionality. Two methods commonly used in value engineering are life-cycle analyses and cost comparisons. In life-cycle analyses, the value engineering consultant compares the purchase, operating and maintenance costs of alternative systems (such as HVAC, plumbing, and electrical) and provides the owner with options based on this analysis. Cost comparison involves recommending alternative building components. Along with the cost comparison, the value engineering consultant usually explains the functional aesthetic differences between alternative components.

STEPHEN A. HESS ET AL., DESIGN PROFESSIONAL AND CONSTRUCTION MANAGER
LAW 262, ABA Forum on the Construction Industry (2007).

Variance/Variation. A variance or a variation is a form of written authorization, usually from a government agency, permitting construction in a manner that is otherwise prohibited by code or other regulations. There are two types of variances: area variances and use variances. Use variances "permit deviation from zoning requirements regarding the use of the property, whereas area variances . . . permit deviation from zoning requirements regarding the construction and placement of structures on the property but not permitting deviation from the zoning requirements regarding the use of the property." *Ferraro v. Board of Zoning Adjustment of Birmingham*, 970 So. 2d 299, 304 (Ala. Civ. App. 2007). The distinction between area and use variances is, "for the most part, a judicially created distinction." *Id.*

Generally, an area variance is not controversial because it is usually granted due to an odd configuration of a lot or some peculiar natural condition that prevents normal construction in compliance with zoning restrictions. WEST'S ENCYCLOPEDIA OF AMERICAN LAW, *Variance*, http://www.answers .com/topic/variance (last visited Feb. 18, 2010).

> Use variances are more controversial because they attempt a change in the permitted use. For example, if a lot is zoned single-family residential, a person who wishes to build a multifamily dwelling must obtain a variance. Applicants for a variance cannot argue hardship based on actions they commit that result in self-induced hardship.

Id.

W

Waiver. Waiver is "the voluntary or intentional relinquishment of a known right. The essential elements of a waiver are the existence of a right, knowledge, actual or constructive, and an intention to relinquish such right." *Great*

Plains Real Estate Development, L.L.C. v. Union Central Life Insurance Co., 536 F.3d 939, 944 (8th Cir. 2008).

Waiver of Subrogation. An insurance carrier's right to subrogation (i.e., to step into the shoes of its insured to recover from others)

> may be waived by the insurer, either by contract or by con-
> duct inconsistent with the assertion of subrogation rights. For
> example, a failure to assert subrogation rights while a tort-
> feasor and the insured enter into a settlement agreement will
> waive the insurer's right of subrogation where the insurer
> had knowledge of the contemplated settlement and purpose-
> fully failed to act.

STEVEN G.M. STEIN, CONSTRUCTION LAW § 13.12 4–13 (Matthew Bender 2009). Contract provisions that provide for mutual waivers of subrogation rights are often included in design and construction contracts, especially with regard to claims covered by property insurance. "The American Institute of Architects ('AIA') provisions operate to shift to the owner the ultimate risk of loss, which is then transferred to the owner's insurer for valuable consideration, leaving the insurer no right to proceed against a subcontractor with respect to property loss." *Id.* A waiver of subrogation is useful because it avoids disruption and disputes among the parties to [a construction] project. It thus eliminates the need for lawsuits, and yet protects the contracting parties from loss by bringing all property damage under the all risks builder's property insurance. *St. Paul Fire & Marine Insurance Co. v. Universal Builders Supply*, 409 F.3d 73, 84 (2d Cir. 2005).

Warranty/Guarantee. A warranty, sometimes referred to as a guarantee, is

> an assurance by one party to an agreement that certain facts
> are truthful and it is intended precisely to relieve the prom-
> isee of any duty to ascertain the facts for himself. Thus, a war-
> ranty amounts to a promise to indemnify the promisee for
> any loss if the fact warranted proves untrue.

Paccon, Inc. v. United States, 399 F.2d 162, 167 (Ct. Cl. 1968).

Generally, a warranty is either express or implied. In the context of a construction project, "a contractor often expressly warrants that title to all work, materials and equipment covered by an application for payment, whether incorporated in the project or not, will pass to the owner no later than the time of payment free and clear of all liens." 3 PHILIP L. BRUNER & PATRICK J. O'CONNOR, JR., BRUNER AND O'CONNOR ON CONSTRUCTION LAW § 9:1 (2002).

In addition, warranties given in connection with construction projects may be implied. It has been held that

> implicitly, every building contract requires that the work be performed in a good, workmanlike manner, free from defects in material and workmanship. Accordingly, jurisprudence dictates that a contractor is liable for damages if it is shown that he did not possess the necessary skill, efficiency or knowledge, or did not exercise ordinary care in performing work and is liable for losses, which the owner suffered because of the contractor's non-compliance with the contract.

Austin Homes, Inc. v. Thibodeaux, 821 So. 2d 10, 13 (La. App. 3 Cir. 2002).

Warranty Period. A warranty period is the time for which a warranty is in effect, which typically "begins immediately upon the issuance of the certificate of substantial completion from the architect. Most contracts require a one year minimum warranty or correction period on most installations on the project. However, many products carry a manufacturers' warranty longer than that." BARBARA J. JACKSON, CONSTRUCTION MANAGEMENT JUMPSTART, 127 (John Wiley & Sons 2004).

> A warranty period is not a limitation governing the assertion of a right of action; rather, it defines the period within which a cause of action for breach of warranty may accrue. The warranty period circumscribes the interval of time within which the warranty exists. If a breach occurs before the warranty expires, a cause of action accrues. Statutes of limitation, on the other hand, bar a right of action. The two may occur at the same time but will not necessarily do so.

Grogg v. Massey & Leonard Construction, 39 Va. Cir. 522, 523 (Va. Cir. Ct. 1996).

Work Authorization. In the construction industry, a work authorization is the verbal or written approval to proceed with contract work or "agreed-upon additions to contract work . . . negotiated during construction." *Lexicon, Inc. v. Safeco Insurance Co. of America*, 436 F.3d 662, 665 (6th Cir. 2006).

Working Foreman. A working foreman (also known as a working supervisor, a straw boss, a gang leader, or a group leader) is an

> employee, that performs the same kind of work as that performed by their subordinates, and also carries on supervisory functions. . . . A working foreman is a supervisor who is not exempt from the [Fair Labor Standards Act] because he regularly performs work that is unrelated or only remotely related to his supervisory activities.

29 C.F.R. § 541.115(a).

In evaluating eligibility under the Fair Labor Standards Act, the "working foreman concept is useful because it helps to distinguish between a manager of a recognized subdivision and a mere supervisor of subordinate employees." *Shockley v. City of Newport News*, 997 F.2d 18, 26 (4th Cir. 1993) (internal quotations omitted).

Y

Yellow Book. Also known as FIDIC E&M form, the Yellow Book provides a form of the

> conditions of contract for electrical and mechanical works. . . . [The Yellow Book] is designed for use in contracts involving the manufacture and supply of large electrical and mechanical systems. While less concerned with the erection of such systems at the construction site, the form does provide for such work.

ROBERT F. CUSHMAN & JAMES J. MYERS, CONSTRUCTION LAW HANDBOOK § 48.03[A][2], Aspen (1999).

"Your Work" Exclusion. A "your work" exclusion is a provision contained within most liability insurance policies that excludes coverage

> for property damage to the insured's work arising out of such work. Liability policies do not insure or guarantee the insured's work. Instead, such policies provide coverage for damages awarded by reason of an injury caused by the insured's work to some other property or person. A work exclusion is intended to eliminate coverage for the cost of repairing or replacing the insured's faulty work, but it does not eliminate coverage for the damage caused by the insured's faulty work.

ALLAN D. WINDT, INSURANCE CLAIMS AND DISPUTES, 421, Shepards/Mcgraw-Hill (2001). "A commercial general liability ('CGL') policy generally protects the insured when his work damages someone else's property. The 'your work' exclusion prevents a CGL policy from morphing into a performance bond covering an insured's own work." *Wilshire Insurance Co. v. RJT Construction, LLC*, 581 F.3d 222, 226 (5th Cir. 2009).